After Dark

BIRTH OF THE DISCO DANCE PARTY

AFTER DARK DISCO · EST. 1971

BY NOEL HANKIN

Cover Design By: Mariana Coello
Cover Photo Taken By: Alix DeJean

Interior formatting by: Jackie Friesen

ISBNs:
Hardcover 978-1-7366149-0-7
Paperback 978-1-7366149-1-4
eBook 978-1-7366149-2-1

Leon Niknah Publishing Company
East Hampton
New York, USA

Contents

Preface

DAVID N. DINKINS
106TH MAYOR, CITY OF NEW YORK

The city of New York has enjoyed many incarnations throughout its history, and each period of rebirth has been celebrated in a fashion unique to its time. As the population has evolved, so have the venues to which each wave of "new" New Yorkers have flocked to enjoy the company of friends — old and new. The Gilded Age of Delmonico's, the Roaring Twenties, its Stork Club, and the Harlem Renaissance its Cotton Club and the Savoy Ballroom. New York of the Seventies gave birth to a gathering place called Leviticus.

During each era, the fashionable clubs served not only as attractions for the rich and famous and revelers of all walks but as locations for political events for the City's officials. Invitations to fundraisers at Leviticus for campaigns and causes didn't need the address; the club was so well-known.

The people of Harlem and its political community, once restricted to locales above 110th Street for gatherings, found our way into the City's midtown through the doors of Leviticus and the ventures it helped spawn. The socio-political movements of the Fifties and Sixties did much to bring New Yorkers together in the workplace, and young entrepreneurs like Noel Hankin and Mal Woolfolk helped to bring us together again at the end of the day.

The melding of New Yorkers under one roof was good for business, good for politics, and good for the cultural life of the City, and Noel and Mal are to be commended for their roles in that process. May they forever remain "The Best of Friends."

Acknowledgments

Much love and appreciation to my wife Gwendolyn and our two daughters, Arana and Loren, for their persistent encouragement and support. Thanks also to Idris Diaz, my brother-in-law, and my good friend Jane Jacob for their editing support as well as Sanford Biggers and Anslem Richardson, my sons in law, for their enthusiasm and guidance.

Special thanks to my former partners in The Best of Friends: Tony, Danny, CP, Wayne, Andre, Harry, and Mal; they all contributed. Thanks also to Harold & Norman Dow, who managed Justine's and contributed mightily to our success.

Finally, I dedicate this book to the thousands of patrons who supported us at Lucifer's, Leviticus, Justine's, Brandi, and Bogard's. Many of you encouraged me to write this book because it was an important part of our lives and none of us want it to be forgotten.

Chapter 1
TURNING TO GOLD

"*It's time.*"

His voice couldn't be heard over the music, so Danny leaned over and signaled to Tony to give the bartenders a heads up. A virtuoso of the vinyl, Danny was so skilled at DJing that he intuitively knew when the frenzied dancers needed a break. Thanks to his turntable magic, the "Theme From Shaft," the hottest song of the day, had been pumping continuously for over 10 minutes, and the dancers were near the point of physical and emotional exhaustion.

A few moments later, Danny slowed down the momentum by playing "Didn't I (Blow Your Mind This Time)" by The Delfonics. The plan worked. More than a hundred thirsty dancers swarmed the bar, but the bartenders were ready for the rush. They quickly quenched the crowd and sent them back to the dance floor.

"Bar sales should look good for the night," Tony pointed out to Mr. Chu, the owner of the club.

Mr. Chu nodded. He was clearly pleased to see so many well-dressed people — more than 300 — jammed into his building on a random Thursday night.

I was at the front door with CP and Andre. When Danny glanced over at us, CP gave him a thumbs up.

The year was 1971. The place was the Ginza, a dance club one flight down from street level on East 58th Street between Madison and Park Avenues in New York City. And it was the first of many soon-to-come events by us, a social club called The Best of Friends (commonly shortened to TBOF). We were eight members doing what we loved, but that night was especially memorable due to the high level of energy generated compared to the dances we had previously been giving with live bands.

Guests, dressed in sharp business suits and stylish dresses, were on their toes dancing the Penguin as multi-colored lights bathed them. It was a young, rather conservative crowd. Still, the combination of powerful, crystal-clear music, rapidly-changing colored lights, and the emotion of dancing created a primal connection to all on the dance floor. The faint aroma of perfume and cologne mixed with that of perspiration from the dancers.

Dancing the Penguin required a lot of energy and stamina. Most dancers were glistening. Some were in a full sweat. The few people who weren't dancing watched intently, mesmerized by the visual and audio spectacle they were experiencing. It was unlikely any of them had ever witnessed anything like this before.

DJing is an art. It requires the DJ to have his pulse on the music scene and to constantly search for new, hip, danceable sounds. Danny and CP could read the crowd and knew when dancers wanted to reach a higher level of energy. There was an unprecedented, somewhat magical communion between DJ and dancers. It led to a tailored-to-the-moment playlist that encouraged non-stop dancing at a level of intensity that was previously impossible. I was one of eight partners that organized this disco dance party, which guests described as new, fresh, and exciting. I asked CP how he decided what record to play next. He responded "You have to decide if this beat goes well with that beat. It hits you."

During earlier dance parties that we gave, Danny and CP taught themselves how to cue up a song, like "I Got the Feelin'" by James Brown on one turntable, then switch to a song with a similar beat, like "Dance to the Music" by Sly & the Family Stone on another turntable — all without a mixer. They used two turntables and had to switch from "phono 1" to "phono 2," but the change was abrupt, so the second record had to be queued up just right to pull it off. It wasn't always exact, but it was usually pretty close.

The equipment at the Ginza was state of the art, complete with two Technics turntables, earphones and a sound mixer so as the volume on one record was faded down, the volume on a second record was turned up. That made it easier to continue the beat from one song to another compared to switching from "phono 1" to "phono 2". Using the earphones, my DJ partners could

Danny Berry, Tony Cooper, Noel Hankin, Charles "CP" Perry, and Andre Smith

listen to the second record and, at the top of a bar, hold the record still while the turntable continued to spin underneath. The second record would then be released at the precise moment to keep the beat going without interruption. This enabled the music to be seamless, and dancers never missed a step. Danny and CP knew the music well, especially how certain songs started and ended, which was crucial in transitioning from one record to the next.

Some songs were short, maybe 3 minutes long, so our DJs not only had to be extremely knowledgeable about the music but nimble enough to match the beat. With certain red-hot songs, like "Theme from Shaft" by Isaac Hayes, Danny and CP used two copies of the record to extend the song by playing the bridge (the instrumental part in the middle of many songs), or other parts of the song, over and over again. This technique was never experienced before — at least not by our crowd — and it drove dancers wild!

Perhaps because of this technique and the extraordinary sound system, we were enjoying an unexpected wave of enormous popularity, not for ourselves personally, although there was some of that, but for the exciting and welcoming atmosphere we created. It was the birth of a movement, although we didn't know it at the time. As Herschel Johnson wrote in Ebony magazine: "For many people, disco patronage approaches religion."[1] From a business standpoint, everything we touched was turning into gold.

After graduating from college in 1968, we formed TBOF as a social club to host dances just like the ones we gave with our college fraternities and social clubs. There was no financial incentive for what we were doing...we just thought it would be fun. There were eight of us, including me, Noel Hankin. We all lived in Queens, New York except for Mal Woolfolk who lived in Teaneck, New Jersey. Mal didn't join us until 1971 when we specifically sought him out because he seemed to know just about everybody in our cohort and everybody liked him. We believed Mal could attract more people to our events. And he did.

Charles "Danny" Berry lived in Jamaica, a predominantly African Amer-

---

[1] Ebony, February 1977, pg. 54 *Discomaniacs get down, style and profile from coast to coast,* by Herschel Johnson.

ican, middle-class neighborhood in Queens, and graduated from C.W. Post in 1968 where he majored in math. He was a quiet force — smart, analytical, and knowledgeable about music, mainly R&B. Danny was one of those guys who could hear a song and not only tell you who recorded it, but he could tell you something about the performer. He was also very observant. These traits made him an extraordinary DJ because he knew how to gauge the mood of dancers and match it with just the right song. After graduating from college, Danny taught math in a junior high school for special needs children. It was a demanding job, but he had enough spare time for other activities. Danny and I, along with a few friends, formed a couple of social clubs that threw successful parties and dances. This proved to be an important stepping-stone for what was to come — the nationwide craze that seemed to grow out of what we started. It was through Danny that I met Tony.

Tony Cooper lived in St. Albans and graduated in 1968 with a degree in psychology and computer science from the New York Institute of Technology. After graduation, he became a 3rd-grade teacher. Tony was savvy, unassuming, and carried himself in such a way that he commanded respect. When he was in high school, Tony played basketball and baseball in local schoolyards and parks. He had an easy laugh and knew a lot of people. All of us had afro hairstyles in the '60s and '70s, but Tony's afro was one of the biggest around.

During our college years, Tony was president of a social club that he formed along with several friends called the Kingsmen. They had a clubhouse in Queens that Tony rented from his father where they gave much-talked-about, popular parties on Friday and Saturday nights. That clubhouse, called the Kingdom, was where Tony's family lived before moving into a new house. The Kingsmen had an attractive and loyal following of mostly middle-class African Americans who primarily lived in the St. Albans and Hollis areas.

The experiences that Tony, Danny and I, plus a few more of our friends, had during the late '60s, prepared us for a journey that dramatically changed the way many New Yorkers socialized. The enormous success of the Ginza was a harbinger of what was to come. But there was no way to anticipate that the impact of our events and the music of the '70s would continue to be so influential to this day, now 50 years later.

Chapter 2
QUEENS TO HARLEM

"*Hey, man! Where are the parties tonight?*"

Andre never knew where the parties were, but he was one of my few friends who had his own car, a VW Beetle. I didn't have a car, but I always had a list of parties. Since we both had something of value to offer each other, we often hung out together. We got along well and grew to be close friends in short order.

Andre Smith was raised by his mother in the Ravenswood Projects in Astoria, Queens. That's a pretty tough environment to grow up in, but he excelled in school and graduated from Fordham University. Andre was smart, savvy, and loved technology. He also loved socializing and going to parties. I got to know Andre in the '60s when we were college students. Although we went to different colleges, we pledged the same fraternity, which is how we met. We bonded over our mutual love of music, dancing, and socializing. I was also close to Danny Berry and hung out with him on occasion, but he didn't always have access to a car. However, Danny was one of my best sources for party addresses. Many parties were in the St. Albans area, which is near where Danny lived.

I lived on the other side of town near Baisley Park in the South Jamaica neighborhood of Queens, a more modest community. During the '60s we never went to parties in my neighborhood, or Andre's for that matter. The parties I am talking about were house parties given by young adults who either knew us or knew of us. Parties were typically held in the parents' homes, often in the basement. We didn't need an invite. We were almost always welcomed when we arrived. Neighborhoods with the nicest houses typically had the best parties. These nicer neighborhoods were St. Albans, Hollis, Cambria Heights, and Springfield Gardens. But there were also many good parties in Manhattan, Brooklyn and, on occasion, in New Jersey or out on Long Island.

Andre wanted to make money. He wanted to earn a comfortable living and afford the nicer things in life, therefore his career aspirations were focused on business and felt this was his best avenue. I suspect growing up in the projects honed his ambition for something better. He had a large, saltwater fish tank in his mother's apartment. He took that fish tank with him when he got his own apartment on the Upper West Side, which was a big project since his tropical fish were delicate and required the water to be just so. I think Andre liked his saltwater fish because they were unique…a bit of a status symbol. Andre also loved technology and delighted in being the first to get the newest, coolest, latest gadgets and devices, such as computers and telephones. He was one of my few friends who owned a reel-to-reel tape recorder, which we used often for fraternity and house parties. His tape recorder was a Teac, the best brand for a high-fidelity sound. Andre wanted only the top-quality electronics.

Wayne Scarbrough was also a good friend. He was smart, practical, and loved to party. As an undergraduate at St. John's University, he was the best breaststroke swimmer in New York City. Not many people were aware of his accomplishment because we didn't have much interest in swimming as a sport. And Wayne was the kind of guy who wouldn't bring it up. But if you asked him, he would tell you about it. Wayne was an only child and lived with his parents in a well-manicured house near Rochdale Village, the world's largest housing co-op when it was built.

Although we all went to college, it wasn't a given. Wayne and I went to Shimer Junior High School, grades 7-9, where only a small percentage of

Wayne Scarbrough

students were college-bound, so an academic-oriented high school was not in the cards for most. However, some of us wanted to go to college and I was among them. I got good grades, so I figured I was on track. One day, though, I was called to the guidance counselor's office.

"Next year, when you move to high school, you will go to Woodrow Wilson Vocational High School," my counselor told me rather matter-of-factly.

"Woodrow Wilson?", my mind was spinning.

"Of course," she replied. "It is the closest high school to your house. You'll be able to choose from many different trades to learn...auto mechanic, carpentry, welding. You should have no trouble finding a job right after high school."

She was right. But I knew that I wanted to take a different route.

"I want to go to college."

I will never forget the look on her face. It was pure disappointment. In the 1960s, guidance counselors didn't encourage everyone to go to college. Their job was to steer people, particularly black males, toward vocational training.

"John Adams is already over-crowded," she explained. "There is no room for you there." John Adams was the closest academic high school to my neighborhood. I didn't know anything about it other than the fact that it had an academic curriculum, which was essential if you wanted to go to college. Students at Woodrow Wilson were rough around the edges and seemed older than high school age like they were already weary of the drudgery.

"But, I want to go to college," I repeated.

I wasn't the only one. There were enough Shimer students on my side of town who wanted an academic education to justify creating a John Adams High School annex at Woodrow Wilson. That fall, about a hundred of us went to the annex for the 10th grade. Since the main building of John Adams was several miles away, we missed out on all extracurricular activities — no band, no track team, no opportunity to write for the school newspaper. I had to wait to do all these things until we attended the 11th and 12th grades in the main building.

Aside from delivering the Long Island Daily Press newspaper to subscribers, my first summer job was with the Great Atlantic & Pacific Tea Company, otherwise known as the A&P. I had to go to their headquarters office in downtown Manhattan to take a test. I did well on the test — so well that my score surprised the administrators. I was only 16 but based on my test score, I was eligible to man a cash register in my local store. But when I reported for duty at my local A&P, all they wanted me to do was take out the garbage and pull and dust the shelves. Pulling shelves meant pulling cans and boxes forward to the front of each shelf, to make the shelves look full and tidy. Looking back, I should have insisted on manning a cash register.

As a senior at John Adams, I took advanced placement (AP) classes in physics, biology, and chemistry to help prepare for a career in medicine. I did well at John Adams and started making plans for college. Once again, I sought the advice of the school counselor. My parents were immigrants from the Caribbean and not good at navigating the college admission system. And once again, I was disappointed by what my guidance counselor told me.

"Don't apply to Queens College. You need a 90 average to get in and you only have an 88 average so you will lose your $10 application fee," the counselor told me.

Queens College was part of the City University of New York (CUNY) and tuition was free if you qualified. My parents had already told me they wanted me to go to college, but they didn't have the money to pay for it. I was not aware of student loans or academic scholarships so going away to college was out of the question. Therefore, when the counselor advised me not to even apply to Queens College, I didn't think to question it. I was deflated but figured I'd work during the day and go to school at night. Fortunately, I mentioned my situation to a friend named Ricky Mangum. Ricky told me that if I applied to Queens College, they would "bicycle" the application to the other CUNY colleges in the order I specified so that each could determine if I qualified. Based on that advice, I applied and listed Queens College first, then the other four-year colleges and finally the community colleges.

I was jubilant when an acceptance letter arrived from Queens College. What my guidance counselor failed to recognize was that my three AP courses pushed my GPA well over 90. Since AP classes are taught at the college level, 10 points were added to adjust them to a high school grade. It was a lesson learned; if you don't manage your own life, others will manage it for you. I felt stupid for blindly listening to bad advice without questioning it. I committed right there never to let anyone else decide what I could or couldn't do.

After receiving the acceptance letter, I gathered up my good friend Big Don, who lived up the street, and we rode our bicycles the six miles to Flushing to see my new campus. Big Don was college-bound, but not at Queens College. He was planning to go to Long Island University. I had never been on a college campus before so I was extremely disappointed when we got there, and the security guard wouldn't let us in. I politely explained that I was

Richard "Ricky" Mangum

accepted to start that fall, but the guard remained adamant about not letting us in. I realized at that moment that I should have made an appointment for a tour. It was a Saturday afternoon, the campus seemed deserted, and here we were on our bikes. Looking back, the guard was just doing his job but at that moment I felt like I didn't belong. Big Don and I settled for riding around the perimeter of the campus and stopping occasionally to peer through the fence.

Forty years later, I contributed to a construction project at Queens College and my name is now on a brick in the Alumni Plaza at the entrance to the campus, just a few feet from where I was refused entry. Around the same time, I was honored by Queens College as one of their top 100 Alumni Stars in the history of the school. Since QC was a large school with 20,000 students, that was quite an honor and it gave me a feeling of redemption.

During our junior year of college, Wayne Scarbrough and I pledged Kappa Alpha Psi Fraternity, a national organization with an off-campus chapter in Harlem. Andre Smith and Ricky Mangum pledged the year before. At that time, colleges and universities in the New York City area had relatively small numbers of black students on each campus so black Greek-letter organizations tended to exist off-campus and allowed eligible students to pledge from any accredited college or university in the New York metro area. Pledging was done under the auspices of the alumni chapters. The alumni big brothers kept tighter reins on us than a college or university would and, importantly, they cared about us personally.

Pledging off campus was not easy. A typical on-campus pledge period lasted six weeks or so. Instead we pledged for six months since we only met on weekends. During weekdays we had projects to work on like making paddles, learning about the fraternity, and memorizing personal information about our line brothers. Wayne and I were part of the "Unshakable 9" so we had to learn about eight other brothers. That meant memorizing the names of all relatives, ages, key dates, home addresses, phone numbers, and so on. Also, traveling from Queens to Harlem for meetings at the Kappa Kastle was time-consuming — over an hour each way by bus and subway. Some days I made two round trips, one for a pledge meeting during the day and another to go to parties. I always got a ride to go to the parties, so I only needed to use public transportation for the meetings.

Prior to pledging, I rarely went to parties because my class load was heavy. The semester I pledged Kappa I had an exceptionally challenging schedule. My courses included physics, German, calculus, biochemistry, and English literature — all difficult courses, especially biochemistry. As a pledge, I was exposed to a whole new world of heavy-duty socializing. There were many activities at the Kappa Kastle in Harlem and all across the metro area. Since my line brothers were going to different colleges, I got turned onto a wide array of new social circles and parties.

The Kappa Kastle was on West 141st Street in Harlem. There was a large shield in the window featuring the diamond-shaped Kappa logo and our secret motto: Phi Nu Pi. As you entered the Kappa Kastle, there was a small entrance foyer followed by a reception room. The walls were adorned with framed photographs of the founders and there was a staircase to the upper floors. The rear room on the ground floor was set up for meetings with theater-style seats and beautiful wood-paneled walls. This is where we held chapter meetings. Pictures of all previous Polemarchs (our name for president) were displayed on one wall. The second floor had two large rooms; one with a bar and café tables, the other was bare and served as a dance floor with a couple of bench seats on one side. The upper two floors were off-limits to non-Kappas. They had a few couches and were used primarily for rituals, pledge meetings, and for brothers who just wanted to hang out for a while or spend the night if they couldn't make it home.

The Alpha Phi Alpha fraternity had a house one block down the hill on Convent Avenue. Their house was bigger than the Kappa Kastle and the limestone exterior was much more impressive. Omega Psi Phi, also known as the Qs, had two houses, one nine blocks north on 150th Street off Amsterdam Avenue and the other in the Bushwick section of Brooklyn. Kappas and Qs gave plenty of parties, but the Alphas…not very often. They were known as the most studious of these three fraternities.

I was having a great time. Too great. I loved my new level of exposure and access to an enormous network of impressive new friends and acquaintances. I guess it's fair to say that I went wild and shirked my real responsibilities. Shortly after being inducted, it dawned on me that it had been two months since I attended any of my classes. The best option for me was to drop all the classes or else suffer a failing grade in each one. But the deadline for dropping classes had passed. As a result, I got a big fat "F" for all 18 credits that semester and failed out of day school. To be re-admitted as a matriculated student, I had to take night classes and get good enough grades to pull my GPA over 2.0. Plus, I had to pay for night classes, which put a strain on my budget. That was motivation enough. I buckled down, earned an A- average that semester of night school, and qualified to get back into day school. That meant no more tuition payments.

Music and dancing were, and still are, an important part of black fraternity life. An entrenched tradition among these fraternities was that we would sing at our parties. Some songs were old and traditional. But we also took contemporary songs and changed the words to praise our fraternity and sometimes disparage rival fraternities. Wayne was good at writing lyrics. He wrote a pledge song to The Tyme's "Somewhere." The original verse was:

Somewhere my love waits for me.
Somewhere beyond the sky and sea.
Somewhere I'll see her and my heart will know
This is the face that I love so.

Wayne's re-write went like this:

Somewhere my pin waits for me,
Somewhere beyond the sky and sea.
I'm pledging Kappa, 'cause my heart has known,
This is the frat that I love so-oo-oo.

After crossing the burning sands, one of our favorite songs was the Temptations' "My Girl." We simply replaced the words "My girl" with "Kappa." We also had custom lyrics to Curtis Mayfield's "I'm So Proud," The Parliament's "I Wanna Testify," Marvin Gaye and Tammy Terrell's "Ain't No Mountain High Enough," and Tennessee Ernie Ford's "Sixteen Tons." This last song had humorous lyrics that abused other fraternities. We sang three or four songs at every party we gave, as did other fraternities. Although we were rivals and often sang lyrics that belittled the other guys, we were all friendly toward each other and extended invites to each other's get-togethers and parties. Some members of rival fraternities became best friends. It was a fun time and fraternity life took on a high level of importance.

The two largest black sororities in New York, Alpha Kappa Alpha and Delta Sigma Theta, also gave dances. I went to almost all of them. On several occasions, Kappa Alpha Psi partnered with the AKAs to give Alpha Kappa Alpha Psi Dances. With my fairly extensive exposure to dances, I learned a lot about how to organize them. I could see what worked and what didn't. I could identify important issues, such as marketing strategies, lead time requirements, venue and band costs, the impact of band selection, crowd flow, etc. A key takeaway was that to get a good turnout, you have to focus on the ladies. If the ladies talk up a dance in advance, the guys will be there.

A successful dance was important because it was a powerful recruiting tool for new pledges. The idea was to price tickets to attract a good-sized crowd to ensure a social success and generate positive word of mouth feedback. Proceeds from the dance had to cover the cost of renting the hall, mailing out flyers, and pay for two bands. The venue took care of the bar since they held the liquor license. Two bands were always needed so that one could play while the other was taking a break. Typically, one band played R&B and the other Latin music.

During a ten-year span, African Americans in the New York area developed a strong love affair with Latin music. That's why Latin bands were so popular at our dances. Roughly from 1960 to 1970, most dances and house parties featured a Latin music set to allow dancers to show off their mambo steps or cha cha cha or merengue. If a host didn't play Latin music, guests would complain. People practiced their Latin steps, mainly the mambo, and looked forward to showing off their moves at parties and dances. Those who didn't learn how to Latin had to sit on the sidelines when Latin music was played, but at least they were entertained. Some dancers were so good, other dancers would clear the floor to give them more room and so that they could watch the show too. The creativity of turns and moves was often amazing.

During our college years in the '60s, the songs we enjoyed included "Acuye" and "Alto Songo" by Johnny Pacheco, "El Molestoso" and "Azucar Pa' Ti" by Eddie Palmieri, and "Oye Como Va" and "Ran Kan Kan" by Tito Puente, among others. To be able to dance to these Latin songs, you had to know what you were doing. It required practice. Many people had fancy moves and turns, but the real challenge was to make sure your steps remained in sync. The male dancer had to dance his steps flawlessly in order to guide his partner. Either you knew it or you didn't. You couldn't fake it.

Tony and Danny had the best Latin moves in our group. They could steal the spotlight whenever they stepped onto the dance floor. Good dancers inspired others to practice more often, and some to not even try. After all, if you didn't dance well, people might talk about you. I was on the cusp. I found the mambo to be difficult and didn't venture onto the dance floor very often when Latin music was playing. Although my mambo and other Latin steps weren't very good, I loved the music, and to this day, I still do.

CP lived in South Jamaica and returned home in 1965 after serving 1 ½ years in the Air Force. He was honorably discharged with a bad back and immediately enrolled in the Fashion Institute of Technology. Everyone loved CP because he was the kind of guy who enjoyed life and made ordinary occasions seem like big fun. He had a natural smile and laughed with an infectious, disarming chuckle. CP, with his tall and wiry frame, was also an excellent dancer and had lots of innovative twists and turns on the dance floor. When he danced, many eyes were on him. Although, like me, dancing to Latin music was not his strength. At least, that was my opinion.

Some of the other popular Latin artists were Ray Rodriguez, Willie

Charles "CP" Perry

Colon, Ray Barretto, Charlie Palmieri, Bobby Rodriquez, Ricardo Ray, and Hector Lavoe. Folks loved to dance to their tunes. Later, as Latin Boogaloo and Latin Shing-a-Ling sounds grew in popularity, groups like Joe Cuba, Joe Bataan, Pete Rodriguez, Mongo Santamaria, and Willie Bobo began to push out the mambo and other classic Latin dance sounds with Latin jazz and Latin/R&B blends. The rise of Latin/R&B sounds was born in clubs like the Palladium where both types of music were being played. Of course, the many college fraternity and sorority dances probably fed into the blending of R&B and Latin musical sounds as well since they also featured R&B and Latin bands.

This newly blended music was wildly popular, but for those who loved to dance classic Latin dances, the crossover sounds were a dilution. Latin Boogaloo and Shing-a-ling music hastened the demise of classic Latin ballroom dances, at least among African Americans. When the new sounds became overly commercialized and mainstream, it lost some of its appeal. Compared to the classic Latin sounds, Shing-a-ling and Latin Boogaloo were a flash in the pan. These new sounds and dances were hot, but just for a minute; their energy faded fast. We would see this happen again, but at the time, all we knew was that the classic Latin dance craze ended among blacks around 1970.

None of us knew it then, but we were on a trajectory that would change the lives of thousands of people in profound ways. It changed our lives, too.

Chapter 3
"IF IT'S FREE, IT'S ME"

"We're the Intruders."

One night, Danny, CP and I went to a party and, although we knew no one, we got in anyway. Not sure who said it, but one of us jokingly said we were "intruders." The Intruders were a hot singing group at the time. Once inside, CP and Danny put on a show on the dance floor and I could hear people whispering to each other "That's the Intruders!"

We all lived in nearby but different neighborhoods and, for the most part, commuted to different local colleges while living with our parents. This meant we were able to stay in touch throughout the year. We were good friends and spent a fair amount of time together during our college years in the '60s. We knew each other from parties or fraternity life. On a few occasions, we would get together to play basketball, paddleball, cards, or go to concerts together as a group. We saw Buddy Miles, the Four Tops, the Temptations' "In a Mellow Mood" concert at the Copacabana, and Johnny Mathis with dates at a club in Newark, New Jersey.

But house parties were our main preoccupation. Every Thursday evening during our college years, we would get on the phone to compare notes about where the parties were for the upcoming weekend and who was going to drive. I didn't party much as a freshman, but after I pledged Kappa, I did. For people like me, who didn't have a car, it made a difference if you knew of a good party. I was always able to get a ride, mostly with Danny or Andre, but occasionally with CP. Most folks in our circle didn't need a formal invitation. Because we were well-known, odds were that if the host didn't know us, he or she probably knew of us. Sometimes just knowing a friend of the host was enough. A commonly held perspective was that being a member of a national fraternity or a popular social club, like the Kingsmen, was an assurance that we were okay. There was a lot of truth to that.

While the parties in Queens were often held in the basement, in other boroughs, they were typically in the living room of small apartments or brownstones. When we had multiple addresses for parties we generally hit the ones we felt were in the nicest spaces first. During the summer months, there were backyard parties, mostly in Queens, and occasionally out on Long Island in towns like Hempstead and Westbury or in northern New Jersey. On at least one occasion, we cruised around St. Albans on a July 4th holiday in the afternoon looking for signs of a party. There were about four of us in the car and, among us, we pretty much knew someone on every block. We would look for smoke from a BBQ grill and an abundance of parked cars to determine where the party was. Then we'd just walk in as if we were invited. If the party was a dud or we didn't like the vibe, we would simply say "Sorry, I think we got the wrong address." We didn't always find a good party, but we found one often enough.

Pledging Kappa introduced me to a lot of new people, places, and parties. It also introduced me to the world of Harlem nightclubs. This was an exciting and new experience for me. Harlem had an array of clubs, most featuring live music. You could tell which clubs had the best music by noting if there were double parked cars in front. When clubs were particularly hot, there were even triple parked cars. I went to every single one of these clubs, most of them only once, just to see what they were like. I felt like I was stepping into another world. Once inside one of these clubs — especially if it had a good band playing — the energy level was high, people were well-dressed, and the crowd was interactive, meaning they responded audibly to what they were hearing. Periodically you would hear an announcement such as "Would the owner of a white Cadillac convertible, license plate number such and such, please move your car." This is how folks who were blocked in would get out.

The most popular clubs that I remember were Big Wilt's Smalls Paradise, the Baby Grand, Jock's, St. Nick's Pub, Red Rooster, Lenox Lounge, Showman's, and Count Basie's. Interestingly, none of these clubs had dancing, at least not on the nights I was there. One of the most memorable live acts I saw was Jimmy Castor at Smalls Paradise. Castor was a real showman, meaning there were triple parked cars and high energy in the room. Even though we booked Castor at several of our fraternity dances, I never got to know him. I was always focused on greeting people at the door and mingling with guests inside.

Going to parties was the bulk of the social life for most of us while we were college students during the '60s because, aside from gas and toll money to get there, they were free. We heard of occasional rent parties in Manhattan but we never went to them. After all, we had so many free party options it made no sense to pay. We also went to Riis Beach and Jones Beach on weekends during the summer where you would see just about everyone. Few of us went away on vacation during the summer and none of us had access to country clubs. Local bars and clubs were expensive, and we generally had no money. Our motto was "If it's free, it's me." Plus, the local bars catered primarily to an older crowd, and fancy downtown bars were predominantly white and didn't feel welcoming to us. In contrast, house parties always had friends or at least familiar faces. Additionally, once you were at a party, you often found out about more parties from other guests. It was not unusual for us to hit two or three parties each on Friday and Saturday nights.

An important ritual we had during that time was to grab a bite to eat after we left the last party. Around 3 or 4 am we would go to an all-night eatery. If we were in Harlem, we often went to Sherman's for ribs. The first time I went to Sherman's I ordered mac and cheese with my ribs. But after noticing that many of my fraternity brothers ordered spaghetti with their ribs, I gave it a shot even though it didn't seem like a good combination. Nevertheless, I became a big fan. All of Sherman's various locations closed down years ago, but to this day, whenever I have a chance to eat some down-home ribs and spaghetti in tomato sauce — I go for it. On occasion, if we wanted to splurge, we would go to the famous Wells Supper Club on 7th Avenue (re-named Adam Clayton Powell, Jr. Boulevard in 1974) and 132nd Street for chicken & waffles – another combination that was new to me. I grew up in a Jamaican household and had never heard of these unusual food combinations but they were so good, you got hooked after one meal.

After going to parties in Queens or out on Long Island, we would go to an all-night diner called TADs on Rockaway Boulevard near JFK Airport, or the White Castle on Hollis Avenue and Francis Lewis Boulevard. We'd order breakfast at TADs or maybe a hamburger and play a few songs on the juke-box terminals that were on some of the tables. We'd often see groups of other friends and compare notes about how good or bad their parties were and who was seen with whom. Sometimes, these sessions were more fun than the parties themselves. We always had big conversations at TADs, but we couldn't compare notes much at White Castle because we typically ate in our cars. What was amazing to me when we went to White Castle, was to watch Andre, who was smaller than average, eat a dozen greasy White Castle burgers with no problem. I had never seen anyone eat a dozen White Castles before. I had a little more height than Andre, but it was a strain for me to eat just six!

Parties were easy to give. During college years, almost all were at our parents' homes. All we needed was a turntable, a place to dance, and something to drink, most often a punch. Nibbles were present, but if you arrived late, chances were all the food would be gone. There were many parties where space was tight, but at that stage in our lives, no one minded. We actually preferred crowded parties because it felt more like a happening. To keep the guests dancing, someone had to continuously man the record player to keep the music going. This was an important and demanding job but it was fun to select the music. The big drawback was that it cut into socializing time. A major advance was the use of a reel-to-reel tape recorder that could provide an hour or two of prerecorded music. Of course, this eliminated the opportunity to "read" the crowd to determine what song to play next. Andre not only had a reel-to-reel tape recorder, but he also had tapes with great music. We used his equipment often at the Kappa Kastle and, on many occasions, close friends prevailed upon Andre to bring his reel-to-reel to their party. Some of us got to know his playlists pretty well. But we never got tired of them.

We went to many parties in neighborhoods that we didn't know. With no GPS, we wasted a lot of time making wrong turns in places where we didn't know the local streets, often in New Jersey, Brooklyn, Hempstead, and other parts of Long Island. On many nights we spent more time in the car than at parties. One night we never even found the party. After searching unsuccessfully for most of the night, we just abandoned the hunt and went to breakfast.

Social organizations were, and continue to be, an important part of African American life, particularly among those with a college degree. That cohort enjoyed socializing among themselves because of their many shared experiences. All ethnic or societal segments tend to socialize among themselves, but none have as many formal social organizations as African Americans. These organizations are a direct legacy of racial discrimination and the Jim Crow era, which blocked African Americans from joining white organizations. Hispanics and other ethnic groups have far fewer organizations because most arrived after many discriminatory policies were removed. Also, some Hispanics joined African American organizations. We had, for example, a good sprinkling of Latinos in Kappa Alpha Psi Fraternity. In New York City, there was a slight overlap between African Americans and Puerto Ricans in terms of social circles.

There were, and still are, literally hundreds of social organizations in black communities across the country. Most were formed in the early to mid-20th century and have survived through many generations. Some are national organizations with local chapters that meet regularly and hold annual or biennial conventions, while others are local clubs and emphasize personal relationships. One might think integration would eventually weaken these organizations or render them obsolete, but to the contrary, they have been growing. An important reason for their allure is the comfort in knowing that members will fit in and be accepted. In my experience, most African Americans find that socializing with white folks informally over drinks is not always a comfortable thing to do. One never knows what will be done or said that creates discomfort or other problems. Plus, there are cultural differences. For example, blacks tend to be more focused on dancing and fashion. While many whites love to dance, it is not as popular an activity as it is among African Americans. These factors help explain why black social organizations have thrived and continue to be an important part of black life.

Another significant benefit of joining one of the national black social organizations is that if you moved to a different metro area, you could simply transfer your membership and plug into a group of people with similar backgrounds and interests… and instantly connect with a comfortable social circle. Membership provided a secure sense of belonging and connection. These organizations existed, and still exist, to provide an array of social events and contacts in welcoming environments. Some have a clubhouse or headquarters where they can meet. Other organizations hold meetings in members' homes or restaurants.

Among African Americans, fraternity members tend to be active as undergrads, less active right after college when many members would get married and raise families. Then, after the kids are grown and leave the house, many become active again. As a result, alumni chapters are larger than undergraduate chapters.

Aside from the Greek letter organizations, the vast majority of major black social organizations are geared toward older adults or post-college and are typically all male or all female. The few organizations that involve men and women are usually dominated by the women such as Jack & Jill of America or Cup & Saucer. For families living in predominantly white neighborhoods, Jack & Jill is especially important since it might be the primary vehicle to expose one's children to other black kids. Once a child passes the age of 18, they are no longer eligible to be a member or participate in Jack & Jill events.

Many social organizations have been around for generations and are still thriving. The Greek letter organizations cater to both undergraduate and alumni men and women except for Sigma Pi Phi, which is a fraternity that has no undergraduate component. It caters exclusively to college graduates who are high achievers in their chosen field. Members of Sigma Pi Phi include many of the most prominent African Americans such as Rev. Dr. Martin Luther King, Jr., Tom Shropshire, Ralph Bunche, W.E.B. DuBois, Arthur Ashe, and Congressman John Lewis. (See Appendix I for a sampling of national and local African American organizations)

In 1967, I was at a party one night when Ricky asked if I'd like to join him and Danny in forming a new social club with two other friends, Reggie Washington and Bob Harris, who were members of Omega Psi Phi, also known as the Qs. We happened to all be at the same party that night. It did seem a bit unusual for me to partner with Qs in a social club since, in a way, they were competitors. But to be part of something new seemed exciting, especially since this specific group of guys was particularly popular, smart, and savvy.

Danny went to many fraternity events even though he didn't pledge any. But because he knew so many people, he was invited to many parties and was always one of the best dancers, which made him even more popular. Many women considered Danny a friend and they all had a lot of respect for him, so I knew he was a good guy. Reggie was the best singer among the Qs and was extremely popular because he helped them shine when they sang at parties and other events. Everyone knew and loved Reggie. Bob had a conservative side but he was smart, witty, and always fun to hang out with. Ricky, of course, was my Kappa brother and close friend. In addition to being a highly regarded go-to man for information, Ricky had a big personality and a great sense of humor. That's why so many people liked him. Ricky was also an organizer and creating this social club was his idea. We all agreed to join. We each had our own set of contacts and somewhat different social circles so I knew that any party we gave would be well attended and a social success.

We called our new social club the Raunchy Five. Ricky came up with the name. I know it's counterintuitive, but as popular undergrads and being well-known among our cohort in Queens and beyond, we had the luxury of having an outlandish, risqué sounding name. Our followers knew that we would only put on quality events and attract desirable people. It didn't matter what we called ourselves.

We played recorded music at our parties. The first one was held in a local dive bar in Jamaica on Sutphin Boulevard. Even though the venue was pretty tattered, and the décor was dated, our crowd was the "in-crowd." They had a ball…and told their friends about it. That helped establish our reputation as a reliable source for great parties. Our second party was held at the American Legion Hall, also in Jamaica. At the American Legion event, the entrance to the party was not obvious. There were three different entrances and they were located in different parts of the building, so we created a poster with directional information and leaned it up against a monument in the front yard of the building. There was a long staircase to get to the side entrance of the building and a few additional steps to get to the door that was our entrance.

About an hour into the party, Ricky told me there was an irate man at the door. Danny joined us as we walked over to find out what was happening.

"How disrespectful!" he was yelling.

The man was old and stooped, and while he didn't pose a physical threat, we were concerned because he was so angry.

"Sir, calm down," Ricky said, holding his palms up to the man. "What's the trouble?"

He was upset that we placed a party poster in front of a memorial for a WWII hero. It must have been a memorial for one of his buddies. The man was so incensed that he tore our poster into little pieces.

"We apologize," Danny explained to the man. "We didn't know."

The vet responded, "Well, you should know!"

After the offended veteran huffed away, we took turns standing outside the American Legion to let guests know where to go. The incident made me think about the enormous pressure veterans must have felt during combat, losing buddies left and right, and the mental toll it must have taken on them.

We followed up the Raunchy Five with an expanded roster of members and changed our name to Low Life Limited. Again, our group was so well-known and popular, that what we called ourselves didn't matter. The Raunchy Five and Low Life Limited parties were strictly for fun. We weren't thinking about making money. The admission fee was simply a way to cover the cost of giving the party and to control the crowd. We didn't want just anyone walking in. The parties were well attended and successful, but the level of energy and excitement was low compared to the glamour of dances we gave as Kappas and Qs. After all, our parties were just in Queens and were a lot smaller. We wanted more. And we were about to get it.

Chapter 4
BAMBOOZLED

"*Excuse me. Were you invited?*"

In the spring of 1968, a friend named Renell Fisher invited me to Barbra Streisand's birthday party. Renell lived on West 95th Street and was big into the arts. He turned me onto cultural events such as the Alvin Nikolais Dance Company. Renell also loved theater, concerts, and the like. As it turned out, Renell, was not actually invited to the Streisand party, but somehow, he had gotten the address. It was a mansion on East 82nd Street, right off 5th Avenue near the Metropolitan Museum of Art — a very ritzy neighborhood.

Since Renell didn't have an invite, we came up with a plan to crash the party. I got Andre to drive that night; Renell sat in the front passenger seat while I sat in the back. We all wore jackets and ties since that was the accepted uniform for just about anything. When we pulled up to the address, a security person was standing next to the open front door, so we knew we were at the right location. Andre hopped out of the driver's seat first and ran around to the curbside to open the door for me and then closed the door after

I emerged. Renell got out of the front passenger seat carrying my jacket. He helped put the jacket on me then dusted off my shoulders in a conspicuous way. The three of us walked up the steps of the Streisand mansion. I was in the lead and Andre and Renell followed as if they were my retinue. As we approached the security guard, I gave him a confident "Good evening!" He nodded and without questioning us, moved aside so we could enter.

The party was in the large, elegantly appointed parlor room of a limestone mansion. It wasn't crowded, but the people who were there were huddled in small groups. This would have been Barbra's 26th birthday, but most people in the room were quite a bit older. I guess they were managers, agents, record company execs, and the like. At 21 and 22, we felt young in that crowd. We could feel eyes on us. And since we didn't mingle with any of the other guests, it made us stand out. The fact that we were the only African Americans in the room didn't help. 5 minutes later, a man came over and asked if we were invited. After confessing we were not, we quickly headed for the door and walked out just as confidently as we walked in. We had been caught, but we bragged about going to that party anyway. It didn't matter that we never even saw Barbra.

That same year, Ricky, Danny, CP, and I partnered with four guys from Manhattan to give a dance at the Manhattan Center. We figured the partnership would make the event more successful than if we gave it by ourselves and we were right. The dance was a great success…well attended and lots of fun. My Queens partners and I anticipated that net proceeds would be several hundred dollars. After all, we had given dances before and knew how to gauge the profit margin. But at the end of the night, our new partners, the group of guys from Manhattan, announced that they paid all the bills but no money was leftover. They controlled the door therefore they controlled the money, but we knew that couldn't be right. We called everyone together in a quiet corner of the lobby, away from the main entrance, and confronted the Manhattan guys.

"What do you mean there's nothing left?" Ricky asked in disbelief.

The Manhattan guys simply repeated their claim that no money was leftover. They explained that the take at the door was just enough to pay the bands and the hall rental…nothing more. No profit. The speech seemed rehearsed.

We eyed the Manhattan guys for a long moment before giving each other a knowing look. We didn't believe them, of course. But we couldn't prove anything because we didn't collect cash at the door — they did. We had been bamboozled.

We had no recourse other than to chalk it up to a learning experience and vowed to never work with the Manhattan guys again. It was this incident that led to the official formation of The Best of Friends. We had been looking for new socializing opportunities, which is how we ended up partnering with the guys from Manhattan in the first place. It started a few months back.

Since Danny, Ricky, CP, and I lived in Queens, and our experience in giving dances was at venues primarily in Manhattan, we decided to partner with the group of guys from Manhattan to help attract folks from Manhattan and the Bronx. We barely knew the four guys but had heard they had a good following. We called our combined group of eight men City-Wide Associates and planned to stage a dance in March of 1968 at the Manhattan Center on West 34th Street. We hired two popular bands: the Manhattans, a hot singing group that had a big hit with "Follow Your Heart" and Latin music star Joe Cuba. Cuba who had a bunch of big hits, like "I'll Never Go Back To Georgia" and "Bang Bang", that helped establish him as the "Father of Latin Boogaloo".

We all chipped in to pay for the bands, which were $600 each, as well as other expenses. From any perspective, the event was a success. It was hard to tell how many people the Manhattan folks attracted, but I recall seeing lots of folks from Queens and some from Manhattan that we invited. We were pleased to see the room full, and that everyone had a good time. We thought everything was going as planned until the Manhattan guys swindled us for our take of the profits. We learned to never relinquish control of the door to someone we didn't know well.

———————————

A couple of weeks after the Manhattan incident, CP, Danny, Ricky, and I decided to create a new social club with friends we felt we could trust. Ricky arranged for us to meet at Maloney's, an old-time neighborhood dive bar on Sutphin Boulevard near Hillside Avenue in Jamaica. None of us hung out at Maloney's, but it was located in the main shopping district that served our part of Queens, so everyone knew the area.

One of the first things I saw when I entered Maloney's was a large jar of pickled pigs' feet on the bar. It looked like a scientific specimen, like the ones that were in my college biology classrooms. I wasn't hungry, but it took away my appetite anyway. I had never been inside Maloney's before but thought it was strange and disgusting to have such repulsive looking food sitting in plain sight on the bar near the entrance. The bartender told me it was always on the bar and that some people loved it — it was a tradition. Years later, I grew to enjoy pigs' feet too, but not the pickled version.

I invited Andre, Wayne, and Big Don to the meeting. CP invited Otis "OP" Perry (CP's brother), Fred Dantzler, and Ted Pettus. Danny invited Tony Cooper, Harry Felder, and Artie Hart. I knew everyone well except for Tony, Harry, and Artie. I had seen them around but didn't know them well. I trusted Danny, and if he said they were trustworthy, that was good enough for me. Plus, based on my conversations with Tony and Harry, our social circles overlapped a lot, which is always a good sign.

Tony and Danny knew just about everyone. When I say "everyone" I mean black folks in our cohort — early 20s and college-oriented. For that group in Queens, we probably had one degree of separation. Andre Smith, Wayne Scarbrough, and Fred Dantzler were not able to make the meeting but told us they definitely wanted to be a part of the new social club. Interest in joining the club was strong because most of us had a track record of giving successful dances and parties and everyone knew it would be fun. The only question was whether everyone had enough time to devote to a new social club.

Maloney's was fairly empty and dark. We went to the rear to be away from any customers who came in after us. We crammed into a large booth under a large moose head hanging on the wall. We ordered beers and spent the first half-hour or so making sure everyone knew each other. We determined that we all had many mutual friends, which made everyone feel more comfortable. When we got down to business, Ricky and I explained the problem we had

Harry Felder

with City-Wide Associates at the Manhattan Center and how the Manhattan guys cheated us.

"For people to put together successful dances, members of the group have to be able to trust each other," CP chimed in.

Ricky added, "It helps if you partner with good friends who you know."

That's when we came up with the name "The Best of Friends." With that, our new social club was born. It was a poignant moment on a day that we will always remember: April 4, 1968, the day Dr. Martin Luther King was assassinated.

Our mission for the new social club, as we envisioned it then, was simply to give dances, not so much to make money, but to have fun and enhance our social lives. The Best of Friends (TBOF) initially began with twelve members. We each chipped in seed money to cover the cost of printing tickets and to place deposits on the hall and bands for the first dance. We knew advance ticket sales would bring in enough money to cover all remaining expenses.

Artie liked the idea of the club but decided not to join. I don't recall his specific reason, but we were all starting, or about to start, our careers and some were getting married. Ted Pettus joined but dropped out a short time later because he started an ad agency called Lockhart & Pettus Advertising that would go on to become one of the most successful black ad agencies in the country. With Ted's departure, eleven members remained. Big Don dropped out next. He had family issues and couldn't devote time to a social club. By the end of 1968, Otis and Ricky also dropped out because of career pressures. Otis had just gotten married and had a high-pressure job in sales at General Foods. Ricky was in law school and he was also married. By 1969, our membership was eight strong: Charles "Danny" Berry, Tony Cooper, Harry Felder, Wayne Scarbrough, Andre Smith, Charles "CP" Perry, Fred Dantzler, and me, Noel Hankin. One key to our successful dances was our comprehensive mailing list. Danny had a friend who was a keypunch operator at IBM. We gave her the names and addresses of all our friends and contacts, and she created

Maloney's where TBOF was founded

The Best of Friends, 1968

a punch card for each person that the computer would then convert to print-ed mailing labels. This was cutting edge technology at the time. We printed invites for each dance, and with the printed labels, mailed out invites to over a thousand socially active folks. They, in turn, helped spread the word. Plus, we all made phone calls to let people know about the dances. But mailing out flyers was our primary promotional tool. Mailings enabled us to control the invites to keep the focus on our college-oriented crowd. The flyers also let our guests know about our dress code. We used the phrase "semi-formal", which meant suits and ties for men and cocktail dresses, suits, or comparable attire

TBOF, 1970 in lobby of Lefrak City: l-r, CP, Tony, Andre, Wayne, Noel, Danny

for women. This dress requirement allowed us to turn away undesirables and random people who just happened to walk up. The Best of Friends (TBOF) gave many successful dances during the next couple of years at venues such as the Hotel Diplomat, the Manhattan Center, the Carlton Terrace, all in Manhattan, and the Concourse Plaza Hotel in the Bronx. Each of our dances made several hundred dollars and enabled us to expand the mailing list. We had lots of fun and goofed around on occasion.

For one dance at the Hotel Diplomat, we added a new feature — a fashion show. Style and fashion were, and still are, important to African Americans. We called our fashion show "Design '69" and recruited a few female friends to help organize the show and assist with rehearsals. "Design '69" was just like our other dances except that during the middle of the evening, we showcased about a dozen young, beautiful, and chic ladies in their finest on a runway. Some modeled their own trendy outfits. Unlike most other fashion shows, our guests knew all of the models because they were part of our inner circle of regulars. So, the crowd reaction was not only for the fashions but also for the ladies modeling them. Carol, my little sister, was one of the models. She wore a fabulous green and white dress with a matching wide brim hat as she strutted down the runway to "Cleo's Mood" by Junior Walker & the All-Stars. The evening was a big success. It generated a lot of talk and helped elevate our organization.

Perhaps the best dance we ever gave was at the Concourse Plaza Hotel, which was billed as "Black Christmas." We didn't plan anything special or unique for this event. It was a straightforward dance, but because it was during the holiday season, folks got dressed up more than usual, and the evening had an especially festive atmosphere about it. People still remembered "Black Christmas" many years later. With the success of these dances, we were able to build up our mailing list to over 3,000 names, and the popularity of TBOF continued to rise.

Chapter 5
CONSCRIPTION DRAMA

"*I need the names of everyone you had sex with.*"

In 1969, I was working with the Public Health Service, and receiving only a small salary — just $6,700 annually — as a Syphilis Epidemiologist. It was a fancy title, but my friends simply called me a "syph sniffer" because that was the goal of the program; I would interview patients with syphilis to find out the names and addresses of all their sexual contacts during the contagious period and bring them in for treatment.

I got this job thanks to Ricky. He pointed out that the job came with a 75% chance of getting an exemption from the draft. I didn't want to be shipped to Vietnam, so I applied. I knew there might have been better job options because the Civil Rights Act of 1964 was beginning to open doors that had historically been closed to black folks. However, the possibility of getting a draft deferment was far more important to me at that point in my life. It seemed every time I turned on the TV or picked up a newspaper, there were reports of hundreds of deaths.

After a year on the job, I realized that civil service work was not for me.

Too many coworkers were promoted based on length of service rather than merit. I began looking at other options. CP worked for Warwick & Legler Advertising, and the ad industry sounded cool and glamorous. So, I asked CP to introduce me to the head of account management at his agency. Through him, I met senior executives at other ad agencies. After a few weeks of networking, I landed a job with Young & Rubicam (Y&R), the largest ad agency in the U.S. It did not escape me that my new job was the result of the riots in the '60s and the major civil rights demonstrations that highlighted racism. Corporate America had very few black employees and, as the largest ad agency in the country, Y&R probably felt vulnerable.

About the same time, Andre left Banker's Trust to accept a position at Irving Trust located right around the corner from Y&R. After work, Andre and I would often meet for drinks. CP worked further uptown and joined us on occasion. We went to a lot of different places but never found one where we felt comfortable. Typically, area bars had large crowds, but we felt somewhat isolated because we didn't fit in too well. Also, these venues did not play the music we liked, and they had few patrons of color. Years later, in a Black Enterprise article, CP put it this way: "We had partied in houses in the 1960s, but when we got to midtown, we were older. We had suits and ties on and we were working. I felt like Dr. Jekyll and Mr. Hyde. I was working for a Madison Avenue advertising agency, and there was no one to relate to. I used to leave the midtown area sometimes to go to lunch in Harlem, just to get away from the scene."[2]

Midtown didn't feel welcoming to me, but I made the most of it. Andre and I would occasionally use an uptown tradition called "bumpin." We'd go over to 2nd Avenue where there were lots of bars and hangout joints and buy an appetizer and drink at one bar, then move on to the next place, then the next. That was enough to make it a full evening — three appetizers and three drinks. Bumpin' was fun, but in midtown, we rarely bumped into anyone we knew.

Ricky was getting married shortly after graduating from Queens College.

[2] Black Enterprise, September 1981, "The Million Dollar Party" by Stephen Gayle, pg. 52

It was the night before his wedding, and we had a bachelor party for him in Harlem. We hit up several clubs and, afterward, a few of us took Ricky to the Red Rooster for our final drink of the evening. We sat in one of the booths against the wall on bench seats that were covered in fake red leather. Above each table was a small chandelier. We had a pretty good buzz from the drinks we had at the other Harlem clubs and it was taking too long for our drinks to come. Ricky spoke loudly: "Where are our drinks?" Then he grabbed the chandelier above our booth, pulled it back and pushed it forward. It swung like a pendulum and crashed loudly into the ceiling. It didn't break, but the noise was loud and got the bar manager's attention. He was not happy.

"What are you guys doing? Trying to break up the place?" the bar manager of the Red Rooster hurried over, shouting at us. "You have to leave!"

We apologized, but the bar manager was adamant. While we wanted to have that last drink, it seemed like a good time to end the night. It wouldn't be the last time I would be kicked out of a place. The Red Rooster had a reputation for attracting high achievers. Men like Congressman Adam Clayton Powell, Jr., a Baptist preacher and fearless civil rights activist. He had a reserved seat at a table right next to the window — no one else could sit there. Powell was wildly popular in Harlem because he used his charismatic charm and confrontational style to fight for the civil rights of African Americans. Many other prominent people frequented the Red Rooster including E.J. Smith, a popular executive with IBM, Dr. Vernon "Doc" Baker a celebrated physician, and Dr. Chester Redhead, a high-profile dentist to many celebrities like Aretha Franklin.

A few years after our short-lived visit to the Red Rooster to conclude Ricky's bachelor party, the Red Rooster closed down. I never got a chance to go back before it closed. At least not back to the original Red Rooster. Marcus Samuelson owns the new Red Rooster, but he says it was not named after the original since he was not aware of it. Anyway, everything went well the next day at Ricky's wedding and it was beautiful. Ricky danced with his bride to "You're My Everything" by the Temptations before heading off to the Caribbean for a honeymoon. I went to many weddings every year, mostly in June, for three or four years before the pace slowed down to one or two per year.

I was against the war and so were most of my friends. The Reverend Dr. Martin Luther King, Jr. and Senator Robert Kennedy, two powerful voices against the Vietnam War, were silenced by assassination two months apart in 1968. As important as Dr. King was, I had a similar amount of admiration and pride for Malcolm X. Maybe more. Malcolm X was a gifted speaker and excelled at the art of disputation. His talent provided a rare opportunity to cheer when he made TV appearances and outwitted an opposing guest or news anchor. Malcolm X, with his frequent references to "by any means necessary", was a scary figure to many whites. However, when Malcolm X returned from a trip to Mecca, he became more moderate and repudiated the Nation of Islam. Some believe he was assassinated by the Nation. Others believe the FBI took him out.

My impression was that Dr. King represented a safer place compared to Malcolm X because of his non-violent stance and, as a result, the news media seemed more sympathetic to his viewpoints. However, within my circle of friends, there was a greater level of interest in Malcolm X than Dr. King. We didn't agree with all of Malcolm X's views, but we supported the idea of standing up for ourselves and being treated as valuable human beings. Plus, Malcolm X's electrifying oratory skills were exciting to witness. I could tell that this was a fairly widespread feeling among African Americans in the New York area, and perhaps beyond, but not in the South. Based on my conversations with southern blacks, Dr. King's influence in the south was monumental compared to Malcolm X.

Nevertheless, the assassination of Dr. King hardened my resolve not to fight in the war. It crossed my mind that, as a Jamaican, I had the option of moving to Canada or back to Jamaica and becoming part of the British Commonwealth. But I ruled that out. The Vietnamese did nothing to deserve the devastation we brought to them. They never did anything to hurt the United States or any of our citizens, but our leadership was scared to death about the possibility of Vietnam becoming communist — they wanted it to be a democracy. Who authorized us to tell Vietnam what kind of government they should have?

My mother was in the kitchen when I broke the news. "Mom, I've been drafted." She stopped stirring the pot she was tending on the stove. I knew she would be upset, but when she looked up at me, I could tell her mind was racing.

When I was younger I had thought about enlisting in the Air Force and becoming a jet fighter pilot but scrapped that thought when I learned that instead of a four-year commitment, you had to serve at least six years. Anyway, that was before Vietnam was raging. To be drafted was not a good option for me. I had a great new job and was excited about my social life. But when the Army sent a bus token with a date to appear, I had to go, or be arrested. The token was to take public transportation to a location on Jamaica Avenue where an Army bus drove a group of us draftees to Ft. Hamilton in Brooklyn where we would be given physical exams. Sonny Dove, the great St. John's basketball player, and I sat in the back of the bus with a handful of other poor souls. To keep the mood light, we told jokes. Sonny knew that with his 6' 7" height, he would likely be deferred, and he was right. After the physical exams, Sonny was out and I was in. I got drafted. They sent me home with a specific date to report for duty.

I was not happy about being drafted, but the news hit my mother particularly hard. My two older brothers were already serving. Errol, my oldest brother, volunteered for three years in the Army. If drafted, he would only have to serve two years, but by volunteering, he had a chance to select his assignment. He was pre-med and requested an assignment at the Walter Reed Medical Center in Washington, DC., which he got. Ivanhoe, my middle brother, was serving four years in the Air Force and was on his second tour of duty in Vietnam as an AP (Air Police).

My mother was a bit of an activist. She knew how to sew and got a job as a seamstress in the garment district. She joined the International Ladies Garment Workers Union and, on several occasions, challenged management by charging them with abuse. When she wanted to get something done, she knew the importance of being aggressive. Nevertheless, given that she had little experience in navigating American bureaucracies, I was shocked to learn that she set up a meeting with the local draft board to challenge my conscription. I don't know where she got the idea from, but my guess is that her union bosses may have helped her. Anyway, on the day of the meeting, we both put on a nice outfit and took the Q6 bus to Jamaica Avenue where the draft board was located. We were ushered into a small conference room with three men on the other side of the table. Mom and I sat down, and she launched into an impassioned speech in which she talked about my two brothers who were currently serving in the military and the fact that Ivanhoe was still in Vietnam. She raised her voice and spoke firmly and with emotion: "You already have two of my sons. DON'T TAKE MY LAST SON!"

The sole survivor policy, which was enacted years earlier, was meant to prevent a sole surviving son from being drafted. Both my brothers were still alive, but theoretically, they certainly could have died in service. My mother's presentation worked. The draft board exempted me. At that point, aside from failing the physical, I never heard of anyone getting out of the draft after receiving a token. I will always be proud of Mom for what she did and how well she did it. There is no question, if it weren't for Mom, I would have wound up in the infantry in Vietnam with an excellent chance of getting messed up in the head or killed.

The U.S. government, including Presidents Truman, Eisenhower, Kennedy, Johnson, and Nixon, justified the Vietnam War by claiming that if Vietnam became a communist country, it would create a domino effect in Southeast Asia and nearby countries would fall to Communism. As it turned out, that fear never materialized. Today, Vietnam is a peaceful and thriving Communist country and an important trading partner with the U.S. Importantly, Vietnam's neighboring countries did not follow suit. Cambodia is a democratic republic and Laos and Thailand continue to be Kingdoms.

In 2016, President Obama visited Vietnam where he was warmly received. Obama said, "Now we can say something that was once unimaginable. Today, Vietnam and the United States are partners." What's also surprising is that today, the Vietnamese people love American tourists. After all the napalm, agent orange, and periodic atrocities brought on by our military, who would have thought they would be so warm and friendly to us today? Would Americans have been that forgiving if the shoe were on the other foot?

After graduating from college in 1968, Andre and Wayne followed Ricky's lead by marrying their sweethearts and focusing on family and careers. Ricky was probably the smartest one among us. He went to Stuyvesant High School where only high performing students were admitted. Ricky was awarded a National Merit Scholarship, received a BA from Queens College, an MBA from Adelphi University, and a law degree from St. John's University. More importantly, he was extraordinarily knowledgeable – he was like an encyclopedia. Many people went to Ricky to get info or advice and he was always on point. Ricky was the one who encouraged me to apply to Queens College/CUNY because he knew they would bicycle my application to the other CUNY schools. In terms of our social life, Ricky was a prime mover in organizing TBOF and identifying candidates for membership, so it was disappointing to me when he dropped out. Of course, at that point, Ricky had no idea what fate lied ahead for us. No one did.

Chapter 6
GOTHAM CITY WOES

"*Call the police!*"

When I stepped out my front door one day to head downtown, the elderly lady across the street beckoned to me with her hand waving furiously. As I crossed the street and walked up to her, she said in a loud whisper, "Someone broke into the house next door!" as she pointed to the house.

"Call the police!" I exclaimed.

"I did about 20 minutes ago, but they haven't come yet."

"Call again!" I shouted as I sprinted to the front of the house in question and rang the doorbell.

I have no idea what I was thinking, but after I rang the bell, I got a little nervous because I thought the burglars might come out and try to harm me. I retreated to the sidewalk, picked up a brick from the decorative border in front of the house, and waited. After a few more seconds, two young boys, probably 14 or 15 years old, scampered through a side window and ran as fast as they could away from where I stood. I threw the brick at them and almost hit one, but they both got away. About 10 minutes later, a green car drove very slowly down the street with the driver staring at the house with the missing brick in front. I wrote down the license plate number and reported it to the police when they finally came — another 20 minutes later.

The homeowners told me later that day that there was a blanket on the living room floor filled with items the thieves planned to take. By ringing the doorbell, I scared away the robbers before they could roll up the blanket and connect with the getaway car. The family that lived in that house was grateful to me for saving their stuff. A few days later, I called the police to find out if they were able to find the burglars from the license plate number I gave them. They said the car was stolen and abandoned about two blocks away. I believe the burglars lived on or near the block with the abandoned vehicle because a lot of unsavory, idle characters lived on that street. However, the police never found the burglars.

In those days, police routinely avoided active crime scenes and drove around the perimeter of an incident to give the bad guys a chance to get away because they did not want to confront them. I knew this was routine in my neighborhood, but found out later that there were many neighborhoods, including much of Brooklyn, where that was the modus operandi. When there was a shooting, the police simply planned to arrive late and pick up the bodies. The cops rarely caught the bad guys, which resulted in a rising rate of crime that didn't subside until the 1980s. As one might guess, neighborhoods with the least police presence were predominantly black.

The Ginza, the discotheque we promoted on E. 58th Street, attracted a crowd that seemed optimistic to me – despite the city-wide economic problems and high crime rate. Many of our guests had good-paying jobs, career possibilities and, thanks to us, a new way of socializing at night. For most other folks, the city was a scary place, especially after dark. With the cuts in law enforcement [3], a rise in citywide unemployment that pushed the rate to over 10%, and over a million households dependent on welfare by 1975, the number of rapes and burglaries skyrocketed. Abandoned blocks, arson, car

[3] *New York Times*, March 20, 2008. "City Police Force Could Soon Be Smallest Since the 90s," by Al Baker

thefts, felony assaults all rose dramatically.[4] Heroin, and the emergence of crack cocaine, also deepened the crime problem. Drugs made people desperate. My family, like most black families, could not flee the city. As a result, we learned to live in an increasingly dangerous environment. Despite our precautions, my family and I were personally affected in a significant way.

When I was still in college, I bought my first tuxedo, which I needed for occasional black-tie events hosted by my fraternity, Kappa Alpha Psi. Wayne had told me about a sale at Alexander's department store — $99 for a tuxedo. It sounds cheap by today's standards, but it was a fair amount of money back then. Being a Kappa was important to me, so it was an easy purchase to justify. I was proud to own a tuxedo. A few months later, however, on a day when no one was home, neighbors saw a truck pull into our driveway and loaded up with things from the house. They later said they thought we were moving out. Nope. We were being robbed!

The burglars took everything of value in the house. The most valuable item the burglars took was a large console stereo with built-in radio, turntable, and speakers. With it, we had a small record collection, a stack of 33 1/3 albums, and a bunch of 45s — all gone. The console stereos of the 1960s were monstrous pieces of furniture. Ours dominated our living room, so we knew there had to be at least two strong men involved in the robbery. They also took a camera, toaster and, worst of all, my new tuxedo. We called the police, but it was a meaningless gesture. We knew nothing would come of it, and we were right. We had to eat the loss.

Under Mayor John Lindsay, who served from 1966 until 1973, New York City experienced many difficult days. He ran as a Republican for his first four-year term, then as a Democrat for his second term. Lindsay was socially liberal, fiscally conservative, charismatic, and well-liked in NYC. At one point, he even contemplated running for President, but then his popularity took a series of hits. On January 1, 1966, Mike Quill, head of the Transit Workers Union, walked off the job along with his 33,000 members. No subways or buses ran. Over a million New Yorkers were unable to get to work the

---

[4] Disastercenter.com, "New York City Crime Rates 1960-2016"

following Monday morning, crippling the city. [5]

Two years later, a comprehensive sanitation workers' strike left thousands of tons of garbage piled up on NYC streets. The mountains of trash created a public health hazard that led the Mayor to declare a state of emergency.[6] And, in 1969, two back-to-back major snowstorms left millions of people snowbound and unable to get to work. People fortunate enough to live near a subway station were in pretty good shape, even though most had to walk several blocks in very deep snow. But many New Yorkers, including much of the residents of south Queens where most of us in TBOF lived, had to take a bus to the subway and the buses couldn't make it through the drifts. Only a few brave, determined souls could walk the two or three miles in deep, heavy snow to get to a subway station, but most could not. By the time the city dug out Queens three to four weeks later, 20 people had died. Obviously, the Mayor did not cause the snowstorms, but he was heavily criticized for how he handled them.

On April 4, 1968, following Rev. Dr. Martin Luther King, Jr.'s assassination, there were riots in NYC and many other cities across the country.[7] The situation was so bad that when the election of 1973 came around, New York City decided to dump the popular Lindsay in favor of someone new. Many New Yorkers felt a new mayor would improve living conditions in the city. But on the contrary, when Abraham Beame was elected mayor, things got worse.

Crime, including murders, robberies, and subway crimes, increased every year from 1960 to 1980.[8] The New York City Police Department reported that 1980 was the worst year of crime in New York City history with more reported murders, robberies, burglaries, and thefts of automobiles and other items than in any previous year since the department began compiling such statistics in 1911.[9] The mid-70s was also the golden age of the mob. They

[5] NY Daily News, August 14, 2017 *Shutdown: John Lindsay, Michael Quill and the New York City Transit Strike of 1966*
[6] NY Daily News, January 27, 1968
[7] The Atlantic, April 3, 2018, *The Riots That Followed the Assassination of Martin Luther King*
[8] New York City Crime Rates 1960 – 2016 via Disastercenter.com
[9] *New York Times*, March 25, 1981, "1980 Called Worst Year of Crime in New York City History", by Leonard Buder

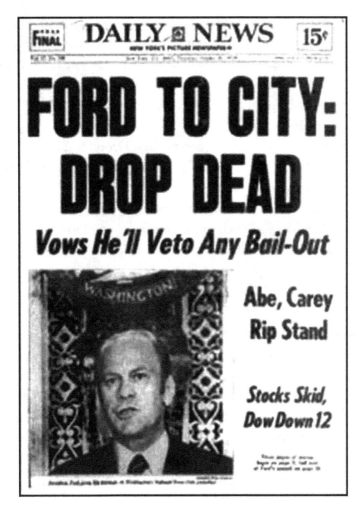

were at full strength and ran unfettered in New York City, the epicenter of mob activity in the country. Michael Franzese, a captain in the Columbo Family, said "I didn't feel New York was ripe for the taking. I thought we already took it."[10] Rudolph Giuliani, U.S. attorney for the Southern District of New York, summarized the mob's influence this way: "The mafia controlled many aspects of legitimate business. They controlled transportation, restaurants, hospitals, shipping docks. They put judges on the bench. I could go on and

[10] *Fear City: New York vs. The Mob*, a Netflix documentary, 2020

49

on."[11] On top of these many problems, New York City experienced a fiscal crisis that was so severe, the city was not only on the brink of bankruptcy, some predicted the city would lose its status as the business capital of the country and become a second-tier city. To stop that from happening, Mayor Abraham Beame sought help from then-president Gerald Ford. But the president vowed to veto any bailout which led the New York Daily News to proclaim in what became a famous headline: "Ford to City: Drop Dead."

Because of all of these problems, white New Yorkers fled the city in droves, settling in the relative safety of nearby suburbs while most African Americans stayed put. Many white professionals kept their jobs in the city then, after work, rushed to catch commuter trains and buses leaving a void in midtown restaurants and nightclubs. This situation opened the door for us to access venues that were previously off the radar.

In November 1970, I was invited to a birthday party after work at a place called La Martinique, located at 57 W. 57th Street, a prestigious part of midtown. I asked Andre to join me. Neither of us had heard of La Martinique nor been invited to a party like this in midtown. About two hundred people were in attendance, and a DJ was spinning records. There was a large dance floor, and the predominantly African American crowd was dancing to records like Diana Ross & The Supremes'"Someday We'll Be Together," and Tyrone Davis'"Can I Change My Mind." Everyone was well dressed and looked sharp. The vibe was especially exciting to us because we had never experienced anything like it; midtown, midweek, right after work, people dancing as if it was Saturday night! In business, when the predominant trend is to zig, there is often an opportunity to zag. We zagged.

[11] *Fear City: New York vs. The Mob*, a Netflix documentary, 2020

Chapter 7

DANCERS COULDN'T GET ENOUGH

"There's nothing else like it."

After our night at La Martinique, I called an emergency meeting of TBOF. We met at Danny's parent's house that weekend in their enclosed front porch. We had an idea that we knew the others in TBOF needed to hear. Andre took the lead.

"We have what could be an exciting opportunity in midtown. There is a captive, growing audience of black folks working in midtown with nowhere to go after work."

Next, Andre and I described the hall itself. Compared to some of the venues where we had dances, La Martinique was in a more upscale neighborhood, on 57th Street, one block from Carnegie Hall. The club was also a step up. It was old, but you could still feel the elegance it once had. Importantly, it was spacious; about as large as some of the halls where we gave dances.

Lastly, since Andre, CP, and I were the only ones who worked in midtown, we explained that an increasing number of black folks were working in various businesses in the area. I chimed in, "We have a captive audience of young, black businessmen and women right in midtown. They're already dressed up, many could walk to La Martinique, they have money in their pockets, and we know they would enjoy this type of scene."

CP chimed in: "There's also plenty of free parking after 6 pm for those who drive in." But the most important revelation was how exciting it was to dance to songs like James Brown's "Mother Popcorn," the Temptations' "I Can't Get Next to You," and Archie Bell & The Drells' "Tighten Up," right after work! We all agreed this was something special and a solid move for us to make.

Tony and Danny volunteered to check out La Martinique to see if they could cut a deal for us there. As teachers, they would be off for the holiday season in a couple of weeks and could investigate La Martinique during that break. A couple of weeks later, we met in my apartment in Lefrak City, which I rented right after joining Y&R.

Tony and Danny reported that La Martinique was exactly as Andre and I had described it — and that it was available. But Tony went on to say: "The room is a bit too large with a capacity of over 600. However, we found a smaller venue right around the corner called the Ginza, located at 40 E. 58th Street that is also impressive and about half the size of La Martinique." Located between Madison and Park Avenues, it was also a prestigious address. Tony explained that "The area has high-end apartments, nice restaurants, and expensive retail stores. And because the Ginza has a capacity of 300, it will be easier to fill than La Martinique. Therefore, it's less of a risk."

Although we were all excited about the possibilities in midtown, Tony was wise enough to push past his initial excitement and look at the opportunity through a logical business lens. He wanted to take advantage of the opportunity, just like the rest of us, but he wanted to do it right...without growing pains. Looking back, I can appreciate Tony's conservative approach. I didn't see Tony's leadership qualities before, but it became clear to us during those discussions that he not only had good judgment, he was a natural leader.

He was also very clever. Tony only found the Ginza because he noticed a newspaper ad promoting a social event for Jewish singles hosted by an organization called Saki Ltd. Tony and Danny simply went to the address and discovered that the Ginza was a perfect venue for us and Mr. Chu, the owner, was anxious to bring in a new crowd. The crowd that Saki Ltd. brought in didn't drink much, so the bar was not very profitable. A promoter named John Juliano controlled Saki Ltd. We found several suitable venues by simply following Juliano's ads for the Jewish singles parties and discovered that they were all anxious to bring in a new crowd.

The entrance to the Ginza was a simple door covered by a rounded black canopy with white lettering that spelled out the word "Ginza." As you entered, there was a small foyer and a narrow staircase leading down one flight to a balcony level overlooking the dance floor that was located one flight below that. The balcony ran around the entire room with a large bar in the back. There was a cage for Go-Go dancers and a DJ booth on the opposite side of the balcony. On the lower level was the dance floor, which was surrounded by café tables. There was also a buffet table on one side of the room that featured chow mein and chop suey, and on the other side of the dance floor was another bar.

TBOF booked the Ginza and began planning our move to midtown. We all agreed that the event at the Ginza should be weekly to give folks who worked in midtown a regular, predictable place to go. This decision proved to be wise.

Danny indicated that the Ginza had sufficient air conditioning as well as an excellent sound system with two turntables, so our events would be turnkey. In fact, the Ginza had a DJ who would spin records for us. We forgot the DJs name, but Danny and CP watched how he operated the two turntables and after a few weeks, they took over the role of DJ. It was a good fit. We all loved music but for Danny and CP it was much more personal. They loved to introduce the crowd to new tunes with a danceable beat. Music with an infectious beat was the key to keeping people on the dance floor and the dancing was the key to getting people to come back for more. In the early '70s, the technology to create non-stop music existed, but it was hardly being used. That was about to change.

The idea of using two turntables was not new to us. Andre and I had experienced discotheques in Montreal where they often had two turntables. But they simply played one record at a time without any effort to blend songs. As undergrads, we checked out Montreal because we heard they had a lot of discotheques (they did) and that they were inexpensive (they were). By the late '70s, Montreal was the second biggest disco capital behind New York City.[12]

There were discotheques in Manhattan — like the Hippopotamus and Sheppard's at the Gotham Hotel — that catered to an older (older than us) white crowd. They didn't dance as much as our patrons did, and more importantly, the music they played was not the same as what Danny and CP played. Danny and CP drove the dancing experience by playing up-tempo R&B, funk, and soul with a heavy beat and mixed records to provide high energy on the dance floor that would build to a fever pitch. They found a way to do this by making the most of the two turntables. The technique they used was slip-cueing, where they would hold a record still at the start of a beat and release it at just the right time, so during the transition from one song to the next, dancers didn't miss a step. Occasionally, they used the two turntables to extend the length of a particularly good song for dancing. My DJ partners were so successful at using this technique at our clubs that we were, no doubt, instrumental in helping to usher in the 12" extended play single that became a staple of discos a few years later.

When Danny and CP took over the DJ booth, the dance experience reached a higher level. The playlists they curated were very creative and focused more on dancing than the music the house DJ had been playing. Our crowd was demanding and they wanted to be challenged. Danny and CP did just that. The experience my DJ partners created was a high-powered dance party that featured carefully curated, non-stop music. To us, these events were an extension of the live-music dances we had been giving. Our customers were dressed up in suits and ties, just like at our previous dances and the admission prices were also similar.

Danny and CP were so in tune with the music that they could build up

---

[12] https://daily.redbullmusicacademy.com/2014/08/montreal-disco-feature, "How Montreal Became Disco's Second City" by Will Straw, August 19, 2014

the intensity to reach a fever pitch several times during the night. The frenzy felt like dancers were climbing the walls. It was a completely different experience than other nightclubs that played only one record at a time. In those clubs, the music stopped and started often, but not so in our clubs. The relationship between DJ and dancer was fresh and inspired a higher level of interaction than was possible with live bands.

When historians and writers talk about the start of disco, they often mention France during the occupation by Germany before World War II when swing bands played the American jazz music that reflected black and Jewish heritage. Adolf Hitler outlawed swing bands, referring to it as "nigger music" and "degenerate music."[13] With swing bands outlawed, young people in France embraced the idea of dancing to another version of the music they so loved…records. However, the European style of discotheques never took hold in this country. After all, swing bands were not outlawed in America, and live music — with its superior sound quality — was strongly preferred over the poor sound quality of records. Following the war, discotheques continued to be popular in France and other parts of Europe. But in the U.S., aside from a few spots like the Hippopotamus and the Peppermint Lounge in NYC, the concept did not take root. While the Peppermint Lounge played records, they relied primarily on live music.

Most music writers and historians acknowledge that the disco craze started in New York City in black and gay "underground" clubs. There are accounts of gay clubs, like the Loft and the Sanctuary, but until now, the role that black clubs played in popularizing this phenomenon has remained untold. Black performers dominated the music that powered the disco era, as did black club promoters and owners. The clubs we promoted and built attracted larger crowds than the gay clubs and our patrons were more diverse. Even though writers and historians often fail to mention the impact of black club promoters, our discotheques played a significant role in the escalation of disco into a national phenomenon that eventually spread across the world.

Back when the German-controlled French government banned jazz clubs

[13] Mibba.com, 2012 by Kurtni

from featuring swing bands during the 1940s, club owners played records by orchestras like Duke Ellington, Bennie Goodman, Louis Armstrong, and Tommy Dorsey that were smuggled in from the United States. That's when the term "discotheque", which means "record library" in French, was born. The first discotheque in France was "La Discotheque," which opened in 1941. After the war, a lush and famous discotheque called "Whisky a Go-Go" opened, which served American spirits and played American jazz. It became a famous and world-renowned establishment.[14]

African American jazz musicians, along with writers and other artists, gravitated to Paris more than any other European city. I think this attraction started with the Parisian love affair with jazz and other forms of American music. Plus, and perhaps more importantly, the word was out among African Americans that Parisians were less prejudiced than Americans. After WWII, African Americans played an important role in liberating France, and the French treated black soldiers with the same appreciation and respect as white soldiers. The French welcomed black soldiers as heroes wherever they went: restaurants, clubs — all public places. That was not the case in the United States. Black soldiers returned home to segregation in America, Jim Crow, and second-class treatment. Even the most decorated black war heroes did not escape the ravages of discrimination when they returned home. Many black soldiers believed that fighting for American democracy would give them full citizenship in the U.S. Of course, that was not the case.[15]

It wasn't just black veterans who were discriminated against when they returned home. Jazz musicians, writers, singers, and actors who were celebrated for their art in France and other parts of Europe, were snubbed by white America. Jazz singer and dancer Josephine Baker, for example, traveled to Paris in 1925 to perform and ended up staying for years because she was finally free of the discrimination she experienced in the United States. Even the great

[14] Lifestyle Lounge, http://lifestyle.iloveindia.com/lounge/history-of-discotheque-6702.html, History of Discotheque

[15] The Military Times, "African American GIs of WW II: Fighting for Democracy Abroad and Here at Home" by Maria Hohn, Vassar College, The Conversation AP, January 30, 2018.

Jesse Owens, whose four gold medals in the 1936 Olympics meant so much to the free world by smashing Hitler's claim of Aryan superiority, was snubbed when he returned to America. Keep in mind Max Schmeling, the German heavyweight boxing champion, knocked out Joe Louis just a few weeks before the Olympics so many around the world believed there was validity to Hitler's claim of Aryan superiority. Despite Owens' spectacular triumphs in Berlin, which did more than anything else to dispel Hitler's superiority claim, there was no call from the White House, no appropriate government recognition, and, importantly, not a single job offer.

After the Olympics, Owens struggled to support his family. He was reduced to accepting various odd jobs, even when they were demeaning. Finally, in 1976, as a way to acknowledge the wrongs that were done, President Gerald Ford honored Owens with the Presidential Medal of Freedom, the highest civilian award. And in 1990, President George H.W. Bush posthumously presented the Congressional Gold Medal to Owens.

In his lifetime though, Owens was a bigger hero in Europe than he was in his home country. Jesse Owens' victories gave the world hope. In the context of 1936, his achievement was massive and on a global scale. He bested Hitler and weakened the Nazi ideology, yet his momentous and significant accomplishments were ignored by Americans. There is an avenue in Berlin, near the Olympic stadium, that proudly bears his name to this day: Jesse Owens-Allee.

After WWII, the popularity of discos in Europe still didn't transfer to America. Americans continued to prefer live music and big swing bands in particular. In the late '60s, technological advances made recorded music more attractive and affordable. High quality, powerful speakers, turntables with earphones, and sound mixers made it possible to create a musical experience that rivaled the quality of live music and, importantly, transported people to a trouble-free state. DJs could curate sounds from a near-infinite array of performers and sounds to inspire dancers. The breadth of options available to a good DJ enabled the development of an exciting new experience on the dance floor. It was an instant phenomenon. The disco era occurred after we created a strong momentum for the experience in midtown Manhattan. Patrons were diverse and came from various cities across the country. Their enthusiasm generated a powerful word of mouth that rippled across the country.

Danny and CP were careful to select just the right music to play to create the mood they wanted. In those days, people could go to a record store and listen to the music with earphones before buying the records. Danny and CP frequented record stores and previewed hundreds of albums to find the ones with cuts that had the right beat and tempo. The pulsating beat and chest-thumping sound created a hypnotic intensity that was broadly appealing. This type of music did not make you want to sit and listen; this music made you want to get up and dance. The dance experience was very different than with live bands because the beat continued without interruption from song to song to song. Strobe lights and mirrored balls added to the hypnotic effect.

When Danny or CP repeated the bridge of a song like "Super Bad" by James Brown or "War" by Edwin Starr, you could hear the audible approval of the crowd. It was mesmerizing, ecstatic, and with all the hot, sweaty bodies grooving in unison, more than a little sensual. When people left the Ginza at the end of the night, they expressed their appreciation for the experience. The vibe in our discotheque embraced people in such a way they couldn't wait to tell friends, family, and co-workers about the euphoric experience. It generated a powerful word of mouth that was more effective than advertising and kept lines outside the Ginza every Thursday for weeks.

New York has always had plenty of clubs that featured dancing. As early as the mid-60s, some clubs began introducing recorded music. However, these clubs didn't resemble what we created. As far as we knew, our Thursday nights at the Ginza were the first dance parties of its type that catered to a young, diverse clientele. What we created was a precursor to the discos that became so popular in the mid-late 1970s. Although our patrons were predominantly African American, we had a good representation of Hispanics, with a sprinkling of white and Asian guests as well. The clubs we promoted on select nights were predominantly white clubs that were not doing well. Our events brought in a whole new set of patrons. At the Ginza specifically, we also had Asian patrons who were regulars at the Ginza but also came on Thursday nights, which was our night.

Dance music, disco style, originated from black urban culture. Our guests wanted to dance to hard-driving music with a strong beat. They were stylish but didn't come to profile, they came to dance. Some white clubs played music by black artists, but it was in small doses intermingled with songs by white artists. Their patrons were a little older than ours, and they did not dance as much. Before Chubby Checker's 1960 smash hit "The Twist", many white clubs and radio stations rarely played music by black artists. Just a few years prior, all music by black performers was called "race music," which was meant to be a pejorative.

Danny and CP pioneered the disco sound by curating up-tempo R&B songs in a way that made dancers want to stay on the floor. Records sounded different at the Ginza than they did at home. The Ginza's state-of-the-art equipment enabled an array of notes and sounds to be heard and felt that were not possible on home systems. Songs like "It's Your Thing" by the Isley Brothers, "Get Up (I Feel Like Being) A Sex Machine" by James Brown, and "Girl, You Need a Change of Mind" by Eddie Kendricks were more enjoyable and embracing than on a typical home stereo player. Even at high volume the Ginza speakers remained crystal clear and brought out sounds and emotions that created a new and engaging experience. Kendricks' song was particularly well-suited for extended dancing because it was over 7 ½ minutes long. The song was not recorded with discos in mind, but the length proved so suitable it opened the door for more long format recordings.

There were discotheques in the gay community in NYC that were note-worthy. Earlier I mentioned the Sanctuary and the Loft, which were perhaps the two most important ones. The scene at these clubs was very different than our events because they were drug-laden with acid, Quaaludes, and LSD. The Sanctuary opened in 1969 and catered essentially to gay men. Women were discouraged from attending, but there was a certain level of diversity: black and white, rich and poor, but primarily male. The Sanctuary had previously been a German Baptist Church in Hell's Kitchen on West 43rd St. The DJ station was on the altar with a dance floor in front of the altar. Many of the pews were still in place. It only had a capacity of 346 people but was remark-able because it was the first, or one of the first, openly gay nightclubs in the city.[16] Francis Grasso was a white, gay man who was one of the first DJs to blend one record into the next with great effect. From all accounts, he was a creative DJ who took the crowd to greater heights than they had ever experienced.

While we were unaware of Grasso's DJ work at the Sanctuary, Danny and CP developed their own DJing skills independently at the Ginza and La Martinique in front of larger, more diverse crowds. There appear to be some similarities in the experiences that these DJs created. At both clubs, DJs transported dancers to a place of freedom and euphoric pleasure. Danny said he learned beat-matching or slip-cueing from a DJ named Gary Brodis, who worked at the Hippopotamus. Of course, knowing how to beat-match does not make someone a good DJ. Danny developed an innovative music selection sequence that worked so well, he got all of the DJs we subsequently hired to use the same technique. Danny's innovation was to gradually increase the energy level on the floor until it reached a climax. Then he would slow it down or switch to a Latin set so dancers could hit the bar, go to the bathroom, or just take a breather. Giving guests a chance to hit the bar was important because it ensured we would meet our bar guarantee. After the break Danny would start all over again, gradually building up the pace reaching four to five climaxes a night. The way Danny curated the music, it created a level of engagement with dancers that was unprecedented. Everyone was on the same ride, and no one left the dancefloor until the trip was over.

The Loft started as weekend house parties held in an apartment owned by David Mancuso starting in 1970. Mancuso was a gay white man from Utica, New York whose parties were so successful, he turned his apartment into a private club and held events "by invitation only" since there was limited space. He played an eclectic array of music, dispensed drugs, and provided free food and juice with an admission price of $2.50. Mancuso was known as a pioneering DJ and, from a music standpoint, a purist, so he played each record from beginning to end with no attempt to provide a continuous beat, so it was very different than our dance party experience. Since he didn't have a liquor

[16] http://www.disco-disco.com/clubs/identify-clubs.shtml

license, Mancuso's parties were more like rent parties. But they were apparently very successful and attracted an influential and passionate following.[17]

Some of the other clubs that could be considered discotheques in 1970 were the Dom (pronounced dome) and the Electric Circus. The Dom was a popular spot in the East Village, but their music was a simple jukebox. Adjacent to the Dom was the Electric Circus. They had disco dancing, but mainly featured live acts and circus-type performances.

The way our DJs played music increased the demand for more danceable recordings. Reflecting on this period, Chic founder and record producer Nile Rodgers said: "We were typical R&B and funk musicians and knew that if we could get people on the dance floor, we could get a record deal. It was exactly that calculated."[18]

Danny and CP were well versed in the available music, so they selected songs with the right beat and emotion to keep people on the dancefloor. Danny was so effective in selecting cuts that many patrons begged to know the name of the records he was playing and where they could buy them. If a record wasn't available at stores, Danny would buy a box from a wholesaler on Jamaica Avenue and sell them at cost to customers who were clamoring for them. Several artists got a big boost when Danny and CP featured their music. Record companies got wind of the hit-making power of our clubs and started sending us promotional copies of new songs. The gradual increase in dance or disco music picked up momentum in 1974, and by 1975 disco recordings took over the Billboard charts.

In the early '70s, our clubs, and presumably gay clubs too, featured soul, funk, and up-tempo R&B.[19] Disco music grew out of a blending of these styles, and by the mid-70s, when disco blossomed, white groups also began to achieve success in this new genre. Some of their top recordings included Wild Cherry's "Play That Funky Music," KC and the Sunshine Band's "Get Down

[17] *The New York Times*, November 19, 2016, "David Mancuso, Whose Manhattan Loft Was a Hub of 70s Nightlife, Dies at 72," by William Grimes
[18] *Vanity Fair*, February 2010, "Boogie Nights" by Lisa Robinson, January 6, 2010
[19] *Vanity Fair*, February 2010, "Boogie Nights" by Lisa Robinson, January 6, 2010

Tonight," Average White Band's "Pick Up The Pieces", and, importantly, the Bee Gees with a bunch of number one hits including "You Should be Dancing" and "Staying Alive". These songs were frequently on the nightly playlist at our clubs along with hits by other groups, like "Disco Inferno" by the Trammps, "Turn the Beat Around" by Vickie Sue Robinson, "Boogie Oogie Oogie" by Taste of Honey, and "Le Freak" by Chic. There were also popular songs that delivered messages relevant to the Civil Rights Movement, like "I Will Survive" by Gloria Gaynor, "Ain't No Stoppin' Us Now" by McFadden & Whitehead, and perhaps the most influential example of a Civil Rights anthem, "Say It Loud, I'm Black And I'm Proud" by James Brown.

By 1978, almost all of the top hits on Billboard were disco records, mostly by black artists. Over 200 radio stations in the U.S. programmed disco music full time as this new style of dance music swept across the country with the power of a tornado. The phenomenon was very much global as the hunger for disco ricocheted through countries all around the world. Despite the "Disco Sucks" mantra of rockers in 1979, music from the disco era remains popular and relevant to this day. Disco songs are still played on the radio, featured in TV and radio commercials, and sampled by hip-hop artists. "Good Times" by Chic was one of the early disco songs to be sampled. Nile Rodgers was given credit on the label of "Rappers Delight" by the Sugar Hill Gang because they simply used "Good Times" like a rug and overlaid the rap on top.[20] Rodgers threatened a lawsuit, and they reached an agreement: Rodgers was listed as co-author of the song and shares the royalties. Overall, Rodgers has become perhaps the most successful songwriter/producer/performer in the business. It all started with disco. The early '70s was a dynamic period, especially for music. We knew we were onto something special with what we created at the Ginza but we had no idea that it would lead to a global phenomenon.

[20] Theguardian.com, July 13, 2019, "Nile Rodgers: I'd Always Talk About Strange Jazz with David Bowie" by James McMahon

Chapter 8
"THE BEST OF FRIENDS"

"*I think we need to ban people who don't act right at our events.*"

After a few weeks, we began to see issues related to guest behavior and called a meeting of TBOF to discuss how to handle them. What do we do with people we catch smoking pot in the bathroom? How do we handle a situation where a guest gets loud and rambunctious? We met at Wayne's parent's house, which was just a few blocks from Woodrow Wilson Vocational High School. The house had attractive shrubs and a beautifully manicured lawn. We were impressed to learn that Wayne's dad received an award from the community association for having the best lawn in the neighborhood. Wayne's mother was a wonder, too. She made an outrageously refreshing lemonade that you knew was going to taste good just by the way it looked. You could see thin slices of lemon floating in a large clear glass pitcher amid the frigid cubes of ice. It tasted even better than it looked. We didn't get this type of treatment at other houses, so there was always a strong preference to meet at Wayne's house. As usual, we gathered in the basement, which was an amply sized, finished space with sofa, chairs, TV, and a card table. Some of us spent hours playing bid whist down there.

We gathered in a circle in front of the couch to discuss the issues and develop specific policies to deal with the problems we saw, as well as a few we anticipated. Tony obviously spent some time thinking through many of these issues because he came prepared with specific recommendations. He suggested that we implement a punishment for breaking the rules and offered a consequence that was sure to make rule-breakers think twice. He said: "I think we need to ban people." Our events were so popular that most of our regulars would shudder at the thought of banishment.

Tony continued, "I say if we catch someone snorting or smoking weed in the bathroom, or elsewhere, we ban them for one month. The same with loud cursing or arguing. If there is an outright fight, they get banned for three months or even for life depending on how bad it is."

Andre chimed in, "Sounds good, but how will the person at the door know when someone is banned?"

Tony responded, "Among us, we know just about everyone who comes to the Ginza, so we need to let all partners know when we implement a ban on someone. We have to make sure we communicate with each other and with our staff, mainly the bouncers."

There was no debate or disagreement. We all felt Tony was right — we trusted his judgment and agreed with his plan. There were not many bans, but there were some, and they proved effective. The Ginza was extremely popular, so the desire to get in was strong enough to deter bad behavior. And just making people aware of the penalties encouraged even some rough characters to behave when they were in the club.

The '60s and '70s were difficult times for New York City. In 1968, the city suffered from the results of devastating sanitation, transit, and teacher's union strikes. Then in 1970, an illegal U.S. Postal Service strike crippled the city further and threatened to close down Wall Street. A few years later, an economic recession hit New York especially hard and the city experienced enormous budget shortfalls. This forced cutbacks in city services, including uniformed police officers, which in turn led to an increase in violent crime and an acceleration of white flight. The suburbs had better schools, more reliable services, and were considered safe. For some, midtown after dark was a dangerous place.

As a result, many clubs and restaurants were hurting for patrons, especially in midtown Manhattan. If it weren't for this dynamic, TBOF would not have been able to afford to venture into midtown. African Americans were generally socializing uptown in Harlem or other black neighborhoods. Aside from the occasional dance, midtown was considered a virtual "dead zone" for African Americans. But despite all the problems plaguing the city, TBOF was about to transform midtown into the hottest new party center.

In planning our events at the Ginza, we focused on how to keep the bad element out. We knew that if we failed, it would ruin our chances for success. We also wanted to establish a certain level of elegance and sophistication to give patrons a feeling of stepping up when they came to our events. We saw what crowds looked like when radio was used to drive invites. Most folks would be fine, but radio-driven events always attracted some people who were obnoxious, rowdy, or just plain troublemakers. So, we developed strategies to keep the bad guys out:

+ *Avoid mass media, especially radio because it would expose us to undesirable characters*
+ *Minimize publicity for the same reason*
+ *Promote the event by utilizing our mailing list and handing out invites to young adults who looked successful and sophisticated*
+ *Implement a strict dress code at the door to help keep out undesirables and to encourage good manners: jackets required, no hats, no sneakers, no jeans*

At the end of each night, everyone in the club — partners, employees, and a handful of close friends — walked out together to ensure that all got to their cars safely. New York City was scary back then due to the high crime rate and lack of police presence, so we had to be cautious.

We shared the dress and behavior policies with Mr. Chu, the owner of the Ginza, and his staff. The staff helped spread the word, which made the club more appealing and welcoming to ladies — and gentlemen too. Having all of us partners walking around was also a deterrent against bad behavior.

The result was that our events were trouble-free. Tony's plan was perfect for our situation. It turned out to be a good idea to let everyone know what we expected and to enforce policies without exception.

Tony not only had an excellent grasp of the business, he also expressed himself with a confidence that made the rest of us TBOF members feel comfortable in following his lead. We all joked around on occasion, including Tony. But he knew when to be serious, and when it came to business, his focus was complete. Tony approached issues in a measured way. His ideas tended to be conservative, which worked to our benefit, at least for the next several years.

Because of our tremendous and conspicuous success, competitors came out of the woodwork. They staged events in various parts of the city and tried hard to attract our following. Some even attempted to pass out flyers inside our events, but we would promptly put them out. Then they passed flyers outside as customers were leaving. But our competitors were never much of a threat because none of them had the consistent quality and elegance of our affairs. Competitors' events were mostly in fringe areas of the city, like the East Village or the far west side. And as far as I knew, only one owned their venue and they didn't have a liquor license or cabaret license. Venues that competitors were able to secure were often not properly air-conditioned or didn't have a good sound system or were simply too small. We had none of these problems. Also, having eight partners gave us a much broader reach than other promoters who were often one or two-man operations. Because of our advantage in terms of social reach, we were able to be more selective at the door. For example, when people showed up with an improper outfit, we could afford to turn them away. That was not always the case for our competitors.

We were also able to provide personal greetings to all who entered our events and again when they left, often calling people by name. Personalized greetings made guests feel special and elevated our events because it made guests feel like they were our friends instead of patrons. However, our main point of distinction was the non-stop, perfectly curated, dance music delivered on a top-of-the-line sound system by DJs who knew how to read the crowd and respond accordingly. Of course, the location was also a draw. We were front and center at a great venue in what was the most important business district in the city, and perhaps the country — midtown Manhattan.

Since CP and I worked for ad agencies, we took responsibility for developing a promotional flyer to be sent to our mailing list and discreetly handed out. We designed the flyer to fit in the inside pocket of a suit jacket so that we would have a ready supply whenever we ran into prospective customers. We primarily focused on inviting ladies because we knew from our dance experiences that inviting attractive, socially active ladies would bring in the guys. Our first flyer had a hand-drawn, stylized rendering of a New York City skyline at night with the headline: "Midtown After Dark." This headline recognized that black folks rarely hung out in midtown after work. They went uptown or to black communities in the outer boroughs, Queens, Brooklyn, and the Bronx. (Staten Island is an outer borough, but we didn't know anyone who lived there). The flyer indicated that the party was every Thursday from 5-9 pm at the Ginza and gave the address. We didn't use the word "discotheque" in the flyer, but the experience we created was exactly that. (See Appendix II)

We planned to cater to the growing number of African Americans who were working in midtown Manhattan and encourage them to stop by before going home. Patrons were thrilled to find a great space with fantastic music, a free drink, and free food. Another key factor was the crowd. Most were college oriented so just about everyone knew a good number of people in the room, which made folks feel comfortable and that they were at a happening. This dynamic was important because socially oriented, young black folks wanted to be where the action was.

Our first Thursday was February 11, 1971. The temperature was in the 30s and it was blustery outside. The almighty hawk, the wind, was racing through the streets. About 100 guests showed up for our first night. The next Thursday, we had about 150 guests. For a Thursday night, this was the only place to be so word of mouth spread quickly. By the third week, we reached maximum capacity, about 300 people, and had to stop letting in people. The line outside went down the block! By April, as the weather warmed up, the line was not just down the block, but around the corner! We didn't have a velvet rope, but guests lined up in an orderly fashion based on when they arrived. They were patient and, as other guests left, we admitted them in the order they arrived.

We realized we were on to something much bigger than an informally organized social club. It was a thrill to recognize that our discotheque was so popular with folks and to realize that the money we collected was beyond our wildest expectations. One night at the Ginza netted more money than a dance — with far less work. Also, since the word was out that we were there every Thursday, our event was quickly established and no more marketing was needed. Of course, as we bumped into good-looking, interesting people, we continued to pass out flyers. Because our crowds were growing so fast, we had another emergency meeting at Wayne's house to map out how to handle such a rapidly growing enterprise. We reviewed and tightened all known and anticipated policies and discussed the numerous issues that arose. Tony and Danny, our president and treasurer, were instrumental in guiding our moves during this important and dynamic period.

One issue that arose, for example, was that some guests worked in outer boroughs and New Jersey and wanted to go home to change clothes before coming to the Ginza. They complained that by the time they arrived, the party was half over. Some of these patrons were service or blue-collar workers, and they needed to go home to put on a suit or jacket. We certainly didn't want to lose these patrons, so within a few weeks, Tony extended the hours to midnight. Eventually, we changed the closing time to 4 am, which is when bars had to stop serving in New York State. For a while, we had two different crowds: one right after work and the other late night. The after-work crowd began to thin out, so we pushed the start time back to 9 pm to consolidate the evening and make it easier for us to handle.

During this period, we didn't just host our weekly events at the Ginza, we continued to give occasional dances. Our dances were always scheduled on a Saturday night, so there was no conflict with the Thursday night Ginza events.

Fred Dantzler was one of our original partners. Recall he wasn't able to attend the meeting at Maloney's where we formed TBOF but he made it clear that he wanted to be part of the group. Freddy, which we all called him, loved the glam lifestyle and was a bit of a ladies man. He dated a lot of the beautiful women who came to the Ginza. On more than one occasion, I remember Tony asking all of us to avoid dating guests who came to the Ginza because when the relationship ended, they stopped coming. Although he was addressing all of us, Tony was primarily talking to Freddy. Maybe Freddy's defiance of our TBOF rule should have been an omen of things to come because a year later, we had another problem with Freddy. It was far more serious, and none of us saw it coming.

Since Andre, Wayne, and I had to be at work at 9 am every morning, the extension of the Ginza's hours of operation to 4 am every Thursday, made for difficult Fridays. For safety reasons, we had to walk out together, so by the time we got home, it was 5 am, or later. With the high energy of the discotheque, it took most of us another 30 minutes or so to wind down before we could fall sleep. It was difficult, but we were young enough to handle it. Later, when we expanded by adding more nights, those of us with day jobs worked every other night collecting cash at the door. Young or not, those virtual all-nighters took a toll.

On the rare occasions when we didn't have to work the next day, we would all show up at the Ginza. Since we had good coverage, a few of us would walk over to the Playboy Club for a late-night breakfast. The Playboy Club was on E. 59th Street, right around the corner from the Ginza. Although it was a membership club, they had a main room that was open to the public after a certain hour, I believe it was after midnight. We would go around 2 am when the Playboy Club was never crowded. Here they served a wonderful breakfast of eggs, bacon, sausage, ham, and the fixings for a nominal price. There were several private rooms with different activities going on, like live jazz, a comedy show, a cocktail lounge, but you had to be a member with a rabbit head Playboy key to access those rooms. The bunnies rotated between work stations, so we got the same waitresses that the private rooms got. The playmates looked cool in their cute bunny outfits, and it made our breakfast a little more special.

The skimpy bunny costumes, while fun and provocative, would have been totally out of place at our events. At the Ginza, the most common dress for our crowd was conservative suits and ties for men and business suits for women because our guests were coming primarily from the office. A couple of years down the road, when the disco phenomenon went mainstream, the style of dress gradually became flashier and more glamorous, especially on the weekends. Men wore bell-bottom pants, loud print shirts, platform shoes, and large medallions around the neck. Some guys raided their mother's costume jewelry drawer to find a broach or pin that they could attach to a chain and wear around their neck. Women wore bell-bottom pants along with shiny, colorful, and sexy halter tops and lots of jewelry. The glitzy outfits added to the glamour of the evening and helped elevate the experience. It was an escape from reality when you stepped onto the dance floor, a sense of total freedom. It should be noted that even when disco was at its height, TBOF customers never came in outlandish or skimpy attire, as was the scene at clubs like Studio 54 or Visage. And although our patrons were certainly not all drug-free, drug use inside the club was strictly prohibited and punished when discovered.

The Ginza had two Go-Go girls dancing in an elevated cage next to the DJ booth. It felt very '60s to us. It didn't contribute to the atmosphere that was so exciting to our patrons, so we asked Mr. Chu to save his money and end that feature, which he did. Go-Go dancers were a rather dated form of entertainment intended for nights when guests were more into watching and less into dancing. What was exciting to our patrons was the power of the music, beautiful outfits, and lighting that changed in a way that gave it a psychedelic feeling.

On occasion, however, there were some minor problems. One Thursday night, for example, a customer got into an argument with Tony. No one remembers what they argued about, but when the customer threatened Tony by saying "I'm going to kick your ass," Harry Felder, who was standing nearby, stepped in. He wrapped his big arms around the customer, pinning the customer's arms against his torso, picked him up, dragged him up the stairs, and threw him onto the sidewalk. By then, CP and Andre ran up the stairs to support Harry. The display of strength had an impact because the customer offered no resistance. Then Harry picked up the customer by his shoulders and, with their faces about an inch apart, said: "Listen to me. Don't come back!" We never saw that guy again. Harry was physically the biggest and strongest partner in TBOF, and he had just recently completed two years in the Army. He was strong, fit, and fearless.

Our following was not just conservative in the way they dressed; they were also conservative in the way they danced. On the dance floor, guests were coupled off, and women didn't dance by themselves or with other women. Dancing in pairs was the cultural norm at all the social events we went to, including college and post-college dances. This aspect of our culture was probably a vestige of the days when all dances involved holding hands with a partner. In any event, on the rare occasion when two women danced together, it led to stares and comments. Even with line dances like the Bus Stop, dancers got on the dance floor in couples. Dancing alone or with a loose group of people was simply not accepted until a few years later. Specific dances were the order of the day. The dance would vary based on what song the DJ played. The rise of dances where you don't hold hands with your partner led to lots of new moves since both arms were freed up. It also meant that each dancer could do their own thing; they no longer had to be closely coordinated. That led to more freedom and creativity on the dancefloor, but it also gradually eroded many of the specific dances where you had to coordinate moves with your partner. All through that period though, the Hustle, or variations such as the Brooklyn Hustle and the DC Hustle, remained in vogue.

Some journalists and pop culture historians have written that the Hustle was invented during the disco era. That is not true. The Hustle was around way before disco came into being. I can't pinpoint when it started, but we were dancing the Hustle all through college in the early-60s. By the '70s, we were still dancing the Hustle, but also a cadre of dances with no hand-holding, such as the Funky Chicken, the Bump, the Bus Stop, and line dances where dancers formed two lines and couples took turns dancing down the middle. With all eyes on the couple in the middle, they put on their best moves to impress the crowd. Some people preferred to dance holding hands and others preferred to dance separately but it often depended on the song. Some songs were more suited for hand-holding, like "It's a Shame" by the Spinners, "What Does It Take" by Junior Walker and the All-Stars, or "It's All in the Game" by The Four Tops. Other songs were more suited for dancing separately like James Brown's "Say It Loud," the Temptations' "Ain't Too Proud to Beg," and "Hollywood Swinging" by Kool & The Gang.

After several months, the Ginza was the talk of the town among African Americans. Even those who had never been to the club knew of it due to the strong word of mouth. Approximately 10% of the audience was white, and another 10% was Latino. The Ginza catered to Asians and whites on the nights we weren't there. As a result, some of them came to our Thursday night dance parties as well. Although the Ginza was open every night, the only night that was jumping was Thursday when we brought our crowd and my partners were spinning records in the DJ booth. Thursday nights at the Ginza were truly remarkable because it was the first time, perhaps ever, that such a diverse crowd gathered in a purely social setting in midtown Manhattan. It wouldn't be the last.

Chapter 9
THE PENGUIN

"*Is that the best you can do?*"

The popularity of the "Theme from Shaft," combined with the clever mixing of Danny and CP, captivated a whole generation of young blacks with a powerful emotional experience that made them feel connected. We decided to capitalize on this enormous wave by bringing Isaac Hayes to Madison Square Garden. His music was so hot that we knew it would be a guaranteed sell-out. We learned that the Garden had available dates during the first half of 1972, which would give us six months to market the event. We talked about the possibility of getting into the concert business since we knew which artists would be a big draw. We even joked about competing with Ron Delsener, one of the top concert impresarios in New York at that time. But to book Hayes, we had to go through the William Morris Agency, the largest talent agency in the country that controlled many of the biggest stars and personalities.

Danny, CP, and I met with a representative from William Morris, in a small, cluttered office in Manhattan. I don't recall the agent's name, but he was heavy set and his girth extended well beyond the sides of his swivel desk chair.

There was no small talk because the agent was very busy, or made it seem that way. We launched into why we were there. We started by explaining who we were, although I don't believe he was familiar with our operation or the level of success we were enjoying. After our brief background presentation, the agent gave his response.

"I can deliver Isaac Hayes for you. He's available on the date you want," he said.

Before we could process his positive answer, he went on to tell us what it would take to get Hayes.

"Isaac requires 90% of a sold-out gate. If it doesn't sell out, you still have to pay 90%," the agent explained.

In other words, the most we could make was 10% of the gate, assuming it was a sell-out, minus marketing. After paying for radio commercials, posters, and flyers, we would hardly see any profits.

We stared at the agent briefly before CP asked, "Is that the best you can do? We helped make his record a big success by pumping it every night at the Ginza." The response was simply.

"That's the deal. Take it or leave it."

After a glance at each other, we left feeling disappointed. We weren't sure who was being greedy — Hayes or the William Morris Agency.

We didn't deliberate the situation because bringing Hayes to the Garden made absolutely no sense, at least not for us. Anything could happen on concert night. We were mindful that NYC had recently experienced a transit strike, snowstorms, blackouts, and a riot, so any one of those scenarios could spell disaster for an event. Interestingly, someone else brought Isaac Hayes to the Garden in the summer of 1973 and used Frankie Crocker, the top DJ on WBLS radio, to promote it. The concert was a sellout.

Our foray into concert promotions was over before it started. Perhaps it was because we were dealing with a dismissive booking agent who was unfamiliar with the success of TBOF, or perhaps it was because we were trying to bring in the hottest performer with the most significant song from the most groundbreaking movie of the 1970s. It all started in the summer of '71.

On July 2, 1971, the movie Shaft was released. The legendary African

American photographer Gordon Parks was the director, and Isaac Hayes wrote the soundtrack. It's difficult to overemphasize the impact this movie and soundtrack had on African Americans — especially those who frequented the Ginza. Shaft was a smash hit that ushered in an entirely new genre of films, often referred to as blaxploitation. Some critics gave the movie a mediocre review, like Roger Ebert, who gave it 2 ½ stars. But Roger, like many other white movie critics, failed to recognize that Shaft was groundbreaking. While Shaft and other films in the blaxploitation genre did include their fair share of racial stereotypes, these movies marked the first time black actors were portrayed as heroic main characters. Shaft was the first movie to capture the spirit of the unharnessed black hero. It was a powerful representation of a strong black, masculine hero who was suave, a ladies man and, importantly, a super clever, kick-ass detective. Black moviegoers embraced the film fervently, as did many white moviegoers. Shaft revealed a tremendous hunger for this type of hero.

Previous black actors were typically not in control of their situation when in scenes with white actors. This was the case with Sidney Poitier in Guess Who's Coming to Dinner or To Sir With Love. Both were good movies but they lacked the three-dimensionality and authenticity of a character like John Shaft. Shaft was always in control as evidenced by how he told white cops what to do and how to do it. This was a major departure from previous black characters who served mainly as sidekicks. Shaft was the embodiment of Black Power, a phrase just starting to be used by activists and some civil rights advocates.

The movie Shaft had added relevance to our followers because it was filmed in Manhattan, mostly in Harlem. The landmarks, buildings, and streets were familiar to the patrons of the Ginza. It also had strong crossover appeal and exceeded expectations at the box office. Shaft was so profitable, it bailed out MGM, which was struggling at the time.[21] The film's financial success led to dozens more films in that same genre.

The soundtrack from Shaft was also groundbreaking. In the summer of

[21] Chicago Tribune, July 2, 2000, *Shaft Then and Now* by Michael Wilmington.

1971, Isaac Hayes' "Theme from Shaft" was the most popular song played at the Ginza for many weeks. It was also number one on the Billboard chart for six weeks, and Hayes won the Academy Award for best song in a movie,[22] the first by an African American in a non-acting role. Hayes also earned two Grammys for "Theme from Shaft." With the enormous popularity of "Theme from Shaft" and its pulsating beat, Danny and CP, our star DJs, would lengthen the song by repeating the bridge over and over again. The bridge was the part of the song that featured rapid playing of the cymbals with piano and horn riffs. The dancers went crazy for it.

The popular dance for this song was the Penguin, a difficult dance to do because you had to get up on your toes and shift your full body weight from one foot to the other, shuffling in time to the beat and then swinging one leg then the other out to the side. Most patrons were in their 20s and 30s and fit enough to dance the Penguin for extended periods. It was a sight to behold.

On Thursday nights, few people left the Ginza early. Patrons in the club had never experienced such a powerful musical experience and were reluctant for it to end. Many stayed until the 4 am closing time. As people left the club, we always chuckled to see a few folks doing the Penguin up the stairs and out onto 58th Street.

The early 1970s was a fun and exciting time for African Americans in NYC. Thanks to the Civil Rights Movement, African Americans were beginning to gain access to areas that were unthinkable to the previous generation. Black men and women in business attire were becoming more common in midtown. The Ginza, and eventually, other TBOF events, helped these newcomers feel a sense of belonging and social connection. We contributed to the feeling of optimism that many felt. This was all good news for our business. Of course, the high cannot last forever.

The most successful and prominent black entrepreneurs were like celebrities to us. They included Earl Graves of Black Enterprise, Ed Lewis and his partners at Essence magazine, and Bruce Llewellyn, who owned Fedco

---

[22] The Independent, August 12, 2008, "Isaac Hayes: Seventies Soul Superstar Who Won an Oscar for 'Theme from Shaft'

Food Stores and Freedom National Bank. There was also Zebra Advertising, Mingo Jones Advertising, Lockhart & Pettus Advertising, and a handful of others. In 1970, my first year working for Young & Rubicam, I was aware of only a precious few black executives in corporate America who were in senior management positions. I can recall Jackie Robinson at Chock Full O' Nuts because they pumped their message heavily on radio. There was also Joe Black at Greyhound, Tom Shropshire at Philip Morris, H. Naylor Fitzhugh at the Pepsi-Cola Company, Herb Douglas at Schieffelin & Somerset and, as I found out later, Lee Archer at General Foods. These men — and it was primarily men in these positions back then — were heroes to those of us who were trying to make it in the corporate world.

With growing numbers of African Americans in corporate positions, we believed this segment would be the sweet spot of our audience and that it would continue to grow. What we didn't realize is that a large number of people who had service or blue-collar jobs also wanted to be part of our scene, so they dressed up in their finest to come to our events. It was often difficult to tell who was a corporate type versus who was simply dressing the part.

At Y&R, my first client was General Foods, makers of Birds Eye Orange Juice and Birds Eye frozen vegetables. I thought everyone in management at General Foods was white because in all the meetings I had attended that was all I saw. I was surprised to learn that there was a black Vice President named Lee Archer. He was on the dais at a luncheon I attended, which is how I met him. In addition to his business achievements, Lee served during World War II as a Tuskegee Airman, a group of African American pilots who primarily escorted bombers to protect them from German fighter planes. Lee flew 169 combat missions and is the first and only black Ace pilot.[23] To be considered an Ace, a pilot has to shoot down five enemy airplanes — a feat that will probably never be achieved again since air-to-air combat on the scale of WWII, will never be repeated. Lee shot down five German planes in Europe, which is a fantastic feat, especially given that many of his superior officers doubted blacks were capable of becoming good pilots.

[23] CBSnews.com, "Tuskegee Airman Ace of World War II, Dies", January 29, 2010

I got to know Lee quite well over the years and learned just how super smart and modest he was. For example, he never told me that he was a Tuskegee airman — he let me find out from others. Many years later, after I thought I knew Lee very well, I learned that he was instrumental in helping to engineer Reginald Lewis' acquisition of Beatrice International. Lee could not take a prominent position in the newly-acquired company because he was an executive at General Foods and did not want to give that up. So, General Foods, recognizing the conflict of interest but acknowledging the historic nature of the deal, agreed to allow Lee to serve as a director of the company but he could not serve as a company officer. Not many people were aware of this. Lee didn't share this information with me until he was well into his 80s. That is not to take anything away from Reginald Lewis' accomplishments; he was the first black billionaire in the United States. In an interview with Black Enterprise, Lewis famously said: "I'm always amused by people who talk about the overnight success of the TLC Group. We've been banging away at this step-by-step for 20 years. I'm often disturbed by the notion of the so-called glass ceiling, but you know, glass can be broken. It's important to be prepared to act and sacrifice, to accept that if this is what you want, just wishing it would happen is not enough. You've got to follow through and take the necessary steps to make it happen."

Although the percentage of blacks in advertising and other industries was small, the aggregate represented a vital customer base for our nightclubs. These junior and middle management executives set the tone at our clubs because many service and blue-collar workers emulated the white-collar folks. As a result, although our clubs were diverse, the overall impact was decidedly upscale and even aspirational.

One side effect of the high crime rate in New York City was that many women, and men too, might shy away from a club if they felt the crowd was rough or dangerous. An important component of our success was that we created an atmosphere that not only felt safe, but attracted people who were worthy of being friends, dates, or even spouses. Even though word of mouth was strong about our clubs, we were always careful about who we gave flyers to. We focused on corporate types or "buppies", the new, trendy term for black urban professionals. Overall, our guests were pre-screened, well-dressed, and earned a good salary.

While buppies were the prime target of our solicitation efforts, there was another segment on the opposite end of the spectrum that proved to be the biggest spenders. We didn't solicit them, didn't want them in our clubs, but they came, nonetheless. Tony said "As long as they behave and dress appropriately, we should treat them just like any other patron." They were drug dealers, pimps, and other assorted gangsters and hustlers. In most settings, these characters would stand out like a sore thumb, but in our disco environment, with its welcoming attitude and everyone dressed up, they were barely noticeable. In the grand scheme of things, these characters represented a very small percentage of guests, which is why most folks probably didn't even notice them. But gangsters are different than most folks. They always notice who else is in the room.

Chapter 10
MIDTOWN AFTER DARK

"A nything from James Brown."

Someone once asked Danny what record was most effective in getting people up on the dance floor. He replied without hesitation.

Since there was no disco music in 1971 — it didn't become a thing until the mid-70s — our DJs, CP and Danny, had to find songs with a prominent dance beat. The tune had to be danceable because that was the essential element to keep folks on the dance floor. James Brown's songs all had a power and an irresistible, infectious beat. It was pure funk. Once dancers got up, it was easy to keep them going. All you had to do was maintain the rhythm. Few of the top disco recording artists, like Donna Summer, Van McCoy, or Chic, were even recording music at that time. The Bee Gees were recording, but not in the genre of disco. That came a few years later. Nevertheless, my partners got their hands on plenty of great music that fit their magic formula for getting people moving on the dance floor.

By the early '70s, the words people used to describe parties in invitations and flyers had expanded significantly. "Discotheque" meant an event or establishment that played recorded music. But more than that, discotheque connoted sophistication, style, and excitement. The word was occasionally applied to various parties and events when the goal was to send a festive vibe. There were other words for a party that also became popular around that time — "cabaret," "fete," and "soiree" — but none was as important as discotheque. The shortened version, "disco", was also used occasionally, but there was more of a fascination with "discotheque." It sounded European, modern, and hip. "Disco" sounded more casual, less sophisticated, and, for our crowd, sophistication was a draw. Guests enjoyed getting dressed up and expected a refined and cosmopolitan experience. Over time, however, the use of the word "disco" usurped "discotheque" in large part due to its wide use in mass media and pop culture.

Most words that refer to parties have roots in the French language. I guess the French like good social gatherings. In any event, the experience we created at the Ginza, and other clubs we operated shortly after that, were true discotheques. Danny and CP became proficient at "reading" the crowd, making an emotional connection with dancers, and using that feedback to take dancers to a higher level than any live music could. The Hippopotamus and the Cheetah in New York City were billed as discotheques. Sure, they played records, but they also relied on live music and other shows to entertain guests. Later we heard of Chez Regine's in Paris but didn't know much about it at that time. Chez Regine was one of the first true discotheques because it featured a DJ with two turntables instead of a jukebox that had been commonly used at other clubs. Regina Zylberberg is credited with creating that first discotheque environment in the 1950s and years later opened a Regine's nightclub in several different parts of the world. These clubs were popular but they did not ignite the disco boom. The disco boom started in New York City and spread from there.

Danny and CP, our first DJs, will probably never get the credit they deserve for creating such a new and exciting musical experience for dancers. The way they curated and blended various recordings was so fresh and intimate that it represented a culture shift. It was a new way to socialize that was at once inclusive and elevating. When our guests were dancing, my DJ partners could tell if the crowd wanted more or if it was time to switch it up. Reading the mood of dancers was an art developed by paying close attention to dancers who were on the floor for extended periods. In the '70s, dancing was viral across the country, but among those who danced the most, African Americans were front and center.

Without Danny and CP's insights and innovations in the DJ booth, it would have been just another party. While word of these events hit the black community with tremendous reach, most white folks were not aware of this new club experience. Gradually, the excitement of discotheques spread into the white community leading to the eventual opening of fifteen to twenty thousand discos across the country[24] plus a good number in countries around the world.

Getting back to the Ginza, we cut a deal where we guaranteed bar sales of $1,000 every Thursday night. We knew we could reach this target given the magnitude of our loyal followers and the fact that the $3 admission at the door included one drink. Patrons also got chop suey or chow mein provided gratis by the Ginza. This was an excellent deal for our customers. At the end of the night, we would pay Ginza management $1.50 for each drink ticket the bar collected. So, our take was $1.50 per person.

By March 1971, the word had gotten out, and the response was beyond our imagination. With the flow of people coming and going, we averaged 400 people every Thursday night. On some occasions, we attracted more than 500 people. Promotional flyers were no longer needed because the crowd showed up automatically. Patrons were typically in their 20s or 30s, single, and often arrived in small groups, but they always danced in couples. Asians came because they were already familiar with the Ginza. White folks and Hispanics came because they loved the music and enjoyed dancing to it. This unique diversity made our dance parties more interesting because it added a measure of discovery and importance. It was the place to be and everybody was there. The

---

[24] *Rolling Stone*, April 19, 1979, "The Evolution of a Dance Craze" by Stephen Holden

events highlighted the similarities among the different groups and, especially, their shared enjoyment of music and dancing, instead of focusing on differences. After all, music and dance are an innate part of the human experience.

Within short order, Danny and CP's DJing skills improved to the point where some patrons could tell who was in the DJ booth by the way records were played. Today, there are thousands of DJs around the world, with some earning tens of millions of dollars a year. A handful of these DJs have huge followings and can legitimately be called superstars.

Danny and CP volunteered to DJ initially because they knew the music better than the rest of us. Danny and CP demonstrated their creativity in putting together imaginative playlists that periodically generated audible sounds of approval from dancers — and even those who weren't dancing. Danny and CP focused on the crowd. They recognized that our customers were demanding, and that kept them on top of their game. However, they were inventive in the way they selected and blended music. They excited dancers in ingenious ways and sent them home feeling gratified at the end of the night. If the DJs didn't curate the music properly, it could cost us the crowd.

TBOF was a social club, not a corporation. With money coming in fast and furious from the Ginza, we had to move quickly to transform ourselves into a business. Until we could make proper arrangements, we buried the cash in a hole in Tony's basement and covered it over with a small table. Tony and Danny then began working to identify a good tax accountant and a lawyer familiar with the nightclub environment. We also had to figure out what type of corporation to form and what type of bank accounts would be most appropriate. It took us about a month, but based on Tony and Danny's research, we hired David Schwartz as our attorney and Jerry Brickman as our accountant. David and Jerry helped us get organized properly by setting up our first corporation and guiding us in opening bank accounts. I was elected Chair, Tony President, and Danny Treasurer of The Best of Friends, Inc.

We held regular meetings to determine policy and manage the business. Transforming our social club into a business created an immediate reorientation of the organization. Tony and Danny were already leaders of TBOF, but now their role became even more important. Tony ran the meetings since he was devoting the most time to the operation and knew more about the business than anyone else. Danny kept track of the money and provided monthly financial reports. Wayne was an attorney, and we all trusted his judgment, so he served as an unofficial mediator when we had disagreements. Since we were all in our mid-twenties and had little business experience, we were cautious and appropriately wary of the many proposals that came our way. That inclination to be cautious served us well during the early years, but a few years later, it hindered our growth potential by discouraging us from pursuing new business opportunities.

Chapter 11
LEAP OF FAITH

"**W**e're ready to take on *La Martinique*."

After a few months of steady success at the Ginza, Tony and Danny suggested we revisit our original idea of hosting events at La Martinique. Tony said, "Our following has grown much bigger. We're ready for La Martinique." This was the venue where Andre and I had visited so many months before and the place that inspired us to host weekly events in midtown. We passed over La Martinique because we were worried that we couldn't fill the large venue, but the worry vaporized after we saw the lines of people waiting to get into the much smaller Ginza.

La Martinique had two heavy glass doors fronting 57th Street right on the corner of 6th Avenue. Like the Ginza, once you went past the glass doors, there was a foyer area then a staircase leading one flight down to the club. While Ginza's staircase was relatively narrow and unimpressive, La Martinique's staircase was wide and grander. There was a gracious landing near the bottom with a booth to pay the admission fee. From there, three more steps led down to the club level, a large rectangular shaped room with a dance floor in the middle, a long oval bar at one end, and seating areas surrounding the dance floor. Adjacent to the bar was the Caribbean room, which formed an L shape next to the main rectangular shaped room.

We decided to take the leap and negotiated with the owner, Bill Becker, to operate La Martinique every Tuesday evening. TBOF would take the $3 admission, and Becker would take the bar. La Martinique was dead on Tuesday evenings, so it was a low-risk proposition for him. Unlike the Ginza, there was no free drink or food with admission, so the door take was our revenue stream. Again, it was a handshake agreement. With no free drink for patrons, our take would be much higher than at the Ginza. Plus, it was more than twice the size. The only issue was whether or not we could fill it.

To help ensure a large enough crowd, we decided to invite Mal Woolfolk to join TBOF as a full partner. Mal was extremely popular, well-liked, trustworthy, and, importantly, he lived in Teaneck, NJ, which gave us geographic diversity. Mal worked at WBLS, the number one radio station in New York City and, as we found out later, he was also a part owner of the station. Mal was everyone's best friend because he had a way of making people feel special and important. When he spoke with someone, even in a crowded room, his focus was entirely on that person. Watching Mal was a lesson in the value of eye contact. But it was much more than that. When he saw people, he remembered what was important to them from a previous conversation, and he would ask about it. Mal's style endeared him to many people. On more than one occasion, Mal would walk into a crowded party, and it seemed as if everything stopped so folks could greet him. You could hear people say, "Mal is here!" He was so charismatic and relatable, we brought him into the group as an equal partner without any financial contribution. We were all confident that Mal could help bring more people into our discotheques. And he did.

La Martinique was a nightclub built for a bygone era, a remnant from the days of big bands, floor shows, and ballroom dancing. Opened in 1941, it originally featured a full orchestra with live shows from performers such as Danny Kaye, Frank Sinatra, Jo Stafford, and Zero Mostel. It closed in 1950 but was re-opened in 1952 by the legendary jazz great, Josephine Baker. Baker fell in love with France so she became a French citizen and took up residence there in 1925. However, her plan to operate La Martinique was short-lived due to an incident at the Stork Club. The Stork Club was a prestigious symbol of café society and the wealthy elite. While there one night, Baker was treated poorly due to the prevailing racism of the time. She ordered dinner but it never came. Walter Winchell was a regular at the Stork Club, and Baker felt he should have come to her defense and said so publicly. Winchell was one of the most powerful men in the country with large radio and newspaper audiences. He was also a strong supporter of Senator Joseph McCarthy and used the same accusatory tactics that McCarthy used on people he didn't like. Unfortunately, Baker's comments angered Winchell, and he accused her of being a communist. The resulting publicity led to the termination of Baker's work visa, and she returned to France.[25] While back in France, Hennessy cognac hired Ms. Baker to be a spokesperson for the brand. France was far ahead of the United States in the area of racial relations. Hennessy wanted her to be the face of their prestigious cognac because she was a hero and a national treasure in France. In the United States, she was just another black person.

In the 1950s, the black press in America routinely covered news of black folks in Paris with weekly columns. In addition to Baker, many other black celebrities spent time in Paris, including writers such as James Baldwin, Chester Himes, Langston Hughes, Richard Wright, a popular nightclub owner called Bricktop, and jazz musicians such as Sydney Bechet, Charlie Parker, Miles Davis, and Thelonius Monk, just to name a few. Black folks flocked to Paris because they had an unprecedented level of access to jobs and education. And while there was discrimination in France, it was not as intense or institutionalized as it was in the States.

After Baker returned to France, La Martinique was re-positioned as a restaurant and operated as such for many years by Mrs. Becker. When she retired, she sold it to her son, Bill Becker. The day Tony and Danny knocked on the door in 1971, Bill answered, and there was immediate interest. Becker

---

[25] Black Star News, October 7, 2015, "The Night Josephine Baker Never Got Her Steak" by David Rosen

had filed for Chapter 11 bankruptcy and probably would have lost the club had we not approached him. TBOF brought in enough revenue at the bar to keep him afloat and bring La Martinique back to profitability.

As a discotheque, La Martinique had a much different vibe than the Ginza. It required more people to reach a critical mass because of its spacious dance floor and seating areas. La Martinique didn't have a sound system suitable for dancing because it was set up for orchestras. So, Danny bought a state-of-the-art sound system with profits from the Ginza. It consisted of four enormous speakers in large black boxes and four Bose speakers that Danny had hung from the ceiling. Danny also bought a powerful amplifier, two turntables, and a sound mixer with earphones. Danny had Mr. Cooper build a special cabinet to hold the equipment so it could be locked up at the end of the night, since we didn't know who would be using that space on other nights. Danny set up the large black box speakers and the turntable cabinet on top of the one-foot high platform that was previously used for the orchestra. This setup made the DJ the central figure in the room. In contrast, the Ginza's elevated DJ booth was difficult to see from the dance floor.

La Martinique had a capacity of 600, twice the capacity of the Ginza. On the very first Tuesday night at La Martinique, we had a full house. Within a few weeks, so many people came that a line formed with folks waiting to get in as others left. Each Tuesday, over 800 guests entered La Martinique on a flow, and it was clear to us that this concept was resonating among an enormous number of people. Many people just couldn't get enough of the dance experience.

When Danny or CP played records at La Martinique, the sound system was so good, each note went through your entire body — you felt totally immersed in it. Travis, a frequent guest, often brought a tambourine and would wade through the crowd of dancers shaking his tambourine to the beat. He came frequently, and palpably raised the level of intensity. Travis, and several other patrons, also had whistles that would heighten the peaks of energy. As corny as it sounds, the tambourine and whistles made the experience interactive and unique. We rarely let anyone in for free, because it was a slippery slope, but Travis brought so much to the experience, we always waved him in. On one occasion, I tried to play Travis' tambourine and discovered that it's much harder than Travis made it look. Even blowing a whistle requires knowing when it's appropriate and when it's not. If you blow the whistle at the wrong time, it's disruptive instead of energizing.

Although La Martinique was more than twice the size of the Ginza, we had no problem filling it. In the early weeks, lines formed every Tuesday night just as they did for the Ginza on Thursdays. We knew that to preserve our agreement with Bill Becker, we had to make sure we ran a problem-free operation. And we did. Bill sang our praises and appreciated the business we brought in. We never took the situation for granted — we were making too much money to do that. We were careful about the strict enforcement of our policies and always stopped admitting people when the room was full. When a line formed, we would only let people in as others left. As a result, we never had any issues with the Fire or Police Departments.

The large size of La Martinique made it feel more important than the Ginza. It exceeded the tremendous success we had at the Ginza and was the talk of the town that spread beyond NYC and even beyond the black community. Given the stress that many African Americans were feeling from having to deal with routine and systemic discrimination, one could say it was even therapeutic. The power of the music was enhanced exponentially by having the best sound system we could buy, and Danny and CP were on top of their game on the DJ platform. Songs like Stevie Wonder's "Signed, Sealed, Delivered" and "It's Your Thing" by the Isley Brothers became more enjoyable to listen to because of the dynamic and energetic amplification and the fact that you were part of a beautiful crowd that enjoyed the music with you.

The Soul Train TV show, which was created and hosted by Don Cornelius, debuted toward the end of 1971 and greatly contributed to the glamour and excitement of dancing to R&B and funk music. Soul Train featured primarily African American performers and dancers, but the music was so embracing and the dancing so entertaining to watch that many whites tuned in as well. When black folks watched Soul Train, it wasn't just for the entertainment value of the show; it was to pick up new dance moves and to check out the fashions that people were wearing. Dressing up for a night club was an essential part of the fun and Soul Train contributed to an interest in dancing and added to the excitement associated with discotheques.

One of the tasks that came with our success was counting and depositing large amounts of cash every few days. It was a time-consuming task so Tony needed partners to help count the cash. And he was exacting in the way he wanted the money handled. Of course, we had to sort the bills by denomination and count each stack twice. If the count was not identical, we had to count the stack two more times. But Tony also insisted that we place all bills uniformly in each stack. So, Washington, Lincoln, Hamilton, and Jackson were all stacked with the head side up and all heads facing in the same direction. The position of the bills made no difference in the accuracy of the count but it conveyed a certain discipline to this important task.

Within short order, we raised the admission at La Martinique to $5. It didn't make a dent in attendance. We were confident enough to begin expanding to more nights and more venues. Bill Becker always gave us an excellent reference when we approached other clubs, which made a huge difference. Many club owners were uncomfortable doing business with a group of young black men they didn't know. Meanwhile, we also increased admission to the Ginza from $3 to $5. Again, there was no loss in attendance. We found that it was relatively easy to line up venues because many clubs were struggling to keep their doors open. Plus, Bill Becker's positive references made club owners more open to letting us take a night. Just about everyone in the industry knew, or knew of, Bill Becker. After all, La Martinique had been an iconic institution in the city for several decades. Once club owners saw our upscale, college-oriented crowd that spent generously at the bar, they were delighted to have us partner with them. At least most of them were.

I should point out that I subsequently worked in the wine and spirits industry for twenty years and learned that, on average, African Americans spend money at the bar differently than whites. African Americans are more likely to call for luxury or premium brands than whites because they are more likely to perceive it to be a statement about who they are. What that means is that when blacks get dressed up and go out, on average, they spend more at the bar than whites.

At La Martinique, Bill Becker preferred to use his own security person, a large Caribbean black man who dressed in a full Scottish kilt and Glengarry hat outfit. His name was Angus MacGregor, and he was friendly, suave, and had a booming bass voice. I think he wore this outfit because, back when La Martinique was a big band ballroom and then a restaurant, the doorman needed to stand out and be readily identifiable. Or, maybe he just liked the look. Either way, the large Caribbean man looked like a Highland doorman, but his real role was security. He enjoyed our events because he never had much work to do. There were very few incidents at the club and never a fight, which is impressive considering the number of people who attended each week.

Angus occasionally walked around the club but was primarily positioned on the platform where the admission booth was. In addition to having a partner inside the booth collecting money, one of us would stand outside the booth with a clicker to keep track of the headcount. Often, several partners would be on the platform since the added presence served as a robbery deterrent. Angus was twice our age, but he enjoyed chatting with us and became a friend. On occasion, he would bring snacks for us as a treat, like a bag of chicharron, fried pork skin and a separate container of lime wedges. Angus would always say: "Squeeze the lime on it," which kicked up the flavor a notch.

With the remarkable success of our Ginza and La Martinique businesses, Mal, along with Tony, Danny, and CP, decided to share our formula for success with black promoters in nearby cities since we had no intention of expanding there. To pull off events like ours, you needed to have a strong local network of followers. We didn't have a network in other cities, but local promoters did. By sharing our formula, we could give these out of town promoters a chance to make some money too.

Mal took the lead in identifying black promoters in several cities in the eastern half of the U.S. and invited them to a conference we put together in a hotel suite near Kennedy Airport. We invited promoters from Philadelphia, Washington, DC, Chicago, and Detroit, but only folks from Philadelphia and

DC showed up. We walked them through a flip chart presentation outlining exactly how we created successful discotheque events as promoters. We described ways to build up a mailing list, how to negotiate for venue space, and how to control the door to ensure a good vibe inside. We discussed our dress code and how we handled behavior issues. Our goal was to encourage promoters in other cities to become more successful by emulating our protocols and procedures. We were not looking to profit from this, rather we simply wanted to share what we felt was a somewhat time-sensitive opportunity that could benefit promoters in other cities. Some cities had a different dynamic than NYC, but they all had an emerging black middle class and available venues.

The folks in DC opened a club in a townhouse where they had a different vibe on each floor: dancing, jazz club, bar/lounge area, etc. They called their business the Foxxtrappe Town Club. It was very successful for many years. In fact, they expanded by adding the LA Café and Mingles. The guys from Philadelphia followed our blueprint more closely and called themselves The Best of Friends as a tribute to us. They owned four clubs: Vine Street Café, Juice, Café Erlanger, and Le Ferry. This last club was on a permanently moored boat. Café Erlanger was hip and cool because it had a waterfall and several infinity mirrors that people still talk about today. While we had no financial ties with either organization, they gave us complimentary admission into their clubs, and we reciprocated. Unfortunately, with our crazy schedule, few of us had time to take advantage of this arrangement.

In 1971, I went on my first business trip to Detroit for Young & Rubicam. My purpose was to conduct store checks to document Birds Eye frozen vegetables pricing, displays, shelf facings, and sizes versus the competition. Many of my coworkers would conduct eight to ten store checks per day, and their bosses were happy with that. I had a different approach. I always wanted to do more than management expected, so I moved as fast as I could to hit a minimum of a dozen stores per day. I was able to complete 24 store checks in two days and still had time on the second afternoon. Instead of trying to hit even more stores, I decided to visit Motown. After all, I was in Detroit.

I had seen photos of the little house where Motown started, but the telephone directory had a different address. It was the Donovan office building in downtown Detroit, a ten-story building that Motown occupied from 1968 to 1972. I didn't have an appointment because my visit was a last-minute decision predicated on completing my store checks early. I figured the folks at Motown knew about our clubs because we had a national reputation, at least within the black community. I entered the lobby and told the receptionist who I was. She was not aware of La Martinique or the Ginza, but the management person she called was. A man came out, ushered me into his office, and called Hamilton Bohannon to escort me on a tour of the facility. Bohannon, they called him, had been the drummer for Stevie Wonder before becoming a songwriter, bandleader, and producer for Motown. As we walked through the halls, he showed me row after row of tiny offices with a small piano in each one. This is where the songwriters worked. We paused in one of the offices where he played a new song for me that he was working on and asked my opinion. It was almost all rhythm with a simple, repetitive melody. But the prominent beat was tailor-made for dancing and I told him that. Later that evening I went to the 20 Grand Club to catch a performance by the Four Tops. A phone call from Bohannon got me a table right down front. The Four Tops became my favorite group that night.

I didn't know it at the time, but Berry Gordy, Jr. had already moved much of his operation from Detroit to Los Angeles. By June of 1972, the entire Motown operation was in Los Angeles. Some ardent fans wanted the Donovan building to become a Motown museum, and there was a valiant effort to make it happen, but it failed. Another tenant moved into the Donovan after Motown, but they departed in 1974, leaving the building abandoned. It remained vacant until 2006 when it was razed as part of the city's preparation for Superbowl XL. The building had lots of artifacts, original music scores, and many other documents, but the demolition destroyed them. Mayor Kwame Kilpatrick pushed to raze the building because it was an eyesore, and he wanted the area for parking during the Superbowl. By some accounts, not one car was parked there for the big game.[26]

[26] https://daily.redbullmusicacademy.com/2016/05/when-motown-left-detroit-feature, "What It Is: When Motown Left Detroit" by Douglas Wolk on May 23, 2016

I knew Bohannon's music would go over well in our clubs, so I invited him to visit La Martinique on his next trip to New York City. And he took me up on the offer. He happened to come on a night when I wasn't there, but CP was. He and Bohannon became fast friends. Bohannon visited our clubs many times and got to know all the partners, but he was always closest to CP. Bohannon was impressed with our discotheques, both the Ginza and La Martinique, and the sounds that turned on our dancers. Perhaps that contributed to his inspiration because he became one of the leading figures in disco music as a bandleader and songwriter. Bohannon's music had heavy, thudding bass accents and aggressive rhythms – just like many of the songs my partners curated when they operated the DJ booth. Keep in mind, disco music didn't even exist in the early '70s, so the focus was on songs with an infectious, danceable beat.

CP and Bohannon remained friends all through the years. Some 30 years after they first met, CP visited Bohannon at his home in Georgia. Bohannon is a devout Christian, and his focus at that time was gospel music. They remained good friends until Bohannon's death in April 2020.

Many celebrities and personalities came to our events, especially after we expanded to La Martinique. One weekday night, Mal relieved me at the door, so I used the occasion to go inside the club. When you work the door, you can't see much of the club, just a glimpse. It was about 3 am, and many people had already left since the next day was a workday.

At the bar, a guy was sitting by himself. I walked over, ordered a drink, and introduced myself. He said his name was Billy. He was easy to talk to and down to earth.

I asked him, "How're you doing?"

"I'm just relaxin' and enjoying the music," he responded.

I motioned for the bartender to give him a drink as we continued our conversation. I told Billy about The Best of Friends and how we got started. We were having a great chat when CP came over and introduced us. I had no idea I was talking to Billy Preston.

Often referred to as the "Fifth Beatle," Billy Preston played keyboard on many of their most popular albums. He also played with Eric Clapton, the

Rolling Stones, and wrote many songs we still cherish, such as "You Are So Beautiful," made famous by Joe Cocker. Preston also wrote the hit song on Stephen Stills' debut solo album featuring the line "If you can't be with the one you love, love the one you're with," along with many more memorable lyrics. Billy Preston was near the height of his magnificent career at that time, yet he seemed so modest and genuine. He was a pure musical genius and an engaging person. We were all saddened years later when he passed away at the young age of 59.

Perhaps the most exciting celeb to stop by La Martinique was boxing great, Muhammad Ali. It was also in 1971 and Wayne was in the booth collecting the admission fee. Ali had already suffered his first loss to Joe Frazier but won the next couple of fights on his way to making a comeback. I was standing outside the booth with the clicker when I realized who was stepping down the stairs. Ali was by himself. He walked down the wide entry staircase and stopped on the platform where I was.

"Welcome, Mr. Ali," I said as I shook his hand.

He responded, "Thank you. How are you guys doing tonight?"

"Great" I explained. "There are at least 600 guests inside having the night of their lives."

"That's good," he replied. "Looks like you got a good thing going on here. I heard about your club and just wanted to stop by to see it for myself."

The club level was three steps down to a wide hallway entrance to the main room about 20 feet away. Red and black patterned carpeting covered the floor. If you walked in the opposite direction from the main room, you could come back to the same spot because the hallway wrapped around the back of the entrance platform where we were standing and led to the Caribbean room, which connected to the main room with a dance floor and bar. There was a steady flow of people walking past the platform in both directions.

I saw Harry walking by and waved for him to meet Ali. As Harry walked up the three steps and extended his hand, I was struck by how similar Harry and Ali were in size and body shape.

"I'm Harry, one of the partners here. It's a pleasure to meet you," he said.

Ali responded, "My pleasure."

97

Just then, a beautiful lady walked by the wide hallway.

Ali noticed, "You have a good-looking crowd here."

"Yes, we do!" I smiled.

Harry said, "Please feel free to walk into the club so you can see the rest of it."

"No, thanks. I'll just look from here," Ali said.

We knew he had converted to the Muslim faith a few years earlier and didn't drink. I guess he didn't want to be seen in the club around people drinking.

"Can we take a photo with you?" I asked Ali.

"Sure."

Wayne was inside the booth, so Ali, Harry and I flanked the booth so we could all be in the picture.

Ali was charming and down to earth, and we all felt comfortable talking to him. I mentioned how I just got back from Detroit, where I visited Motown and met Hamilton Bohannon, who turned me on to the hatter that all the entertainers in Detroit use.

I pointed out that I bought my hat from that hatter. "What do you think?"

"Yeah, it's sharp," he responded.

I was proud of my maroon fedora with a wide brim and I liked the way it made me stand out. The photo we took with Ali also memorialized my favorite hat. I could wear it on the platform, but not inside the club. After all, we had to adhere to our own rules, too.

After chatting for about half an hour, Ali said, "Great to meet you guys. Good luck with your business," and started walking up the stairs. As James Brown's "Hot Pants" filled the air, I walked Ali to the door and watched as he got into a waiting car.

Ali visiting La Martinique was a big deal and it made us feel proud of the environment we created. A few weeks later, someone else walked down those same stairs and changed my life forever.

Chapter 12
GWEN

"*S*orry, I just wanted to see if it was really your hair."

One September night in 1971, I was in the booth on the platform at La Martinique, collecting the admission fee as guests entered. Three ladies walked down the steps, and I recognized one as an acquaintance from the parties I used to go to in Queens. But it was one of her friends who caught my attention. She was a stunning young woman with a large, perfectly round afro and a super sexy halter top. I thought she might be wearing a wig because it was so large and perfectly round. I rarely left the booth before — only to take a quick bathroom break or for photo ops with special guests such as Muhammad Ali — but I asked Andre to take over the door that night. I wanted to meet the young lady with the gorgeous afro before she entered the club. I didn't want to lose her in the crowd. I left the booth quickly and caught up to her while she was still on the platform.

I don't know what came over me, but I pulled her hair.

"What are you doing?" she hollered.

Sheepishly, I said, "Sorry, I just wanted to see if it was really your hair."

"Of course, it's my hair!" she responded.

I don't recall what I said after that, but she didn't seem mad. In fact, we spent the rest of the night getting to know each other. I escorted her into the Caribbean room, which was away from the dancing and loud music.

The Caribbean room was just a large alcove area next to the bar, but it was roomy enough to hold about 50 people at café tables and a row of booths along one wall. Only a handful of people were there because virtually everyone wanted to be on or near the dance floor, where the action was. I needed a quiet place to get to know the fine young lady whose hair I had just yanked. I learned that we had similar backgrounds, her father was from Honduras, and her mother was Creole from New Orleans. My parents were from Jamaica, so we both had immigrant parents and grew up with the culture of the Caribbean. I graduated from Queens College, and she had just transferred to Queens College from Hampton Institute.

She told me her name was Gwendolyn, but most people called her Gwen. She also told me that her girlfriend, Danita, brought her to La Martinique that night to introduce her to a friend. Gwen had just gotten over a relationship and didn't feel like meeting anyone, so she was reluctant to go. Danita finally convinced her. But before Danita could introduce Gwen to her friend, I came along. We found out later that the person Danita planned to introduce Gwen to, was me! What a coincidence. After our long conversation, I pulled out my little black book and opened it to the "D" section, because Gwen's last name was Diaz. I could fit three names with phone numbers on each page. I handed the book to Gwen with a pen and asked her to jot down her phone number. She wrote her name and number so large that it filled the entire page.

"Why did you write it so big?" I asked, somewhat annoyed.

"So, you won't forget who I am!" she answered coyly.

All I could say was, "Okay. Sounds good to me."

I arranged a date to see Gwen again. We didn't do a whole lot; we just hung out together and talked. We saw a lot of each other over the next several months. Gwen was always happy, thoughtful, and made ordinary occasions exciting. It didn't take long for us to fall in love. But our relationship was interrupted and came close to ending. It was indirectly related to TBOF.

The late nights at the clubs and the early morning at the office equaled some moments of sleep deprivation. One morning, while driving to work in rush hour traffic, I nodded off briefly and rear-ended the truck in front of me. I had worked the night before at La Martinique and only got two hours of sleep. I was already exhausted before I even got up to get ready to go to the office. My exhaustion caused the accident. I was unharmed but my 1966 Mustang wasn't so lucky. The Mustang already had some problems, so I decided to junk it and ordered a new car. It took eight weeks to get the delivery of my new car, a Chevrolet Monte Carlo. During those eight weeks, I had no wheels. I couldn't go to see Gwen. I called and talked to her on the phone, but I couldn't ask her out on a date without a car. With no transportation, it was challenging to get to Hollis, where Gwen lived. It was a long two months for me and for Gwen. She began doubting whether I was serious about her. It took a while to win Gwen back. But I did.

When Gwen invited me to her house to meet her family over dinner, I knew I was on the right track. Gwen's family had the same dynamics as mine in that we each had three boys and a girl. That meant I had to deal with Gwen's three brothers. I was a bit nervous about that and I fully expected some scrutiny and ribbing from them. As it turned out, they were very friendly, and we got along well. Gwen's Creole mother served up some New Orleans style gumbo. I never heard of gumbo before, but it tasted great, and I asked for seconds. Afterward, I thanked Mrs. Diaz for the delicious dinner, and she replied, "Oh, we haven't served dinner yet. That was just the appetizer." She then brought out large platters of baked chicken, potato salad, corn and dinner rolls. I learned that day how important food is to Creole culture. I also learned how delicious their food is.

Three years later, Gwen and I were married. And I've been eating gumbo ever since. We have two beautiful grown daughters and two wonderful sons-in-law. Gwen and I joined the ranks of a large group of people who met life partners at our clubs. Andre, Harry, and Wayne also met their wives at our events. Andre met his wife at one of our Black Christmas dances. They married right after Andre graduated from Fordham University, moved into a townhouse in Teaneck, New Jersey and had two daughters. Harry met his wife Shelly at Leviticus, our first club in Manhattan that would be our flagship. Harry and Shelly had a boy and a girl and lived in a house in Springfield Gardens, Queens. Wayne met his wife at the Manhattan Center, where we staged a dance as City-Wide Associates. They moved into the Cunningham Apartments in Jamaica, Queens, and had a son and a daughter. Wayne seemed very happy. Since he was the first one among us to have a wife and children, he was a role model for us. It turned out that the view looking in was very different than the view from the inside because Wayne's marriage didn't last long.

Gwen and Noel

Chapter 13
BLANKET THE CORE

"*How do you feel about Saturday nights?*"

"Given our success at the Ginza and La Martinique and the overall strong demand for discotheques, we need to expand" Tony explained at one of our meetings. Our first step was to increase the number of nights at the Ginza and La Martinique. Within a few months, we added Friday and Sunday nights to La Martinique, and Friday and Saturday nights at the Ginza. We had a full house every night, and profits were ballooning.

With our successful nights at La Martinique, Bill Becker, the club's owner, approached us.

"How do you feel about Saturday nights?" he asked. "I can offer you a deal to take over Saturday nights here, too."

We were interested, but there was a catch. Bill wanted us to pay for it. It meant we would be sharing the door proceeds. We called a meeting of TBOF to discuss Bill's deal. We decided not to do it. We were interested in expanding, but only if the move made good financial sense. We were realizing the ups and downs of being dance promoters.

That still left Bill with a void to fill on Saturday nights. Eventually, he agreed to let John Juliano take over Saturday nights. We knew Juliano because he frequented La Martinique on our nights and seemed to be monitoring it. He asked lots of questions about our operation, so we thought he was looking to improve his Jewish singles events or perhaps enhance a club he owned in another part of town. We had no idea that he was looking to compete with us as a promoter at La Martinique. Juliano got Frankie Crocker and Johnny Allen, two top DJs from WBLS, to promote the club on radio. By taking over Saturday nights, Juliano got a good number of our guests to attend. In fact, he was probably banking on it. When people heard there was a Saturday night dance party at La Martinique, there's no doubt many of them assumed we were the sponsors.

However, the vibe on Saturday nights was not the same as when we controlled the door. It was a whole different experience and the guests felt it. Juliano and his staff did not know the people who walked through the door. As a result, they were unable to identify troublemakers and, importantly, they did not enforce the dress codes or behavior policies we had in place. That made Saturday nights at La Martinique differ greatly from TBOF events. However, Juliano saw that the African American audience was a better audience for social events than his Jewish singles format. As a result, he eventually bought the Copacabana, Red Parrot, and Ecstasy. The Copa that Juliano bought was a different location than the one where Tony saw the Temps and Tops at a front row table. The new location lacked the prestige and glamour of the original Copacabana.

A few years later, Juliano used a clever technique with some of his clubs that impressed us. He would use a space for a restaurant serving lunch and dinner and cater to a primarily white audience. Then around 10 pm, he would transform the space into a nightclub. He actually changed the name of the venue by simply covering up the day name with a temporary fabric featuring the night name and re-organizing the furniture. His nightclubs catered primarily to a black audience. His strategy worked.

In 1972, we got bad news from Mr. Chu at the Ginza. His lease was up and he decided not to renew. I suspect there was an increase in rent that he was not willing to accept. So, our successful run at the Ginza came to an end. It was bittersweet. The Ginza was our first venture in midtown and helped launch our successful reputation as promoters. It was a bit sad to see it go, but Tony had good news for us. He was able to secure a club on W. 73rd Street off-Broadway called Casa Blanca. We were able to have Thursday and Sunday nights for a bar guarantee. We charged $4 admission and it did not include a free drink. Plus, with a capacity of 350, Casa Blanca was larger than the Ginza, so it was much more profitable. Our events at Casa Blanca were also well-attended and, due to its location in the upper west side, pulled in a slightly different crowd than La Martinique.

Also, in 1972, there was a restaurant near the corner of Madison Ave. and 37th Street that closed down. An Egyptian entrepreneur bought it, remodeled the space, and called it Al Mounia. It was still a restaurant, but he turned the back room into an area for dancing. He had a primarily white clientele and realized only a marginal success. Tony and Danny negotiated with the owner for Thursday nights. Although it was relatively small, we attracted a consistent after-work crowd that spent generously at the bar. Al Mounia continued to extend the reach of TBOF. Later that year, we added Wednesday nights at Barney Google's located on 86th Street off 3rd Ave. Barney Google's was a large, popular restaurant/nightclub, so most folks knew where it was, and the TBOF crowd arrived after the dinner crowd was winding down. Again, because of the upper east side location, Barney Google's attracted a different crowd than the other clubs.

We were at our peak as promoters in 1972. We had seven events a week, all in midtown or near midtown. Essentially, we blanketed the core of the Big Apple. La Martinique and the Ginza, before that event ended, were open from 9 or 10 pm and closed anywhere from 2 to 4 am. Casa Blanca, Al Mounia, and Barney Google's had earlier hours. Some patrons came to our events right after work, while others came late. Hence, on many nights, we had a flow of patrons that exceeded the capacity of the venue. For example, we averaged more than 450 guests at the Casa Blanca even though the legal capacity was only 350. La Martinique had a capacity of 600, but we averaged 800 guests per night. There were a couple of nights, during holiday weekends, when we had over 1,000 guests at La Martinique. Our reputation spread widely among club owners in the midtown area. Nightclub owners all had high regard for Bill Becker because he operated La Martinique successfully for many years. So, when Bill sang our praises, people took notice. Not always the right people.

Word of our success even reached the mafia. They heard about us and the high-quality, heavy-spending crowd we controlled and wanted to see if there was an opportunity to partner with us. Matthew Ianniello, a gangster known as "Matty the Horse", owned a number of clubs in the area and began eyeing TBOF clubs as a potentially profitable partnership opportunity. Two flunkies from Matty's organization approached Tony and Danny one evening at La Martinique.

"You boys are good at promoting events," one of them said. "We'd like to show you some of our nightclubs to see if any would be suitable for you to bring in your crowd."

It was an intriguing offer. Later that week, Matty's men arranged for a limousine to take Tony and Danny to four different clubs. After the visits, which took about two hours, Tony and Danny concluded that none was suitable because they were all juice bars. Tony and Danny were somewhat leery about declining Matty the Horse's offer. But, even more leery to accept it.

Juice bars were common in New York City at that time. It was not easy to get a liquor license, much less a cabaret license, which allowed dancing. For many, juice bars were the only viable alternative.

The two mafia guys ended the night on a cordial, friendly note and expressed their appreciation to Tony and Danny for taking the time to look at the four clubs. The entire time, Tony and Danny conducted themselves with calm confidence and professionalism. The way they handled this encounter helped establish a level of respect and decorum that came in handy a few years later when we had a scarier encounter with a different pair of mobsters.

We were at our peak as promoters with extensive coverage in Manhattan.

After La Martinique, Casa Blanca was our biggest moneymaker.

"We had to stop admitting folks on most nights", recalled Harry, who worked the door at Casa Blanca.

Harry went on to say, "Some people were so desperate to get in they offered multiples of the $4 admission price." Of course, we couldn't let them in, but it was an indication of how strong the demand was.

Casa Blanca lived up to its name. It was a large, irregular shaped room off the lobby of a large apartment building on West 73rd Street with white stucco walls and several arches. It had a sexy, international atmosphere. As our second most profitable club, we averaged 450 people per night, two nights a week. Al Mounia and Barney Google's, both on the east side, were considerably smaller, averaging 100 and 150 guests per night, respectively.

If you aggregate attendance across all of our events, we entertained more than 2,500 guests per week in Manhattan. Because our relationship with these club owners was often a simple handshake, we knew we had to run a smooth, trouble-free operation, or else they could kick us out at a moment's notice. One aspect of that was to make sure we never had a problem with the fire department. We knew from our days of giving dances that the FDNY would shut down an event quickly if too many people were in the building. Therefore, we always had someone with a clicker counting each person that came in. The clicker was also a way to monitor and confirm the amount of cash collected at the door. Fire department officials stopped by our discotheques on occasion, but they saw how controlled the environment was and never had a problem with us.

There were other discotheques in the midtown area, and we knew all of them. I can say confidently that, within Manhattan, we had the largest share of business…by far. That success…at least the money we were bringing in… caught the attention of other unscrupulous people. Even some we knew well.

We experienced a serious internal problem that rocked the Best of Friends. Danny always had a rough idea, from the size of the crowd, how much money should be in the till each night. The clicker we used also served to monitor the cash intake. On one particular occasion, Freddy volunteered to deposit the weekend take. Danny noticed that the deposit was short by about $10,000. He brought it up at our weekly meeting that Monday night.

"What happened to the money Freddy?" Danny asked.

Freddy responded in a rather flip and irreverent way, "Oh, I borrowed some of it, but I will replace it."

That didn't sit well with any of us. After a few expressions of surprise and outrage, we decided Freddy had to go. We could no longer trust him. This was a shocking situation for us because we thought we could trust each other completely. It shook us, but we were unanimous in getting rid of Freddy.

As we all listened intently, Tony said: "Freddy, what you did was not acceptable. You have to repay the $10,000 immediately and you can no longer be in The Best of Friends."

Freddy sank in his chair. He didn't know what to say. Finally, in a soft voice, he said "I told you I'll pay it back. But we can still be friends, right?"

Tony spoke for the rest of us. "Sure, Freddy. We can still be friends." Freddy got up and left the meeting.

Freddy did repay the money and a few months later, accepted a new job in San Francisco. He worked there for a couple of years before returning to New York. When he got back, Freddy was disappointed that his relationship with the guys was no longer the same. He felt we were avoiding him because of what he did, and it depressed him. But that wasn't the case. We were just all so busy, we didn't have time for the type of socializing we did before we owned clubs. We didn't even meet with each other very often because we had already fully discussed virtually every possible scenario and eventuality. Plus, Tony and Danny were seasoned managers by then and didn't need to review every issue with the rest of us. As a result, we got together a lot less than we did in the beginning. But Freddy didn't buy it. He thought we were hanging out together behind his back and excluding him. By then, we owned a couple of discotheques. Freddy would stop by the clubs to complain that we were ignoring him. We explained that none of us were as social as we had been a few years ago. Since we were not hanging out together we'll never know if we would have excluded Freddy. However, we could never forget his betrayal of our trust or forgive him for what he did.

After Freddy misappropriated our funds, everything was different. Actually, things started changing before Freddy left the group. We were all pretty close at one point, but with the stress and pressure of multiple nightly operations, that closeness of the social club days gave way to the realities of business relationships. Plus, by this time, we had opened two more discotheques, a second in Manhattan and one in Brooklyn. As a group, we were highly proficient as a social club, so we excelled at promoting the clubs. As a business enterprise, however, some of us struggled with running this all-consuming business. To be fair, Tony and Danny had learned the business well and were effective. The rest of us, not so much. That put extra pressure on Tony and Danny.

Within a year of his return to New York, Freddy developed a serious health issue. I believe one of his organs was failing and the doctors were unable to fix the problem. He died a short time later. We'll never know if Freddy's mental state contributed to his illness, but I've heard it's possible. We all went to Freddy's funeral and were saddened by his tragic ending. Freddy was not married, but he had an identical twin and a younger brother and sister. Freddy's twin was married with kids and was very different than Freddy in that we didn't see him at many parties or at our clubs. Whenever I hear Curtis Mayfield's "Freddie's Dead," I can't help but think of our former partner and the many good times we had.

As we continued to promote specific nights at additional clubs, CP and I created a new flyer for each. As always, fliers were mailed out to the master TBOF contact list and also handed out to well-dressed sophisticates. It only took a few weeks to establish each club with a crowd that came automatically after that. Word of mouth worked well for us and was our strongest form of advertising. Patrons had their favorites and knew when and where to go for a fun night of dancing. In each case, TBOF collected admission at the door, and the club owner took the bar. The only expense we incurred was the cost of printing a flyer, which was often a one-shot deal, and a bouncer for each event. Every club was a success, both socially and financially. And our profits were astounding. To us, it was a windfall. Of the five club locations, La Martinique was not only the most profitable, to me it was also the most exciting. It was our largest venue, and it was located in a prestigious midtown location that contributed to making guests feel special. Other people also noticed how profitable La Martinique was.

One night three men came into La Martinique and got into a disagreement and argued with some of our regulars. A couple of these regulars went to Tony and complained that the three guys were threatening them. Tony knew who the three guys were. They were part of a dangerous street gang in Brooklyn. Tony, Mal, Angus the bouncer, along with several other partners and staff backing them up, confronted the three characters and told them they had to leave. After a few tense moments, they agreed to leave, but on the way out, they told Tony and Mal they would be waiting outside for them at the end of the night. When closing time came, the partners gathered to walk out together, which was routinely done for safety. Tony and Mal walked up the staircase with Bill Becker and Angus the bouncer close behind them. When they reached the top of the stairs, they could see out the glass doors. Five black cars were parked across the street. A group of tough-looking black men was standing on the street side of the cars, starring into La Martinique. It was not a good time to leave.

"Move away from the door," Mal extended his hands outward and took a step back.

They all retreated down the steps and gathered to discuss the situation.

"Well, Bill," Mal joked. "Can we all sleep here tonight?" That broke the tension a bit and everyone let out a little chuckle.

Bill calmly said, "Wait here until I come back."

He and Angus went into Bill's office. After about 15 minutes, they emerged, walked to the top of the stairs to take a peek outside, and beckoned for my partners to come up. There, in front of La Martinique between the gang members and the front door, were three limousines. Several men had gotten out and were talking to the men gathered across the street. Mal and Tony later said that they couldn't hear what was being said and couldn't read their body language. Both sets of characters were cool and confident...at least temporarily. Two of the longest minutes in history passed before the group of guys across the street got into the five cars and drove away. Two of the limousines also pulled away. The third limousine stayed. A man standing next to that limo walked over to Bill and the rest of the guys and said, "You boys get home safely tonight." And they did. Whew!

My partners didn't know who was in the limos, but they did know that Bill used to write the police blotter for a newspaper and got to know the top brass at NYPD. Bill was a soft-spoken, unassuming man. But he was well known and extremely well respected. Some months later, when we were looking to expand into other midtown venues, Bill got phone calls asking about us and what kind of guys we were. He always gave us a stellar review, which enabled us to access clubs that many competitive promoters could not.

Toward the end of 1972, a series of events brought our successful business enterprise to a screeching halt. Some of it we saw coming. Some of it caught us by total surprise.

Chapter 14
FROM LUCIFER'S TO LEVITICUS

"*It's been great working with you all, but all things come to an end.*"

La Martinique was a cash cow for us, so we were stunned when Bill Becker, the owner of the venue, announced that he was going to move in another direction. It was 1972 when he gave us a couple of months' notice before our days at La Martinique screeched to an end. We knew, of course, that all of our agreements with club owners were temporary, including our relationship with Bill and La Martinique. Bill had been one of our biggest cheerleaders… maybe that's why it stung so much when this chapter of TBOF closed. Bill still appreciated the business that we brought his way and respected how we ran a trouble-free operation. He offered to continue to give us glowing recommendations, but he explained, "All things come to an end." Still, it was a shock.

TBOF had always stayed away from radio advertising. Radio was broadcast to the masses and we preferred to be more selective about our guests. After TBOF left, Bill worked with a new team of event promoters who staged dances at La Martinique. The new promoters advertised on the radio, plus, more importantly, they didn't know the crowd. They failed to follow the dress code and behavior policies we developed and did not implement effective rules. As a result, the vibe was not the same anymore. That group of promoters didn't last too long. Shortly after, our old pal, John Juliano, took over as promoter. During that time, there were a few violent incidents at La Martinique, including a stabbing, that tarnished the venue's reputation. The regulars that we so carefully cultivated gradually went elsewhere. Within a few months, our crowd stopped going to La Martinique.

We were still reeling from the loss of La Martinique when Mr. Chu, the owner of the Ginza, also ended his relationship with us. It had nothing to do with us. Like Bill Becker, Mr. Chu sang our praises. But he, too, wanted to explore other opportunities. We were disappointed but not surprised by this blow. Even though the Ginza had become a little less important to us after we started at La Martinique, especially since we were making much more money at other venues, it was still emotional to end our run at the Ginza. This was, after all, our first foray into midtown.

Then came the final straw. Bob Tirado's lease at Casa Blanca was up. He decided not to renew, presumably because the landlord wanted too much money. We never were completely sure that was the reason, but either way, it spelled the end of Casa Blanca for us. In a short time, we lost three of our key clubs. We had handshake agreements with all of our club owners so we knew the good ride would come to an end one day. This eventuality was something that Tony and Danny had previously discussed with TBOF so we all understood what the next step would be. We had accumulated over a million dollars…it was time to build our own clubs. But before we could execute this plan, we had to endure more upheaval.

The Egyptian owner of Al Mounia told us he had to end our Thursday nights at his club too. He explained that his white patrons were complaining about us and threatening to stop coming to his club on other nights if he continued to let us take one night each week. They didn't want black folks in what they considered to be their club. The owner was in a tough spot. He really appreciated our crowd and he respected our strict standards, but we were only there one night a week. He was concerned about his other six nights and, as a businessman, he needed to look out for his best interests, even if it meant cow-towing to his other patrons, so he ended our parties. We were disappointed because we had built up a nice crowd of regulars at Al Mounia. But we didn't resist or lodge a complaint. The bottom line was that this situation just reinforced what we already knew — we had to build our own clubs.

In the meantime, we added more discotheque venues to replace the ones we lost. They were all successful, but not to the degree of La Martinique and Casa Blanca. The events we promoted included discos at the Dom in the East Village and the Prince George Hotel on East 28th Street in Manhattan. We also continued to put on the annual holiday dance that we themed "Black Christmas," since it had been so successful. We put on that dance for five straight years with the last one held in December 1973.

Wisely, Tony said we needed to learn how to operate and manage a bar before building a large discotheque in Manhattan. Even though we had plenty of experience hosting and promoting our dances, he knew there was much more to owning a club than that. He suggested we start with a small club in Queens, which would be convenient for all of us so that we could learn the entire operation — hiring, ordering liquor, managing the bar, setting up proper bank accounts and accounting systems, and so on.

To get our arms around all the issues and ensure that we all knew what was going on, we built a TBOF office in Queens behind a run-down storefront on Farmers Boulevard. It provided a place where we could meet to discuss management issues and plan to build our business. The outside of the storefront was left untouched, so it looked like an abandoned building. We kept it that way to avoid calling attention to our office, so burglars wouldn't think valuables were inside. Behind the front door, the interior was built out nicely by Mr. Cooper, Tony's father. The front room was a plush carpeted lounge area featuring a bar and living room type furniture. The backroom had a large, round, Formica-topped table that filled the room. It was a custom table that Tony's dad built based on Tony's direction. Eight comfortable chairs surrounded the table. We had plenty of ashtrays because seven of us smoked. No one had heard of second-hand smoke in those days, so without recognizing the risk, we managed our business in this smoke-filled conference room. We debated policies, developed plans to expand our nightclub involvement, and, with the always impressive financial reports that Danny presented, we discussed venturing into other business areas. We wanted to diversify, but none of the ideas seemed to have the traction or profitability we were getting from the club business. We also had lots of parties in this office, including a wedding reception, a bachelors' party, and several New Year's Eve parties.

For our first club, Tony recommended we start small. He found a site where we could build in Queens on the corner of Linden Boulevard and 217th Street in Cambria Heights, near where most members of TBOF lived. Tony had already come up with a name for our first club that we all loved — Lucifer's. There was no rationale for that selection; we just liked how it sounded. The Cambria Heights area, which is adjacent to St. Albans and Hollis was, and still is, a middle-class African American community. Many prominent African American entertainers lived nearby in Addesleigh Park, an upscale section of St. Albans. Residents there included Lena Horne, James Brown, Ella Fitzgerald, Jackie Robinson, Joe Louis, Miles Davis, W.E.B. DuBois, Count Basie, and others. Count Basie, who had one of the few pools in the area, invited all the neighborhood kids to swim in his pool every Saturday, which I thought was very impressive.

The neighborhoods of Cambria Heights, Hollis, and St. Albans had a relatively high percentage of college graduates, including doctors, teachers, and entrepreneurs. These residents comprised our key target audience in Queens. There was a young man who lived in Hollis that we didn't know at that time but would meet a few years later. His name was Russell Simmons.

Linden Boulevard was a long commercial strip running through St. Albans to Cambria Heights with over a dozen bars. They all catered to the local community and were casual. But Lucifer's was a test business for us, so we implemented the same dress and behavior codes that we had in Manhattan, which were enforced by a bouncer at the door. After the first year, the dress code was relaxed except for Saturday nights because, after all, Lucifer's was a neighborhood club. Like the clubs in Manhattan, Lucifer's was designed for dancing, although on a smaller scale.

TBOF in Queens office; l-r, Wayne, Noel, Andre, Mal, CP, Harry, Danny, Tony

TBOF in Queens office; From front clockwise: CP, Andre, Harry, Noel, Wayne, Mal, Danny, Tony

Danny, Tony, Andre at office

Tony bought two large NYC code books that identified the few specific locations that were zoned for a cabaret license. You couldn't even apply for a cabaret license if you were not in one of the approved locations. Tony researched the entire area and learned that there was only one block in our target area that was zoned to accept applications for a cabaret license. That was how Tony selected the building that would eventually become Lucifer's. Initially, we planned to apply for a cabaret license, which would allow legal dancing but we decided not to because the primary purpose of Lucifer's was to learn the bar business. We actually had dancing but the authorities never came by to stop us.

The building we leased for Lucifer's had been an old, run-down Irish pub. TBOF signed a long-term lease, and after reviewing several construction bids, we decided to hire Mr. Cooper. He was a carpenter primarily experienced in finishing residential basements in Queens. We liked his work, but more importantly, we knew we could trust Mr. Cooper. This decision reflected the skeptical nature of our group. There were many building code requirements for a structure where people gather to drink and dance, e.g., we had to use fire retardant wood, fire code sheetrock, floors had to meet load-bearing standards, and so on. We knew Mr. Cooper could be trusted to build our club right, which was not the case with any other contractor.

Since Tony's dad had never built a nightclub before, Tony and Danny came up with a simple template for all clubs we would eventually build. The template included white stucco walls, white bar, red and black patterned commercial carpeting, elevated platform for tables to add visual interest and to make it easier to see the dancers, and, importantly, a dance floor with black and white checkerboard tiles. In the case of Lucifer's, the outside of the building was also painted white with large black three-D letters spelling out the club's name. We kept the original bar that was in the pub and had Mr. Cooper cover it over with white Formica. It turned out to be a magical transformation.

Tony quit his teaching job to work full time for TBOF and to focus on constructing Lucifer's. Shortly afterward, Danny made the same decision. Initially, we simply matched their teacher's salary. However, they were doing a great job and working such long hours that we raised their salaries. But even after receiving a raise, their compensation was still relatively modest considering that, in short order, our business grew to a multimillion-dollar a year operation. Those of us who kept our day jobs did not pull a salary, but we did get reimbursed for expenses. As our first full-time employees, Tony and Danny became the de facto leaders of TBOF. And it only made sense. After all, they had been effective in running the Ginza and La Martinique and in guiding our expansion to additional nights at each club.

In planning the creation of Lucifer's, Tony took the lead in hiring staff. He went to area bars to observe their operation and procedures. When Tony received good service or saw someone who knew what they were doing, he offered that person a job. Bars in the surrounding area tended to cater to older people. Our crowd was quite a bit younger — and more stylish. We offered a fun, attractive place to work. Plus, we featured dancing while area clubs generally did not. So, although there was some overlap with other bars, we largely had a different clientele.

The grand opening of Lucifer's was on June 20, 1973. About a week later, as a way to continue the excitement, we featured Jon Lucien, the Grammy-nominated singer. This level of energy and excitement was rare for area clubs, so Lucifer's immediately became the hottest ticket on Linden Boulevard. Our regular followers knew TBOF owned Lucifer's, so they understood that it would be special. The club was a destination, with patrons coming from as far as Connecticut and New Jersey. Four months after the opening, the Arab oil embargo created a massive nationwide gas shortage that led to panic, fights, and even people stealing gas from parked cars. Some gas stations had lines that were hours long. Despite that environment, our followers continued to come, many from far distances. And they dressed up to go to Lucifer's, just as they did for our Manhattan events.

Arnold Randolph was one of our first employees at Lucifer's. He was very friendly and outgoing, ideal for helping us promote our first discotheque. He also served as a bouncer. Arnold was not very tall, but solidly built. You could tell by the way he carried himself that he was not someone you would want to mess with. But he was also a very giving person and wanted to please his friends - especially the ladies. Friends gave him the nickname "Candyman." This was not a reference to drugs — Arnold didn't even drink. He earned his nickname because he literally had candy in his pocket that he would share with people. He was especially generous with the ladies. As Tony put it, "If he had $3 in his pocket, he would spend it all on a lady."

Tony did a good job of hiring top bartenders in the area. We all knew that bartenders are a clever bunch. They had creative ways to siphon off profits and redirect them from the till into their own pockets. Most frequently, it was in the form of giving away free drinks. Free drinks relate to increased tips so that was a part of the bartenders' incentive. But there were many other tricks that they used. A bartender could put a full bottle of liquor in the garbage. Toward the end of the evening, they would take the garbage out and retrieve the bottle when no one was around. Some bartenders would even sneak a bottle into the bar, sell drinks from it, and pocket the cash. Staying ahead of these various scams was a challenge in running a bar operation.

To thwart the many bartender tricks and give ourselves a certain measure of confidence, Tony found a way to control the bar with a fairly high level of

Tony at Lucifer's

bottom row Tony, Noel; middle row, Andre, Mal, Danny; top row, Harry, CP, Wayne

assurance. He recommended purchasing a metering system called Auto Bar, which consisted of a small meter attached to the mouth of every frequently poured bottle. The metering system was expensive, approximately $8,000, but it put bartenders on notice. We were the only ones in the area to have Auto Bar, which made our operation seem more sophisticated and modern than other establishments. Auto Bar allowed exactly one ounce to pour with each tilt, and the meter would advance by one digit. By reading the meters at the beginning and again at the end of the night, we could estimate the amount of money that should be in the cash register. Some popular drinks, like the Golden Cadillac, that required more than one shot of liquor, or a shot of a rarely served liquor that didn't have a meter, meant that the amount of money expected in each cash register was not exact, but it was close.

Tony and Danny monitored the meters and, after a few months, even before reading the meters they could tell the approximate amount of money that should be in the till based on the size and composition of the crowd. Tony and Danny fired many bartenders because their receipts were short. They were also careful to vet new hires.

In one interview, an applicant told Danny, "I want you to know I am a ten percenter."

"What do you mean by that?" Danny asked.

The candidate explained, "It means I take 10% of my bar receipts."

Needless to say, Danny didn't hire that guy.

Eventually, we ran out of bartenders and had to re-hire some of the ones previously fired. It sounds weird, but these bartenders begged to have their jobs back and promised to be honest.

Based on trial and error and talking to other club owners, we determined that a 15% loss was tolerable. In other words, bartenders could turn in 85% of the amount of cash projected by the meters. This policy recognized that, on occasion, there is a benefit to buying a good customer a drink, and the 15% allowed bartenders to do so. The problem with the candidate who announced that he planned to take 10% is that he made that decision on his own. Not a good idea to have employees going rogue and making their own rules.

Tony and Danny got to know all the bar owners along the Linden Boulevard strip. We were sensitive to the fact that Lucifer's took business from many of them, so we always participated in the bar owners' softball league and Round Robins. The Round Robin was a way to show support of area bars by visiting them and spending money across the bar. Round Robins brought energy and excitement to clubs that might otherwise be slow on a particular evening. Because Lucifer's was the most successful club in the area, Tony always ran the bar while visiting other clubs during the Round Robin. This was to demonstrate that we were not trying to put anyone out of business and it also helped to maintain good relations.

On occasion, one or two nearby bar owners would call on a weekend night to ask if they could borrow a bottle of Hennessy or scotch or whatever because they ran out. Even though this is technically illegal, we always complied because we wanted to maintain good relations. Interestingly, Tony and Danny were obviously new at managing a bar, and the other bar owners were in business for many years, yet our bar ran more efficiently. That's a credit to Tony and Danny's organizational strength and diligence, as well as their good business sense. Compared to other neighborhood bars, Tony and Danny probably had more money to work with, but it was also obvious that they were effective in running the business.

We were so busy running Lucifer's that we were unaware that others were watching our success. Danny and Tony, in particular, had a spotlight shining on them, even if they didn't see it at the time. That spotlight was not always welcomed.

Tony was dating a young lady and decided to take her to the Copacabana to see a Motown show featuring the Four Tops and Temptations. Tony invited his friend Ambrose Brown to join him with a date, which made it a foursome. They were seated in the middle of the room where they ordered drinks and dinner. While they were waiting to be served, a waiter came over and said they were going to be moved to a table right in front of the stage. A table for six was rolled out. Tony and Ambrose took seats facing the stage while their dates sat with their backs to the stage.

As they were being seated Tony's date waved to someone further back in the room. Tony turned around and said "Oh, that's Cheryl. Who's with her?"

She replied: "That's Frank Matthews." "Oh shit!" exclaimed Tony. A waiter brought three bottles of Dom Perignon in ice buckets and six flutes to the table. Tony recalls that Frank Matthews was all over the news during that time. Frank had been arrested in Las Vegas and transferred to New York where he was out on bail.[27] Frank Matthews was, "the biggest drug dealer in the entire United States...."[28] The street nicknamed him "Black Caesar" and "Pee Wee" because he was rather small but stocky. Just then Frank and Cheryl moved up and sat at Tony's table.

There wasn't much conversation because the show started shortly after they all sat down. After the show, Frank paid the full tab, which included dinner. To pay the bill, Tony noticed that Frank pulled out an enormous stack of cash from his pocket and fumbled with it a bit. He had to work hard to control the massive wad of bills. He was probably figuring out a suitable tip, or maybe he was just showing off his impressive bankroll. Frank asked Tony where he parked. "In the lot directly across the street," replied Tony. Frank said he parked in the same lot. While waiting for their cars to come out, Tony thanked Frank for sporting the table. Then Frank invited Tony and Ambrose to bring their dates and join him as his guests at a private club on E. 48th Street. Tony was not familiar with the club...and thought he knew every club in midtown. Frank's offer was intriguing, but there was no way Tony was going to accept. When Frank Matthews was arrested, he was identified as one of the top ten drug dealers in the history of the United States, with an operation that stretched across the country. By FBI accounts, he was responsible for bringing in one third of all the heroin brought into the country. Later, Tony said "I knew he was being watched so there was no way I was going to hang out with him. I didn't want to get involved in something I had no control over."

Tony made up an excuse to politely decline Frank's offer and thanked him. Frank was in a difficult position. If convicted, he would be facing life in prison, so no doubt he was desperate. It was also known that the mafia was

[27] *New York Daily News*, "Justice Story: 'Black Caesar' Frank Matthews Made Off With Millions in Drug Profits", by David Krajicek, April 22, 2012
[28] "The Frank Matthews Story", 2012 a documentary directed by Al Profit and Ron Chepesiuk

123

not happy with Frank since he circumvented them by buying drugs directly from international drug cartels. So, both good guys and bad guys were out to get him.

Police arrested Frank in January 1973, and the judge set bail at $5 million, the highest ever set in the U.S. at the time.[29] But in April 1973, a federal judge reduced his bail to $325k. Prosecutors warned that he had a lot of money and would probably flee. While on bail, Frank was required to make weekly appearances, which he did. That night at the Copa, Frank certainly didn't look like he was trying to hide or blend in because he wore a red plaid sport jacket and flashed around a lot of bills. According to the NY Daily News, Matthews used his time as a temporarily free man to get his finances in order, possibly by creating accessible off-shore accounts in the Cayman Islands or the Bahamas. Clearly, he was a man with a plan. On June 26, 1973, he disappeared, along with Cheryl Denise Brown. Rumor had it that when Frank met Cheryl, she was married so Frank paid off Cheryl's husband so he could date her. When Frank disappeared, he apparently took Cheryl with him and left behind Barbara Hinton, his previous, long-term girlfriend, with whom he had two young sons.

According to media reports, after all these years, the authorities did not have a single sighting or lead — not a trace of Frank Matthews. Frank left a bag with $325,000 with his family to pay off the bail so they wouldn't lose their houses. When he vanished, Frank Matthews was 29,[30] which was just two years older than Tony and the rest of us in TBOF, so it's possible he is still alive today.

Tony's encounter with Frank Matthews was brief, but it wasn't the end of the story. A few days later, Tony was visiting his girlfriend at her apartment. There was a knock on the door.

"FBI! Open up!"

When Tony heard this firm announcement through the closed door, he

[29] Burbank, Jeff. "Did Frank Matthews get away with it?". www.themobmuseum.org. Retrieved 29 March 2020.
[30] New York Daily News, "Justice Story: 'Black Caesar' Frank Matthews Made Off With Millions in Drug Profits", by David Krajicek, April 22, 2012

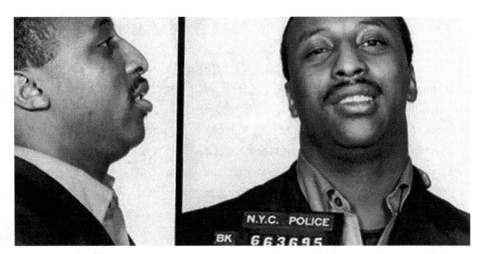

Frank Matthews police photos

ran into his girlfriend's bedroom. Tony's girlfriend opened the door and saw a black guy and a white guy who identified themselves as federal agents. They questioned Tony's girlfriend for a few minutes and showed her photos of different people that they wanted her to identify. Then one of the FBI guys said,

"Tell your boyfriend to come out of the bedroom."

Hearing that, Tony reluctantly came out of the bedroom. The FBI guys began asking him where Frank was. Neither Tony nor his girlfriend had any idea.

"Why would I know where Frank is?" Tony asked.

The FBI guys pointed out that they saw Tony leaving the Copacabana the other night with Frank Matthews, so they assumed they were friends. Apparently, the FBI got Tony's license plate number that night and tracked his every move. Unbeknownst to Tony, the FBI had been following him for a few days. We were not the type of guys who were used to looking over our shoulders. It seems the FBI was following up on everyone who had been with Frank in hopes of finding him, but Frank Matthews was never found. According to the DEA, he fled the country with between $20 and $30 million. But word on the street was that he was worth over $600 million. Presumably, he moved much of that offshore. As the FBI guys were leaving the apartment, Tony asked,

"How did you know I was in the bedroom?" The black agent responded, "We saw your car parked outside."

According to the NY Daily News, "Eight of [Frank's] narcotics confreres were convicted of federal charges in 1975, including girlfriend Barbara Hinton, although the court subsequently overturned her conviction. Several other old pals were killed in mash-ups over the newly available drug turf."[31]

The encounter with the drug lord and the FBI agents, however brief, rattled Tony. It brought home the fact that the business of owning nightclubs put us in the path of some unsavory and potentially dangerous characters. Although Frank Matthews never came to Lucifer's, which was the only club we owned when Tony met him, he still knew who Tony was. Had Frank not been arrested, he probably would have been a customer at Lucifer's because everyone came through there, from corporate types, celebrities, and elected officials down to blue-collar workers, messengers, and various hustlers, mostly numbers bankers and numbers runners. Interestingly, about 35 years after Frank Matthews disappeared, a friend told Tony that he saw Frank at a basketball game. There was even a local newspaper article that indicated Frank Matthews was in town to attend a funeral. If he was, the authorities never caught up to him.

Tony and Danny got to know all the customers who frequented Lucifer's. While some guests came from other boroughs in the city, the majority of customers were from Queens. All the hustlers who stopped by Lucifer's were local guys. They tended to be involved in the numbers racket — runners and bankers — both from south Queens and north Queens.

After several months of managing Lucifer's, Tony and Danny were confident enough about operating a bar to turn their attention back to Manhattan. They found a space on the east side on 49th Street that would have been perfect. It had been a gay club. However, the owner refused to let Tony sign a lease. Tony believes the landlord didn't want a young black group as a tenant. We had a good track record and good references but, apparently, that was not

---

[31] *New York Daily News*, "Justice Story: 'Black Caesar' Frank Matthews Made Off With Millions in Drug Profits", by David Krajicek, April 22, 2012

Leviticus canopy   *Leviticus dance floor*

enough. After more searching, Tony found a space at 45 W. 33rd Street that had been a Chinese restaurant. In fact, some of our acquaintances were giving occasional parties there. The restaurant was large enough for a good-sized nightclub and the rent was acceptable given the location. Interestingly, it was owned by the same person who owned the east side gay club who refused to allow Tony to sign a lease. The difference was that the owner was personally handling the rental of the east side venue, but a broker was handling rental of the space on the west side. So, because of discrimination, we wound up on the west side. The east side was more prestigious, but the west side had easier parking and no residential neighbors to complain about noise or crowds so the west side had a silver lining. Tony signed a long-term lease on behalf of TBOF and once again Mr. Cooper, Tony's dad, was hired to build out what would become our flagship club, Leviticus.

Tony's dad was an excellent carpenter, but he preferred to work alone. Leviticus was going to be much bigger than Lucifer's, which meant a long lead time for completion. Mr. Cooper's price was reasonable and he was trustworthy. We had heard so many nightmare stories associated with crooked contractors, especially in Manhattan, that we were willing to wait longer to open the club and to work with someone we could trust. Our rent was about $4,000 per month so it was concerning to have a large expense with no revenue coming in. We also worried that we might be losing the impressive momentum we gained at the Ginza, La Martinique, and the other clubs we promoted. The delay was aggravating, but we had no choice but to be patient once the job was awarded.

Leviticus was built using similar guidelines as Lucifer's: white stucco walls, white oval-shaped bar, red and black patterned commercial carpeting, platforms for elevated tables, and a black and white checkerboard dance floor. The platforms made it easier for guests sitting at tables to see across the room and to watch folks on the dance floor. It also made the room look visually appealing. The bar was built so that people standing on the side closest to the dance floor were at the same height as people seated on the other side of the bar, which was elevated.

David Schwartz, our attorney, represented more clubs and restaurants in midtown Manhattan than any other attorney, which was the primary reason Tony recommended him. He advised us to set up a separate corporation for each nightclub we owned so that if there was an incident at one club, any liability would be restricted to that corporation and not the others. We also hired Jerry Brickman, an accountant who also had a client list dominated by midtown licensees, with many similar clients as David Schwartz. Hence, they knew each other and worked together on occasion.

An application for a liquor license was generally straight forward. For example, we applied for a license for Lucifer's and it was received in a timely manner. However, a liquor license for an establishment the size of Leviticus that also allowed dancing was another story. In addition to a state liquor license, it required a cabaret license from the city. This was the most challenging type of license to get. We had to apply for the cabaret license for Leviticus when construction was near completion because an on-site inspection was required. It took nine months for Leviticus to be built and a frustrating additional six months before the cabaret license was issued. We thought the club would never open.

While we had a lot of cash, paying a large monthly rent with no income created a loss that could never be recovered. Apparently, the city had difficulty believing a group of young black men could legally come by the money needed to build such a club. We were all in our 20s and it was a period when drug dealers and gangs were looking for ways to launder their cash, so our application was viewed with suspicion. Hence, the delay.

A few years later, I learned that only a small number of cabaret licenses were issued. "Out of the city's nearly 25,000 spots that could be considered nightlife establishments, only 97 had proper cabaret licenses" according to The New York Times. Getting one, advocates say, "is cost-prohibitive and lengthy; a bureaucratic obstacle that few want to jump."[32]

Even Studio 54 did not have a cabaret license when they opened three years later. Steve Rubell and Ian Schrager, the owners of Studio 54, got around the licensing issue by taking out one-day permits every day for several weeks. But these permits were supposed to be used exclusively for special occasions such as a wedding or festival. The head of the State Liquor Authority, Michael Roth, conducted a raid and had Studio 54 closed for selling liquor without a proper license within a month of their opening. Rubell, Schrager, and two bartenders were arrested and police seized cash from the discotheque. Roth was quoted in the New York Times as stating, "The one-day permits had permitted the sale of liquor while Studio 54 awaited action on its application for a liquor license. But such permits are intended for a special function or event, such as a wedding or political affair, and the State Liquor Authority has been getting stricter about their use."[33] After spending a few hours in jail, Studio 54 opened the next day without liquor. They only sold juices and other soft drinks. This went on for several weeks before they finally received a cabaret license. Despite their legal trouble, they still got their license a lot faster than we did.

Interestingly, the cabaret license was created in 1926 during prohibition to ban dancing in bars and restaurants. According to Vibe magazine, "Its purpose was to provide the city with more authority to 'crackdown on African American jazz clubs.' The regulations that were bundled with the law were

[32] Vice, November 1, 2017, "The Repeal of New York's Racist Anti-Dancing Law Was a Dance Party" by John Surico
[33] The New York Times, May 22, 1977, Liquor Authority Head Stops Discothèque's Music, by Eleanor Blau

racist including the banning of 'black' instruments like the saxophone in venues that didn't obtain the license in question. Since the regulations have been repealed or found unconstitutional due to their discriminatory implications." However, the need for such a license was not eliminated until 2017.[34]

We could not have a full opening of Leviticus without dancing since that was the focus of the club. We did have a few special events there, but we were careful to adhere to the legal requirements. We were not about to test the authorities since we believed they would use any excuse to shut us down. The State Liquor Authority looked into the background of each member of TBOF. They talked to family members and neighbors to find out what kind of people we were. It was frustrating to complete the construction of Leviticus then have to wait for six more months to open. It was even more frustrating to pay big rent with no income. To the thousands of patrons that followed us, we were originators of the discotheque environment yet we were missing out on the opportunity we helped to create. It was tough to see other club owners profit from the trend we started while our hands were tied. Based on our knowledge of other nightclubs, a short life was common. We felt New York City was deliberately dragging its feet hoping we would run out of money so they could avoid having to issue a cabaret license. But that didn't happen. Our long wait eventually paid off in a big way.

[34] *Vibe*, April 3, 2017, "Historically Racist NYC Law That Prevents Dancing in Bars is Being Petitioned", by Ashley Pickens

Chapter 15
BUSINESS MUSHROOMED

"*Grab a hammer! Let's get it done.*"

We finally received a cabaret license from New York City in November 1974, not realizing how big a deal it was at the time, and made our final preparations to officially open what would become our flagship club. On the night before Leviticus opened, we all scrambled to get ready. To save time and money, Mr. Cooper hired a carpenter to build short stools out of wood that would be seating for the small café tables that we had in place. We had ordered cushions to go on top of the stools to complete the seat. Unfortunately, the carpenter was unable to finish building the stools. All he managed to do was to cut out the four sides of the seats and the tops, which meant we would have to nail them together.

"Grab a hammer," Tony said. He was confident that we could hammer together the stools in just a few hours. As it turned out, it was a bit more of a struggle, especially for a few of us.

All eight TBOF partners, plus a few unlucky employees and friends who just happened to be hanging around and were recruited to help, were up until

3 am nailing stools together. Some of us barely knew how to hold a hammer, but somehow, we managed.

The ones who struggled the most with a hammer were usually the ones who grew up in an apartment instead of a house. Andre, who grew up in the projects, was clueless with a hammer. He held it awkwardly in his hand and tentatively tapped at the nails. We all had a good laugh watching him trying to drive nails straight into the wood pieces. He kept hitting glancing blows. The nails either popped wildly into the air or they went in crooked. Our tedious task took longer because we had to re-do many of the seats he assembled. Andre was a good sport, even as we ribbed him and made jokes at his expense. Although it was late when we finished, the experience was fun and helped strengthen our bond.

We trusted each other completely, maybe too much. We knew every one of our partners was working as hard as they could to achieve our goal. Over the years, we got to know each other extremely well. All those meetings and extensive communications helped build personal relationships that pulled us through what could have been a stressful situation. Our friendship was probably the key to our success.

We had already announced the opening of Leviticus with great fanfare. We produced a record that featured Vaughn Harper interviewing us about our business. The recording was printed on a thin, flexible piece of plastic that could be played on a 33 1/3 record player. This recorded interview was accompanied by a beautifully designed printed piece with details of the club, address, hours, price, etc. We had mailed this out to thousands of our loyal followers, so we had to do whatever it took to open on time, or else our reputation would have been damaged. We made ourselves into a well-oiled, high-performing team because we had to rely on one another. We understood each other's strengths and weaknesses and supported each other by appreciating everyone's efforts. And through it all, we had fun.

Leviticus opened the next night, Thursday, November 14, 1974. We dressed in our best suits and were ready to welcome our followers. I felt the delay in opening wasted a tremendous amount of momentum and worried that the level of enthusiasm might not be as high as it had been at La Martinique. I was wrong.

Leviticus was on the ground floor of a six-story building. The Chinese restaurant that was there had lots of kitchen equipment in the rear of the ground floor. Next to the main entrance was a windowless side door that provided access to a hallway and staircase that led to the upper floors. We had the kitchen equipment moved to the basement, a space that was also included in our lease. The basement was huge but unfinished. Luckily, we had Mr. Cooper, a professional basement finisher. We asked him to build a row of offices down there so Tony, Danny, and the management team had a place from which to run the operation. A few assistants were also hired to help run the operation; Vivian Shaw, Marilyn Hubbard, and Lynette Taylor were hired to assist with ordering liquor, managing payroll, paying taxes, filing license renewals, developing promotions, and so on.

At the entrance to Leviticus, we replicated some of the features that existed at La Martinique because we liked the way it facilitated crowd flow. The entrance lobby had red and black patterned carpeting and an enclosed booth to pay the admission fee. As you entered the main room, a coat check counter was on the right side. Past the coat check counter was an elevated area to the right with café tables and seats. On the left was a large dance floor and straight ahead was the large, oval, white bar. There was more seating on the other side of the bar and dance floor. In the rear of the room, the dance area opened up to another room that was set up as a lounge. This is where the kitchen equipment had been. We put in a pool table, sofas, lounge chairs, and backgammon and chess boards. A Pong machine was in the corner. Pong was the first popular video game, and while it was rudimentary by today's standard, it was state-of-the-art in 1974. Having the Pong game in our club demonstrated to our guests that we were on the cutting edge of modern technology.

Steve Roberts worked at a bank but because he was good behind a microphone, he served as our MC on weekends. He and I were among the best Pong players in the club. Maybe we could be considered early gamers. Steve and I never played against each other. Instead, we boasted and bragged to each other, in a good-natured way, about our Pong prowess. Our playful banter brought out the competitive nature in both of us. One evening, when we were both available, we decided to play each other. About a dozen people gathered around to watch the match. Like all good competitors, we tried to psyche each other out with trash talk, but it was all in good fun. Steve was an excellent player; I had never played against anyone of his caliber before, so it elevated my game. We had several extraordinarily long rallies, which kept the onlookers cheering and holding their breath. The longer the rallies, the faster the ball moved. There was no time to think about where to move the paddle, it was all instinct and speed. If you didn't anticipate where the next shot was going, the point was over. After many exciting and long back-and-forth rallies, Steve beat me. Even though I joked with him about the win, I knew it was a fair fight. He was the better Pong player that night.

We were extremely pleased with Leviticus. It was perfectly designed for handling the large numbers of guests that came almost every night. Word of mouth about the club spread quickly through black America. Leviticus was a destination…the place to see and be seen. Our guests enjoyed being there and our reputation grew to national proportions. Patrons were genuinely proud that Leviticus was black-owned. I know this because guests made comments to me as they paid their admission fee at the door. Years later, Vaughn Harper, the popular DJ on WBLS radio, was quoted as saying, "Leviticus was the place to be. The only place to be." And Steve Roberts, our weekend MC said, "If you came to Leviticus on a given night, you might see Sidney Poitier or Harry Belafonte or Calvin Lockhart, so you didn't want that to be your off-day. So, the ladies — and gents too — came dressed exceptionally nice."

When patrons walked into Leviticus, many paused when they approached the dance floor because they were in awe of the show they were witnessing. People took pride in their dancing skills and relished showing them off at Leviticus. Plus, we had extraordinary dancers like Tu Sweet who would routinely light up the dance floor. The freedom of dancing without holding hands unleashed a high level of creativity that spawned innovative moves, spins, and gestures — all coordinated to music with a hot tempo. It was a joy to watch. (See Appendix III for frequently played songs.)

Publicity can have a powerful impact on a brand. Even though we did little to encourage it, Leviticus was frequently featured on society pages in the black press, and in magazines such as Ebony, Essence, Black Enterprise, City Lights, and several community newspapers. Leviticus was so popular that you could hop any taxi in NYC and get there without having an address. All taxi drivers knew where it was. Eventually, we received coverage in mainstream publications such as the New York Times, Time Out, CUE, The Village Voice, and other general audience publications.

Although just about everyone who was socially active in the black community knew about Leviticus, we remained guarded about widespread publicity, especially on the radio. This was a reasonable position to take when we first started at the Ginza. But Leviticus was already so well known, there was no reason to hold back media coverage. Crime continued to be a big problem in New York City, and we knew there were plenty of bad characters out there,

Tu Sweet   *Tu Sweet with two partners*

but all the bad actors probably knew about Leviticus already. Nevertheless, we continued to market our clubs primarily through the social "grapevine" and with personal invitations. We figured that people would invite friends who had similar interests and experiences. Since this strategy had been working well for us, we continued to promote the club in the same manner.

None of our clubs served food. We were reluctant to enter into food service because we had no experience in that area. When patrons got hungry, we would simply stamp the back of their hands so they could leave to eat and return. We discussed subcontracted food service but didn't feel comfortable involving an outside entity in the operation. Plus, there were too many unknowns about the food industry, including liability, health, and vermin issues. A few years later, when the idea seemed less complicated, we did add food — via an easy-to-prepare, limited menu.

One night, we introduced a drink called the Blue Whale. It was made with vodka, white rum, pineapple juice, and blue curacao. Served in an all-purpose wine glass, the Blue Whale shimmered in nightclub lights and was an instant success. It cost twice as much as a regular drink and made a lot of money for us. Guests wanted it because it glowed and looked cool. That one drink increased the bar take significantly during its initial year because it was new and trendy. TBOF featured other novelty drinks like the Golden Cadillac, which was also popular, but it did not replicate the level of success we had with the Blue Whale. (See Appendix IV for popular drinks in the '70s at our clubs).

The success of Leviticus created many new challenges for TBOF. It was a much more complicated business model than when we were simply promoters. Now we had to manage employees, pay salaries and insurance, order liquor, and maintain the appearance of the clubs. Our meetings were often long because we talked through each issue in great detail. It was true on-the-job training. Throughout that process, Tony and Danny's leadership skills became apparent and valuable. Their style was conservative and cautious and the rest of us followed their lead. The result was that our business thrived. Our operation ran smoothly with virtually no incidents, and we were all astounded by the magnitude of our financial success. Danny's financial reports quantified our success and made it easy to justify the sacrifices we were making.

As one might expect, the level of success brightened the spotlight that was already on the partners, especially Tony and Danny since they were at the club full time and obviously in charge. In one of the late-night sessions at the round table, Tony pointed out that, for our own safety, we needed to avoid sporty cars and flashy jewelry. We wanted to be less conspicuous to potential robbers. We all immediately agreed with Tony's suggestion without discussion because we all felt the same way. In fact, none of us was into flashy cars or jewelry anyway but the large amounts of money coming in had the potential to push us in that direction. The good news is that none of us was ever robbed. Interestingly though, some of our bartenders wore flashy jewelry and drove fancy cars, which made us wonder if they were helping themselves to more than the 15% we permitted.

The first big holiday after we opened was Thanksgiving. We assumed that everyone would be spending time with their families, therefore we did not expect many people would come out. I manned the booth to collect the admission and prepared for a slow night. But a steady stream of people kept pouring in. I was stunned. When I finally had a breather, I looked inside and saw that the dance floor was crowded with folks celebrating the holiday. It turned out to be one of our biggest nights. It surprised all of us. Many folks spent the day with family and then, after dinner, they were looking for something to do. More than 1,400 people flowed into Leviticus that night. Had we known, we would have scheduled another two bartenders and another security person. The patrons were having so much fun, though, they didn't mind waiting a bit longer than usual for a drink.

When Christmas Eve and Christmas night rolled around, we weren't sure if we should anticipate low attendance or a big crowd. Again, those nights were among our biggest and busiest of the year. I guess it helped that we were open until 4 am. That gave folks plenty of time to hang out with family, enjoy a leisurely dinner, and make it down to our clubs afterward. I also learned that quite a few folks didn't spend important holidays with family at all. In some cases, it was because their family lived in another city while others simply chose not to. On a holiday night, there was a special feeling of intimacy among the guests who came. After all, they were spending Christmas night in a friendly, festive atmosphere. Many became good friends. As patrons got to know each other, the regulars at Leviticus became like family.

The music my DJ partners played was a departure from what the top radio stations played. Our focus was on dancing, and all songs played in our clubs had to have a strong danceable beat. Our patrons loved the tunes they heard and enjoyed dancing to them. Radio stations started getting calls from our guests requesting songs that had never been played on air before. The radio DJs couldn't accommodate them because they didn't have the music that Danny and CP had. Radio station program directors began sending their DJs to our clubs to scout out the songs that turned on the crowd. G. Keith Alexander, a popular radio personality on WBLS in New York City, said, "At one time, radio determined the hits. Now the situation is such that a record can become a hit at the discos and force its way onto the radio. In some record companies, now there are employees who just service discos."[35]

In short order, all the top radio DJs, as well as radio and record company execs, started hanging out at our clubs. They heard songs that were wildly popular with the crowd that had never been played on radio such as "Scorpio" by Dennis Coffey, "Soul Makosa" by Manu Dibango, and "Love to Love You Baby" by Donna Summers (before it was formally released). There was a delay in releasing "Love to Love You Baby" because some felt the song was obscene. It was risqué for those days, so it was not played on radio at all, at least not at first. Eventually, it turned out to be Summers' first big hit and helped establish her as the "Queen of Disco." Another song that was popularized at Leviticus was "Flamingo" by Jimmy Smith. Danny would play "Flamingo" as his signature end of the night song. It was a very slow, sexy tune that signaled the night was over as we gradually turned the lights up. Frankie Crocker picked up on this and ended his broadcast each evening with the same song.

We always had a bouncer at the front door of each club. At Leviticus, we had a number of different bouncers over the years — all were experts in martial arts. Most of our waitstaff also had martial arts skills — many were

[35] Ebony, February 1977, "Discomaniacs get down, style and profile from coast to coast" by Herschel Johnson

black belts. We never needed their special skills, but it represented extra security that made us feel safe. Bob Cherry had worked as a bouncer at the Dom nightclub, but because of his good people skills and savvy, we hired him as a manager. Bob was a big man who used his experience as a bouncer and martial arts skills to keep an eye on the front door.

We were successful in creating a safe and comfortable environment at our clubs. Since Leviticus was the talk of the town, at least in the black community, Gwen's mother heard about it and said she wanted to go. The night she came, she was accompanied by Gwen, her son Idris, and Eloise, a neighbor. I was working that night and proud and delighted to wave them in. They all had a great time and were impressed with what we had built. Gwen and I were already married by then, but it was nice to know that her mother and brother enjoyed themselves and felt comfortable in my club.

Leviticus, along with Lucifer's and the other clubs we subsequently opened, accepted cash only, at least for the first several years. Credit cards were viewed as an unnecessary complication plus the card companies took a percentage of the amount charged. Although many patrons had credit cards, they had no problem paying cash because in the 1970s America was still a cash society. Many businesses did not accept credit cards. Years later, Ken Chenault, CEO of American Express, told me that credit card customers spend more on average than cash customers and American Express cardholders spend more than MasterCard or Visa cardholders. Had I known this back then, I would have pushed to accept the American Express card in our clubs. A few years later, we did accept American Express as well as Diner's Club. But in the meantime, some customers took note of the fact that we accepted cash only. Lots of it.

TBOF had an unplanned and unexpected symbiotic relationship with the drug kingpins and other gangsters who frequented our clubs, primarily Leviticus. Under Tony's leadership, we treated underworld characters with respect while keeping them at arm's length. Most straight people (people who play by the rules) look down on gangsters and treat them as less than. In contrast, when they came to Leviticus, gangsters were treated with respect – just

Jeanne Moutoussamy-Ashe and Arthur Ashe in entrance lobby of Leviticus

like everyone else. But Tony still needed to know who these gangsters were so he discreetly made inquiries. He learned who was who, but he also learned that gangsters never admit to knowing someone. They would often simply say "Oh yeah, I heard of him." Tony explained that "We were in a world that we didn't know anything about." But because of Tony's approach, we never had problems with any of the gangsters who came through our clubs. In fact, Tony was more concerned with straight people acting up than he was with the gangsters. If a straight guy confronted one of the gangsters the wrong way, there was only one way that could end. That was a concern, but fortunately, we never had that problem.

The only incident we had with a gangster was when Black Ronnie started shouting at one of his women. Thankfully, after a few moments, Black Ronnie calmed down and the drama ended. As Tony put it: "We were alright with every level of society. We were alright with gangsters, we were alright with corporate types, celebrities, elected officials, and everyone else."

There were few places gangsters could go to have an enjoyable evening and feel comfortable. Our clubs enabled them to fit in without feeling conspicuous and, because they were treated with respect, they showed respect in return. They viewed Tony and the other full-time partners as friends. Gangsters want friends, just like anyone else. But they can't afford to let friends get too close to their operation. That worked out well for my partners since that is exactly how they felt also.

Lots of interesting people came through the door at Leviticus. I had a chance to meet some of the folks who had been regulars at the original Red Rooster in Harlem. They were quite a bit older than us but they fit in comfortably with the diverse crowd we attracted. This is when I first met "Doc" Baker, Chester Redhead, and E.J. Smith. "Doc" Baker was on the dance floor a lot while Chester and E.J. danced less often. These men were well-connected and very active socially. In the early 1960s, "Doc" Baker helped found a popular social club with friends from the Red Rooster called The Fellas, which remains active to this day. E.J. Smith and Chester Redhead joined The Fellas shortly after it was founded. All three of these men were also members of the Guardsmen, a national organization whose sole purpose was to create high-

Lola Falana dancing with a guest

end social events for the members. E.J. was also a member of Alpha Phi Alpha while Chester and Doc were Qs, aka Omega Psi Phi. I mention this because many of our guests were members of various social organizations and just about all of these organizations had occasional dance parties or dinner dances. The more often you dance, the better you get. Leviticus had great dancers.

Chapter 16
SOMETHING HAD TO GIVE

"*Who's your friend?*

One day after work, Andre stopped by my office. We planned to hang out together since it was the last week before the Christmas holiday shutdown. My department at Y&R had a holiday party going on right near my desk, so we stayed for a while to enjoy a quick drink and nosh on the munchies. At some point, my boss asked me about Andre, like where he worked and where he went to college. Then he asked for an introduction. Andre came in for a job interview a few days later, and two weeks after that, he joined Y&R as an Assistant Account Executive.

Advertising was a glamorous industry to be in, especially in the 1970s. Working for a high-powered ad agency was a terrific job. Account Executives had to dress impeccably because of the many interactions with clients. We felt stylish, sophisticated, and creative. For Andre, CP, and me, it was exciting to work on Madison Avenue in plush offices filled with smart, well-educated people. However, we soon found out that some of the people with impeccable education credentials, were not as smart as we thought.

Andre said, "Some of the them are simply educated fools."

We encountered a good number of Harvard MBA types who wound up getting fired because they believed they should be in charge and make all the decisions, yet they simply couldn't perform. Still others who were very bright had poor social skills or lacked leadership. Andre once observed, "Many 'A' students wind up in research working on projects that we 'C' students give them." But in fairness, many of the people we worked with were super smart and some were conspicuously brilliant. Working with these folks kept us on our toes and made the job interesting and fun.

Wayne, Andre, and I were all on the same page: Despite the enormous success of our clubs, we viewed discotheques as a short-term opportunity that should be used as a springboard into other businesses. We were not about to compromise our careers, which were off to a good start, by jumping into the club business full time. After marrying Gwen and having two daughters, my priorities began to shift. Danny and Harry were married, but had no children at that time, while Tony, Mal, and CP were all single. The schedule was difficult for all of us, but Andre, Wayne, and I had children and were less willing to hitch our future to nightclubs.

Wayne, our unofficial mediator within TBOF, had to resign to accept an appointment as Bureau Chief of the Office of the Bronx District Attorney since it was a conflict of interest for him to hold a liquor license. Wayne's departure changed the dynamic within the group. TBOF splintered into two factions. Tony, Danny, CP, Harry, and Mal were focused primarily on sustaining our nightclub interests. Andre and I, on the other hand, were more focused on our day jobs, which we viewed as the best route to provide for our families. We wanted to see TBOF get involved in a business that we could have faith in as a long-term endeavor, but this proved to be difficult.

After a couple of years, it became obvious that our schedule was not sustainable. The nights we worked meant virtually no sleep. We walked out of the club together at 4:45 am and, aside from Mal, we all lived in Queens. By the time we got home, it was around 5:15 am and often we had to work the next morning. That next day, I was so exhausted from the night before, I typically left the office at 6 pm and went straight home to crash. I believe my partners with day jobs all had a similar routine. Chores had to wait until the weekend. As the months rolled by, it became drudgery. Despite the impressive success we were enjoying, this was a difficult time for those of us with day jobs. Something had to give.

CP, Harry, and Mal solved the schedule problem by quitting their day jobs and joining Tony and Danny working full time at the clubs. CP had been working at Warwick & Legler Advertising. Harry was a public school teacher, and Mal was working at the top R&B radio station in NYC, WBLS. Those who decided to work full time for TBOF had a great sense of commitment to the nightclub industry and believed it could be sustained for the long haul. They felt that Andre and I were not as committed to the business. We weren't.

Danny arranged for us to develop a buy-sell agreement so that if something happened to any of us, the insurance company would buy out the estate of the deceased partner. This way, we wouldn't have to deal with a former partners' family, which would be messy.

To implement the buy-sell agreement, we all had to take a cursory physical exam. We arranged to meet at an office we rented on W. 21st Street at 6 pm one evening for the exam. A couple of us had blood pressure readings that were slightly high.

"How about you boys have a seat and relax," suggested the examiner. "I'll recheck your blood pressure in 20 minutes or so. I'm sure you'll have better numbers then."

We tried to relax as much as possible by taking deep, slow breathes and trying to clear our thoughts. It worked. We all eventually passed the exam, but after we described the business we were in and the lifestyle it entails, the medical examiner seemed concerned.

He said, "You're all doing okay now, but with your lifestyle, you'll be lucky to make it to the age of 60."

None of us was getting enough sleep, we weren't eating well, and most of us smoked and drank. That assessment stuck with me and was a factor in my decision years later, in consideration of my wife and two daughters, to resign from TBOF.

Once CP started working full time for TBOF, he enlisted the help of a chemist friend to create a new women's fragrance called Lawless. Lawless had a pleasant, feminine scent and was packaged in a small black bottle that came in a black pouch with a drawstring. It seemed like a great idea to all of us, but there were lots of issues in the fragrance business, including competition that blocks out newcomers, manufacturing problems, and pre-existing industry relationships that made it difficult to get on enough store shelves. Although it never achieved a meaningful share of market, Lawless was a brilliant product that showcased CP's creative talent.

I was always close to CP and spent a lot of time with him. But I was also close to Wayne and Andre. I was the best man at Wayne's wedding and Andre was mine. I was drawn to these men because they were smart, ambitious, and willing to do new things. For example, shortly after joining Kappa Alpha Psi back in 1965, I suggested to Andre that we drive up to Montreal to check out their discotheques. Andre was down for it and we left that same day. And when I decided to learn how to play tennis, Wayne immediately agreed to learn also. Wayne was a good athlete, but not particularly fast. While our tennis matches were always close, he tended to win more often than I did. After graduating from St. John's Law School, Wayne told me he met a fascinating woman named Joyce who lived in the Bridge Apartments in the Washington Heights section of Manhattan. When I first met Joyce, she told me she was a member of the Ronettes. For a minute, I believed her because she had a similar physical appearance to the Ronettes, but she was just kidding. Anyway, everyone liked Joyce because she liked to joke around and always had an easy smile. Wayne married her and in short order they had a daughter and a son.

We talked a lot about diversifying our TBOF business but without much success. To help spark some ideas and get us off the dime, Tony arranged a two-day meeting for us in Atlantic City and asked each TBOF member to come with at least one new business idea. We all loved the thought of a retreat and had big fun while we were there; however, our brainstorming session wasn't as productive as we had hoped. When we left Atlantic City, we had a list of several potential business options but we weren't exactly jumping up and down over any of them because none seemed as promising or exciting as our nightclub business.

One of the ideas we decided to pursue was a travel club, which we started in 1976 to take advantage of our vast network of contacts. CP and Mal took the lead in pursuing this idea and arranged charter trips to Puerto Rico, the Bahamas, and other parts of the Caribbean. These trips were all successful, and participants had wonderful experiences, but they were not significant revenue generators.

Another business we discussed was an executive search firm, which could also tap into our network. Andre and I decided to pursue this business idea as a new division of TBOF. We received guidance from Andy Harris, a friend who was doing well as a partner in a successful search firm. Andre and I decided to focus on the manpower needs of packaged goods companies since that was an industry we understood fairly well. Andre was developing advertising for Proctor & Gamble and I was doing the same for General Foods. We conducted primary research by calling 50 packaged goods companies each to find out what types of jobs would be in the highest demand over the next five years. The answer was engineering. Although we knew nothing about engineering, Andy Harris assured us that we could learn the jargon quickly and determine which candidates had the right experience for each job.

We also knew, based on the social climate and business environment at the time, that when client companies saw us, they would assume we could only refer black engineers. If that were the case, the business niche would be too small to make a go of it. We needed to place engineers regardless of their color. So, we concluded that our best strategy would be to conduct the business exclusively over the telephone. If client companies didn't know we were black, we would be in a better position to fill all engineering positions. With this basic business plan in place, we quit our advertising jobs and opened Hankin & Smith Consultants, TBOF, in 1976.

Andre and I developed a basic organizational strategy for operating Hankin & Smith. We separated all major packaged goods companies into two groups: one we would treat as client customers where we would place prospects, the other group would be our source of talent. We decided to conduct all our business via telephone to avoid being relegated to "minority placements." After all, black owned ad agencies were viewed that way. Our reputation grew fairly quickly, and several client companies approved us to fill open positions. We had a decent rate of placements for a start-up but knew it would take years to build up the business to a significant revenue level.

Based on the number of placements we made, our revenue stream after six months was just enough to cover expenses and pay ourselves a modest salary. We projected that it would take another five years to build up the business to a level where we could make decent money for ourselves and TBOF. Since we avoided meeting with clients and candidates in person, we quickly realized that we created an unintended consequence. Armour-Dial was my most important client. I placed five engineers there, and the head of HR repeatedly invited me to come to Phoenix to see their operation so that I would know first-hand about the environment and the types of people who would fit into their corporate culture. I would have loved to go, but I didn't want to risk losing their business by revealing my skin color. Instead, I kept coming up with excuses about why I couldn't visit them. Eventually, they stopped inviting me and approvals to fill their job openings dried up. Looking back, I should have gone since I demonstrated that I could deliver high quality engineers regardless of color. However, I stuck to our business plan, which meant we had to work the phones even harder to replace the lost business.

Tony had rented a two-bedroom apartment on a high floor in a new residential apartment building on East 34th Street for Hankin & Smith to use as an office. This replaced the office we had on W. 21st Street. We also used the office for occasional TBOF meetings to discuss issues such as operations, staffing, lease terms, proposals, and diversification ideas. The location was ideal because it was reasonably close to our midtown clubs. Andre and I continued to work the door at the clubs but on a reduced schedule. Even though we had hired some excellent employees, it was always preferable to have a partner collecting the cash. Andre, Wayne, Mal, Harry, and I had a schedule to work the door at the various clubs. Admission to Leviticus was initially $5, but we eventually increased it to $7, then $10, so the cash receipts were substantial.

One Monday night, during a meeting of TBOF partners at the East 34th

Street office, Tony got a phone call from Bob Cherry, our manager at Leviticus, who said, "The club is jumpin' with hundreds of people." Typically, Monday nights were slow. We quickly wrapped up the meeting, so Tony, Danny, and Mal could rush over to help deal with the larger than expected crowd. When they got there, one of Tony's acquaintances nicknamed Gopher, told Tony that there was a lot of money in the room, and he pointed out several millionaires. Gopher knew all the area hustlers and gangsters so he was helpful in pointing them out. None of us knew it at the time, but Gopher had a specific reason why he wanted to get close to our business. It wouldn't take long for us to find out.

The crowd size was unusually large that night because of a private party for a young lady. No one remembers her name, but she was obviously well connected. Tony and Danny thought the private party participants would fill up the VIP section of the elevated platform area that had café tables and chairs, but guests filled the entire room.

Many celebrities and notable personalities went to Leviticus and felt at home. Although we had our share of hustlers and drug dealers, we never had a problem with them because they didn't conduct business in our clubs. During that party, one of the most notorious gangsters in the country, Leroy "Nicky" Barnes, walked in. Gopher told Tony, "You better lock the front door. The FBI is trailing Nicky. You don't want the feds coming in here!"

"Okay, this will be a private party tonight," Tony replied.

Just as Tony walked to the front door to turn the lock, the door opened, and two white guys walked in. They never identified themselves as FBI, but Tony believed they were. The two men walked over to the bar and took seats. One of the men asked the bartender where the bathroom was. Tony overheard the question and walked quickly ahead to the bathroom to make sure all was in order. No one was in the bathroom, so Tony pretended to be using a urinal. The white guy walked in a moment later.

"Nice place, isn't it?"

Tony responded, "Yes, it is."

"Is it always like this?" the white guy asked.

"No," Tony replied. "This is a big crowd for a Monday night."

After about an hour, Nicky Barnes left the club. The two white guys followed, hot on his tail. A few weeks later, news broke that the FBI arrested Nicky Barnes. About a year after that, he was convicted and sentenced to life in prison for drug-related crimes.

To protect his operation and optimize profits, Nicky Barnes had formed an organization called the Council. Modeled after the Italian mafia, the Council consisted of seven major drug lords, each with a separate operation. The Council's code forbade members from sleeping with other council members' wives or mistresses. While in prison, Barnes found out that his money was not being used for his legal defense and that his mistress was sleeping with another council member, so he turned state's evidence. That led to the indictment of 44 drug traffickers. In exchange, Barnes was placed in a witness protection program and released from prison in 1998.[36] He lived anonymously until he died of cancer in 2012.[37]

Our operation continued to be demanding as we added features and increased staff. One of the significant issues was that liquor salesmen called on locations like Lucifer's in the morning. Many transactions were COD so liquor sales representatives had lots of cash on them and feared being robbed. Robberies were more prevalent in the afternoon than in the morning so the sales reps' pattern was understandable. Several salesmen had been attacked, beaten, and robbed. Since our clubs were open until 3 or 4 am, it meant Tony and Danny had to get to the club early enough the next day to catch all the salesmen. If they missed a sales rep, it meant more phone calls, more paperwork, and delays in getting the products we needed.

One of the steps Tony and Danny took to make the operation more efficient was to reduce the number of brands in each category to minimize the number of sales reps they had to order from. For example, they cut back on

---

[36] Sam Roberts (March 4, 2007). "Crime's 'Mr. Untouchable' Emerges From Shadows". The New York Times.
[37] Wilson, Michael (April 26, 2019). "Her 'Prince Charming' Turned Out to Be a Crazed Hit Man on the Run". The New York Times. Retrieved May 8, 2019.

Leroy "Nicky" Barnes

the number of scotch brands, only ordered Tanqueray for those who wanted gin, and only Smirnoff in the vodka category. Fewer liquor sales reps made it a little easier to manage the bar.

One aspect that could not be simplified was dealing with the wide array of guests coming through the club. As Harry put it, "You never knew who was going to come through the door." Some were harmless, yet eccentric characters and some were potentially dangerous. Tony was the right person to run the operation and be our front man. He carried himself in a confident way that commanded respect. Tony's cordial relationship with various individuals was an essential factor in preserving the success we were enjoying. With a different person in charge, our club could have quickly deteriorated under pressure from outside influences.

When you own nightclubs, whether disco or not, you will likely have an array of unsavory characters in the environment. If they don't respect the establishment, they could try to infiltrate the business, use the venue to conduct business, or find other ways to wreak havoc. Tony, Danny, and CP deserve a lot of credit for their excellent people skills. They were respectful and friendly to the various gangsters but never got too close. Naturally, our high volume of guests meant we were presented with some unusual issues and unique situations. But perhaps our biggest challenge was the one that came from organized crime.

For Tony and Danny, there was a big difference between the clientele at Lucifer's in Queens and a nightclub like Leviticus in midtown Manhattan. Lucifer's attracted a handful of hustlers who were involved in the numbers racket, which was a local operation. But Leviticus attracted some of the biggest gangsters in the country. The ones at the top of the heap were drug lords who operated across a large geographic area. We never hung out in bars and certainly not in midtown, so dealing with this element was new to us. Tony and Danny had to figure it out and learn how to manage our operation in that environment. They had to rely on judgment and instinct. And they had to make adjustments based on the various personalities they encountered. If they mishandled those relationships, it could mean a short life to our operation. Thankfully, their judgment and people skills were effective. They earned the respect of the big-time mobsters who viewed our clubs as a comfortable place to relax and spend money. The mobsters blended in but if you paid attention you could tell who was who based on what they ordered and the amount of money they spent. At Leviticus, most of the drug kingpins drank Dom Perignon. Straight people ordered Dom Perignon too but, you could tell who was who based on the amount of champagne they ordered.

One evening, two well-dressed men came into Leviticus — a white guy named Johnny and a black guy named Gopher — the same Gopher that cautioned Tony about Nicky Barnes the night of the unexpectedly large private party on a Monday night. Johnny asked to speak to the owner. Tony was called to the front door. Instead of taking the two men to his office, Tony decided to walk them around the block to get away from the loud music. Gopher said, "Tony, I want you to meet Johnny. Johnny here is a friend — he can help you."

"Good to meet you, Tony," Johnny said. "You boys have a nice operation here. Looks like you're doing good business."

"Thanks," said Tony as he nodded affirmatively.

"There's a lot of things that can interfere with your business, you could have lotsa fights, bad behavior, problems with the facility, ya know what I mean? We will protect it for you." Johnny continued, "The cost to you is $500 a week. Gopher here will make the collection."

Tony understood exactly what kind of protection Johnny was talking about. He knew Gopher and the world he was from, but that didn't make the moment any less scary. Tony did not know the white guy but got the sense that he had some serious bad guys backing him up.

"I can't make this decision by myself," Tony said in a controlled voice. "I need time to consult with my partners." Johnny said "Okay, I'll come back in a couple of days. It's up to you if you want this place protected — or not."

The next morning, Tony called David Schwartz, our attorney to discuss what to do — call the police? Or the FBI? David told Tony, "Write down this phone number. When those guys come back again, call the number. When someone answers, say 'This is Tony Cooper. Please hold on,' and hand the phone to Johnny. Afterward, I want you to destroy the number."

When Johnny and Gopher came back a couple of days later, Tony took them to his office and did precisely what David had instructed. When he passed the phone, Johnny said in a loud, aggressive voice, "Excuse me. Who's this?" Then his tone changed completely. Now he was humble.

"Oh, I'm sorry! I'm sorry! I apologize!"

There was a long pause.

"Don't worry about it. It will never happen again. No problem."

Another pause.

"I understand. I will never see them again."

Johnny hung up and handed the phone back to Tony.

"Okay, everything is alright. I meant no harm," he stammered. "I will never see you again."

Tony destroyed the phone number, then called David Schwartz to thank him. To this day, Tony doesn't know who was on the phone.

Chapter 17
LEVITICUS

"Goons with tire irons."

While Tony didn't know who was on the phone, we learned that Matty "The Horse" Ianniello, controlled approximately 300 restaurants, bars, and sex shops in the Times Square area. "Some establishments were owned outright by Mr. Ianniello's organization. In most cases, though, the profit came in the form of payments for 'protection,' which establishment owners paid as supposed insurance against police raids, union demands for higher wages or, explicitly or not, visits from goons with tire irons."[38] During the 1970s, organized crime was near its peak in terms of power. The mob controlled many police officers, prosecutors, businessmen, and even judges, which meant they could operate with a certain amount of impunity.

There's a back story here. When Tony found the space we leased for Othello's, he signed the lease in the presence of Matty "The Horse" because Matty was an owner the building. Matty was an underboss to Vito Genovese, head

---

[38] NY Times, August 22, 2012 "*Matthew Ianniello, the Mafia Boss Known as 'Matty the Horse,' Dies at 92*" by Paul Vitello

Matthew "Matty the Horse" Ianniello

of the Genovese crime family,[39] one of the "Five Families" of New York City, the most powerful crime syndicate in the nation. Genovese succeeded Charles "Lucky" Luciano as boss and renamed the family after himself. At the time Gopher and Johnny tried to shake us down for weekly protection payments, Genovese was actually in prison but still running the business from his cell.[40] While we'll never know who sent the two guys to shake us down, we made sure we were good tenants and never asked for any favors from our landlord. During this period, mobsters didn't mess with squares (slang for law abiding people.) But if you were doing something illegal that the mob could detect or asked for a loan or a favor, you were fair game. Once you were in their grasp, it was all over. The Genovese Family was known for never reneging on threats and never backing down. They were known to break legs or burn businesses

[39] NY Times, August 22, 2012 *"Matthew Ianniello, the Mafia Boss Known as 'Matty the Horse,' Dies at 92"* by Paul Vitello
[40] American Mafia History, January 22, 2020, "Genovese Family - One of the 'Five Families'"

down when people didn't cooperate with them. The Tamburlaine, a restaurant/nightclub owned by Mr. Chu who also owned the Ginza, was the latest to be torched, so we knew things could get rough. We were fortunate to get out of what could have been a bad situation. In the end, it wasn't the mob that hurt our business. It was Steve Rubell's braggadocios public comments and a vindictive radio DJ from 800 miles away.

Tony, Danny, CP, Mal, and Harry got to know just about all of the drug dealers, pimps, and assorted gangsters that came to Leviticus. On many occasions, drug dealers would put a $100 bill on the bar, order a bottle of Dom Perignon, which cost $65, and tell the bartender, "Keep the change." We had approximately 35 silver ice buckets that were used exclusively for serving champagne. We also served Piper Heidsieck, but Dom Perignon was by far the brand of choice among patrons who wanted to make a statement. When a waitress brought Dom Perignon and a silver bucket with half a dozen flutes to a table, or when the bartender set it up on the bar, it created instant excitement and glamour that was visible from across the room.

One Saturday night, a hotshot stepped up to the bar and ordered four bottles of Dom Perignon. Then he invited all the beautiful ladies in the area to have a glass of champagne with him. A few moments later, another guy came in, sat on the other side of the oval bar, and ordered five bottles of Dom Perignon, just to outdo the other guy. It was an ostentatious display of one-upmanship. Neither of these players were corporate types. As long as they didn't conduct their business in the club and remained polite, they were welcome to enjoy themselves in our clubs. Given the huge sizes of our crowds, the small handful of drug dealers were not conspicuous, except of course, when they were engaging in a champagne duel. After all, we typically had several hundred patrons who simply came to dance.

Some years later, when I was a Senior Vice President at Schieffelin & Somerset, the company that imported Dom Perignon, I learned from the sales guys, that back in the mid-70s, Leviticus was the number one Dom Perignon account in the entire country, thanks to the drug dealers, pimps, and showy gamblers.

Many people played the numbers, which was an illegal lottery-type game that was popular among African Americans and Latinos. In some neighbor-hoods, it was so popular, it was ingrained as part of the culture. Numbers runners collected the money, but numbers bankers were the ones who made most of the money. They, were right up there with pimps and drug dealers in driving up Dom Perignon sales.

One small-time drug dealer known only as Trevor was a frequent visitor to Leviticus. He was a friendly, likable guy with a ready smile and a thick Ja-maican accent. When I mentioned that I was born in Kingston, he opened up and told me about how he grew up in the countryside in Jamaica. He said he was so poor, he didn't have a refrigerator. But in the mid-70s, in New York, he had plenty of money. He wasn't very fashionable, but always neatly dressed and drove a Mercedes Benz. He was the first person I met with a small re-mote-control device that could start his car and turn on the heat from inside the club! Quite a remarkable innovation for back then.

One Halloween night, Trevor stopped by Leviticus, as usual, to discover that we had asked guests to wear a costume. Some did, some didn't. I rented an Indian raja outfit, complete with a turban while Danny and Tony were more creative. Danny dressed up as Fonzie from "Happy Days." Tony put on his mother's dress — complete with wig, stockings, panties, and for a short while, high heel shoes. We knew Tony had on panties because he sat like a man with legs wide open. Trevor was beside himself when he saw Tony; he couldn't stop laughing! Tony had a mustache, goatee, and hairy legs, which made him look preposterous in his mother's clothes. It was a memorable eve-ning made even more so because of Trevor's laughing fit. He had an infectious laugh that rang through the club. We were shocked when a few months later, we heard the news that Trevor had been shot and killed. His body was found rolled up in a carpet. Although Trevor was involved in criminal activity, he always seemed happy and had a great personality. It saddened all of us to learn of his tragic ending.

We garnered a lot of buzz around Leviticus when we hosted a bathing suit party in the middle of winter. It sounded absurd to many people and there was plenty of skepticism. Not surprisingly, the men were less skeptical than the ladies. Many of the women brought their bathing suit to the club in a bag to see if people were actually wearing their bathing suits. They were. There was a steady stream of ladies going into the bathroom in dresses and coning out in bathing suits. Some women, perhaps the ones who were more confident, simply showed up in bathing suits under their coats. It was a big success in that it generated lots of talk, but I don't believe we ever repeated that event. Sadly, no photos exist from that night, so you have to use your imagination to envision a bunch of folks on the dance floor in February dancing in bathing suits!

Bob Cherry had two bouncer colleagues from his days working at the Dom: Tom LePuppet and Frank Judge. We hired both of them to work the door at Leviticus. Tom was renowned in martial arts circles and considered by some as the greatest karate fighter to come out of New York City.[41] Because of his success in karate tournaments, admission to the Black Belt Hall of Fame, and mentorship to thousands of karate students, Tom had a huge reputation. He was a celebrity bouncer. Much later, he worked as a bodyguard for Donald Trump. Tom passed away in 1999 after a four-year battle with cancer, but he continues to be a source of inspiration to many students and fans of karate.

Frank was a big, somewhat overweight, guy whose size served as a deterrent as a bouncer. Frank became infatuated with disco roller skating and skated four to five times a week, often going to an all-night rink after Leviticus closed down for the night. Frank's frequent skating transformed his physique so much, after a few months, he looked like a bodybuilder. Disco roller skating became so popular, we had roller skating nights at Leviticus where we had some of the top skaters demonstrate their moves on the dance floor.

Bob Cherry was also involved in martial arts. He was known as an "Iron Palm," a martial arts designation for someone who can deliver a powerful blow with their palm without hurting their hand. I never saw Bob use this technique in person and, thank goodness, he was never pressed to use it at Leviticus. But I did see Bob use his hands in another awe-inspiring way. One

[41] *Black Belt Magazine*, September 20, 2016 "Thomas La Puppet: Remembering a Pioneer of American Karate and Fighter from the Legendary Tong Dojo" by Floyd Burk

of his routines was to eat dinner at Wolf's, the upscale deli at the corner of 57th Street and 6th Avenue. Since Bob was a frequent customer, they knew exactly what he wanted when he walked through the door: a bacon cheese-burger with several slices of brisket, several slices of corned beef, onion rings, coleslaw, a pickle, and french fries on top — all between a large Kaiser roll. It was a custom, fully loaded hamburger that they made exclusively for Bob. An ordinary person couldn't even begin to eat such a tall sandwich, but Bob squeezed it together with his powerful hands and somehow got it into his mouth. As a bouncer and manager at Leviticus no one ever challenged Bob, which was the best outcome. His sheer size plus calm demeanor helped to

Bob Cherry in the office

keep the peace. Bob's soft-spoken style and good people skills enabled him to diffuse even high-tension situations.

Ron and Lionel Austin, brothers from our part of Queens, were both sanseis (teachers of martial arts) who worked for us as bouncers a few nights a week. They owned a barbershop and a karate school in Hollis. Both were small men and not visually intimidating. I recall when they first started working for us, one of them asked me what the name of our organization was. I told them "The Best of Friends." Ron responded:

"I knew it! You guys don't own Leviticus. Our paycheck says 'AnCo Planning.'"

On the advice of our attorney, we had set up a separate corporation for each nightclub. The corporation for Leviticus was AnCo Planning, an abbreviation for Anthony Cooper, i.e., Tony Cooper. It took awhile for the Austin brothers to believe that we owned Leviticus, but they got there eventually.

Lionel was working the door one night when a well-dressed man in a sharp-looking white suit came to the entrance, but Lionel wouldn't let him in. He was banned for a month because we busted him for using drugs in the bathroom the week before. I don't recall if he was caught snorting cocaine or smoking marijuana. I suspect he figured that if he had an impressive suit on, we would let him in, or maybe he thought we wouldn't remember his ban. But we did, and Lionel was not about to let him in.

The man in the white suit was just average in size but he was bigger than Lionel. Next thing I knew, the man in the white suit grew so angry and frustrated that he took a swing at Lionel. Gracefully, Lionel moved to the side to avoid the punch and retaliated with a blow to the side of the man's head with a restaurant chop stick that he used to keep in his lapel. Obviously, Lionel was prepared for a physical encounter based on the man's level of agitation. Blood poured out the side of the man's head like a faucet, ran down his face, and reddened his white suit jacket. He looked awful, and scary too. The bright red of the blood stood out in contrast to his dazzling white suit. The man paced around for a few moments before realizing that he was truly not getting into the club. Maybe he realized his appearance was no longer appropriate. Maybe he felt defeated by Lionel's blow. Or, maybe it dawned on him that we really intended to enforce his ban. Anyway, he didn't have much to say after that and left. Mission accomplished. But I doubt he would have taken a swing at a big guy like Frank Judge or Bob Cherry.

Sensei Ron Austin also had a memorable night at Leviticus. There was a guy snorting coke in the bathroom and he refused to leave, so CP called Ron. Ron had a remarkable technique where he could put pressure on a specific part of your neck, and it would render you unconscious. Ron asked the man in the bathroom to leave, and when he refused, Ron used his pressure-on-the-neck technique and put the man to sleep. Then he and another staffer carried the man outside through a side door and plopped him on the ground. A few moments later, the man woke up, terribly confused, sitting on the sidewalk. He kept asking, "How did I get here?! How did I get here?!"

I had my own share of memorable experiences while working the door at Leviticus. One night, a B-level celebrity came to the door and was stunned that I wouldn't let her in. I can't remember who she was, but I believe she was an actress. Despite her celebrity status, I refused to allow her into the club because she had on jeans albeit an expensive pair of designer jeans with rhinestones and glitter. Jordache and other designer jeans were just becoming popular by then, and even though they were far more expensive than traditional jeans, we still maintained a strict "no jeans" policy in our dress code. She could not believe that I wouldn't let her in because of her jeans and stood in the lobby area for a while. Eventually, Mal and Andre came to the door and reinforced what I told her — no jeans allowed. She was pissed off and eventually left. The next night, she returned to Leviticus, this time in proper attire, and all was forgiven. Our customers knew the deal, and they accepted it. In a subsequent TBOF meeting, we recognized that enforcing our dress code could get more challenging because fashions were becoming more relaxed and the line between casual and designer were blurring. Nevertheless, for the full life of Leviticus, we enforced our dress code.

Mal had his own encounter with a jeans wearer that could have led to disaster. Mal wouldn't let a man in because of our policy, and the man became angry, loud, and belligerent.

"I don't care what you say, I'm coming in," he told Mal. "I know Tony Cooper, so step aside!"

Mal had left the booth and stood in front of the guest to block his passage.

"I respect the fact that you know Tony, but I can't let you in because you're not dressed appropriately," Mal calmly explained.

The man, who was much larger than Mal, put a big, meaty hand on Mal's chest and pushed him back a foot or two.

"If you don't let me in," he yelled, "I'm coming back to get you!"

Mal was the smallest partner in TBOF, so it was a complete mismatch if it came down to strength. The situation was escalating, and it was not looking good for Mal. But to his credit, he did not back down. Just then, Bob Cherry walked into the lobby and quietly told the angry man he'd like to have a word with him outside. Bob gestured toward the door, and they both exited the lobby. Bob returned a few minutes later by himself. Only then did he tell Mal that the man was "New York Freddie" Myers, the heroin kingpin based in Harlem. Freddie had a massive operation that brought heroin in from various parts of the world for distribution in the metropolitan area. It's not clear what Bob said to Freddie, or how he got him to leave, but the next couple of weeks, because of the threat he received from "New York Freddie," Mal was on his toes. Mal had no idea who Freddie was until after the incident. Had he known, he might not have been so resolute. As Mal put it, "It was the joy of ignorance."

Chapter 18
DOW TWINS

"*Andy Warhol was just another guest.*"

Andy Warhol enjoyed frequenting nightclubs and discos, so when he heard about Othello in 1977, he stopped by. Harold Dow remembers that it was on a Thursday night. "Andy Warhol was just another guest," he recalled. "No one made a fuss over him." Warhol had such a good time, he brought Elizabeth Taylor and fashion guru, Valentino, to Othello on the very next Thursday night. Even with those big names, no one acted star struck over them. Othello's crowd was not into celebrities. They were into dancing and having fun. After a few minutes, Elizabeth Taylor, Andy Warhol, and Valentino got out on the dance floor and enjoyed themselves, just like the other guests. Taylor got into it so much, she danced in her bare feet. When they were ready to leave, Harold and Norman Dow, aka the "Dow Twins", walked them out to make sure they had a safe departure. As they were leaving, Alix DeJean, the photographer we hired to capture celebs and special events at our clubs, was just arriving and captured the moment.

Othello was our newest club. Not long after Leviticus opened, Tony and

Foreground, l-r, Harold Dow, Andy Warhol, Valentino, Elizabeth Taylor, and Norman Dow in front of Othello

Danny found an available space on 8th Avenue and 35th Street — only eight blocks from Leviticus and about the same size. It had been the Jack Nicklaus restaurant. We hired Tony's father to make modifications to the restaurant but left the bar the way it was. We called this new club, Othello. It had a capacity of approximately 500. To minimize cannibalization of Leviticus, we hired the Dow Twins, Harold and Norman Dow, to manage and promote Othello. The Dow Twins were successful and highly regarded promoters. The deal was that they could continue to produce their own popular special events and concurrently market Othello to their following.

The Dow Twins both graduated from St. John's University and developed a strong client base. They were about five years younger than us, which meant they attracted a different crowd. We were in our late 20s and the Dow Twins were in their early 20s so, from a marketing standpoint, the age difference was significant. The Dow Twins not only had an established group of followers, we knew we could trust them. In many ways, they were like a younger version of ourselves. They lived in Jamaica and were proficient and consistent in the events they put together. They promoted dances, Father's Day racetrack parties at Belmont, boat rides, trips to the Bahamas, and so on. But perhaps they were at their best when they put together dances in a variety of interesting venues such as the Intrepid Sea and Space Museum, South Street Seaport, and the Copacabana.

Harold and Norman Dow were identical mirror twins. Mirror twins means one is a righty and the other a lefty...Norman was the lefty. If they weren't in their specific element, most people could not tell them apart. Their reputation for being honest and consistent was precisely what TBOF needed. The twins complemented each other in many ways. Harold was the behind-the-scenes guy. Norman was upfront "shaking hands and kissing babies," as Harold would say. Harold explained his role this way, "My goal was to make sure Norman always had a smile on his face by eliminating distractions and

The Dow Twins

solving problems that might make him unhappy. This way, Norman would remain effective in dealing with the public."

At that time, within the black community, particularly among those in their 20s and 30s, the Dow Twins were arguably the best-known black men in the New York area. Even today, although Norman passed away a few years ago, Harold continues to stage special events under the Dow Twins name. As a result, the Dow Twins continue to enjoy a high level of awareness within that same, now older, cohort. As it turned out, the Dow Twins became extremely valuable managers for TBOF. They worked hard and never let success go to their heads. Also, they were more egalitarian in their approach to marketing than we were. TBOF delighted in attracting high achievers to Leviticus. On the other hand, the Dow Twins wanted everyone to attend Othello and to experience the vibe they created. They got to know most of their guests personally, which gave Othello an intimate feeling even though it was a large club.

Since Leviticus was our flagship club, we wanted to create and promote an aspirational atmosphere. We liked the idea of creating an environment that felt exclusive and reserved for a somewhat elite crowd. Leviticus had glamour and sophistication. It was a place to see and be seen, while Othello was more down-to-earth and relaxed. Because of this difference in orientation, both clubs thrived. In keeping with our goal of continuity, Othello had a similar physical appearance to Leviticus and our other clubs, except for the bar. We kept the same bar that the restaurant before us had. But Mr. Cooper added our signature black and white dance floor, white stucco walls, red and black commercial carpeting, and elevated areas to add visual interest to the room. Like Leviticus, Othello also had a back room with sofas and soft chairs surrounding tables with board games. These backrooms provided a break from the high energy dance floor area.

The success of Othello strengthened our TBOF platform and contributed to our dominance of the nightclub scene in NYC, at least among African Americans. As promoters, we had lots of competitors who also attracted large, predominantly African American crowds. But none of our competitors owned clubs in midtown as we did. As club owners, we had a more consistent presence and ran the operations in a way to sustain long term appeal. That meant physically refreshing the clubs every so often and evolving the programs and activities to align with shifting interests and trends. It also meant staying abreast of new music and upcoming artists so that we could enhance the dance experience with a good blend of older favorites and the latest hits.

White folks who attended our clubs included record company and radio executives, business people looking to have a fun experience without the high drama that existed at some discos, as well as people who lived or worked in the neighborhood. We always had diverse crowds, and everyone who came was made to feel welcome. Given the low police presence, we took a few liberties. There were a few occasions when a group of hustlers would drive up and couldn't get in because they weren't dressed properly. They were respectful enough to not want to break our dress rules, so, when they ordered Dom Perignon to be served in their car, we obliged.

Alix, our photographer, had also worked for Leroy "Nicky" Barnes and Frank "Black Caesar" Matthews — as noted earlier, two of the most notorious drug dealers in the country. Alix said he didn't know what they did for a living, but he accepted the offer when they asked him to photograph some of their lavish parties. Nicky and Frank were competitors, but they ran in similar circles. When Nicky Barnes was on trial, the prosecution subpoenaed Alix. Apparently, they wanted to see his photographs and maybe get him to share conversations he overheard.

Othello canopy

Othello dance floor

In 1978, Harry supervised the remodeling of Othello, which was then renamed Justine's. Although Leviticus was our undisputed flagship, the newly remodeled and renamed Justine's was a close second. The crowd was large almost every night at Justine's, and it generated lots of talk. The Dow Twins were extraordinary managers, and successfully kept their special events going as well. One of their most remarkable events was an annual party at the Intrepid Air & Space Museum. The Intrepid is a massive aircraft carrier that's permanently moored on the Hudson River at the foot of West 46th Street in Manhattan. No other promoters were able to reserve the Intrepid for a party, only the Dow Twins. The Intrepid management felt comfortable with the Dow Twins because they had a track record of good, clean parties. The Dow Twins attracted 2,500 people to these annual parties, which lasted for 25 years. Dancing on the deck of the Intrepid, with spectacular views of the Manhattan skyline as a backdrop, was a magical and exclusive experience. There was dancing on two floors. The top level had a hot DJ playing R&B and disco music and the lower deck featured Latin music with a DJ alternating with a live band such as Ruben Blades, Eddie Palmieri, or Bobby Rodriguez.

Some years later, there was an effort to move the Intrepid for a major renovation. Despite six tug boats straining with engines at full tilt, the Intrepid only moved about two feet. It was stuck in deep mud. Popular DJ Ken "Spider" Webb went on air and exclaimed, "Those Dow Twins' parties, with all those folks dancing, drove the Intrepid down into the mud."

The Dow Twins didn't book the Latin bands through Ralph Mercado, the high-profile booking agent, as most organizations would do. They got to know the bands personally and scheduled with them directly. As a result, the bands made more money than they ever made from gigs arranged by Mr. Mercado. Based on that relationship, the Dow Twins were extremely popular among the members of the various Latin bands. According to Harold, as the Twins traveled around the city, they would occasionally be stopped by a band member who wanted to thank them for the bookings.

The Dow Twins used their popularity with Latinos to arrange Salsa Fridays at Justine's. These events featured live music from 6 to 11 pm. Salsa Fridays appealed to both Latinos and African Americans who, historically,

*Dow Twins fundraiser for the Norman Dow Scholarship
Fund on the Intrepid Sea, Air, and Space Museum*

attended separate events and danced separately. But on Salsa Fridays at Justine's, they danced with each other. None of us knew of any other occasion where blacks and Hispanics danced with each other on such a regular basis.

The Dow Twins hosted many other annual and periodic events that contributed to their reputation, such as parties at the South Street Seaport that attracted over 2,000 people. These parties were held on Friday nights after work during the summer when many New Yorkers left the city to head to the Hamptons or the country. As a result, South Street Seaport had few customers on summer weekends. The Dow Twins' events stirred up the quiet summer weekends and injected excitement into the Seaport. When management of the Seaport tried to end the Dow Twins events, the merchants signed a petition demanding that they be allowed to continue hosting their parties there because attendees brought good business to the restaurants and shops. It's not clear why South Street Seaport management tried to end the events, but you have to wonder if they would have acted the same if the Dow Twins brought in a white crowd. Either way, South Street Seaport management complied, the parties continued, making the restaurants and vendors happy and profitable.

The Dow Twins also supported charitable causes. They supported the Jackie Robinson Foundation by promoting their jazz festivals in Connecticut that attracted over 8,000 people. They also worked with the highly regarded Dave Winfield Foundation and several other organizations to help raise funds for worthy causes. These events provided good cash flow for the Dow Twins and were separate from TBOF operations. The magnitude and quality of the Dow Twins events, combined with their management of Justine's, contributed to their remarkably high level of awareness.

With Leviticus and Justine's operating on all cylinders, the road ahead seemed smooth but we were about to hit some serious speed bumps.

Chapter 19
DISCO BOOM

"*Empty your pockets!*"

When the shotgun was fired, it sounded like someone took a sledge hammer and hit a large sheet of steel. The sound ricocheted through every corner of Leviticus. On Saturday, January 9, 1977, our worst fears were realized — Leviticus was robbed. The robbers probably knew we had a cash business and that on a busy night, there was an abundance of money sitting in the club.

"This is a stick-up! Everyone freeze!"

It happened around midnight when approximately 400 patrons were enjoying a carefree evening. Mal was in the booth collecting the admission fee, a position I often worked. There was a commotion near the front door so Mal left the booth to find out what was happening. Six armed men had gathered there and entered the club. One fired a shotgun into the air causing immediate chaos. Patrons started running in all directions, but mostly toward the back of the room since that was the furthest point away from the robbers. All this was happening to the strains of "Sing a Song" by Earth, Wind, & Fire, blaring on the speakers. In a moment, the music screeched to a halt when the DJ ran out of the booth. He escaped through the back door and kept running all the way to Justine's.

Tony and Harry were at the far end of the bar. When the shotgun was fired, Tony hit the ground along with everyone else in the area — except for Harry. Tony pulled Harry by the pant leg and shouted, "Get down!" The man with the shotgun must have heard the commotion because as soon as Harry dropped down, he moved over to where Tony and Harry were. Tony had his eye on the man with the shotgun who was walking right toward him. The man put the shotgun right in Tony's face and said: "What are you looking at?" Tony immediately looked away. He subsequently said: "I was so scared, I couldn't even tell you if the guy was black or white!"

Over the next 20 minutes or so the robbers took money from the cash registers, waitresses, and jewelry and cash from some of the customers. They made several of the men drop their pants, presumably to slow them down if anyone had the idea of chasing them. Don Cornelius, creator of the Soul Train television show, was there that night with a lady friend. He was one of the guests who ran to the back of the club, so he was not personally robbed. Yes, he grabbed his lady friend and made sure she got to the back of the room also. In the room that night were a few mobsters who took note of who was robbing the club. The robbers did not cover their faces and, apparently, were not aware of who they were robbing.

When the robbers finished, they headed for the back door. Ron Austin, our bouncer, ran after the robbers. The robber with the shotgun turned and fired at Ron's chest, almost point blank. Everyone thought Ron was gone, but he didn't go down. It quickly became apparent that the shotgun had blanks. No bullet hit Ron but it stopped his pursuit. We later confirmed that the shotgun definitely had blanks because, after careful examination, there was no damage to the ceiling from the first blast.

The police actually arrived early, which was a shock. While the robbers were still inside Leviticus, the police were outside. It seems the robbers knew the police were close behind so they made a speedy departure and, presumably, stashed the shotgun and cash. The robbers probably escaped by climbing to the roof of the McAlpin Hotel which was directly behind Leviticus and escaped onto 34th Street. Leviticus was on 33rd Street. A bag with cash and jewelry was found days later on the roof of our building. However, the items were never returned to our customers. We were told that somewhere between the Police Department and the Fire Department, the bag mysteriously and inexplicably disappeared.

A few months later, Tony and Danny got word that three of the six robbers were found dead. The other three were never seen again. Many notable Harlem gangsters visited Leviticus, including "Goldfinger," "Big Jack," "Little Jack," "Macaroni," "Black Ronnie," and the notorious Flewellyn brothers, to name a few. We couldn't recall who, specifically, was in the club the night it was robbed so we'll never know the full story, but none of our Manhattan clubs was ever robbed again. And word got out that the robbers were never seen again, at least not alive.

Anyone who thought about robbing our clubs had to know that they were going up against the power of drug kingpins and other big-time gangsters. I believe that's why Leviticus was never robbed again, even though during that period, there were frequent bar robberies throughout the city. These types of crimes were common because there was very little police presence at night, especially in neighborhoods with black bars. Our locations were in midtown, but even there the police presence was very light.

In the fall of 1976, about a year before the opening of Studio 54, TBOF expanded into Brooklyn with a new club called Orpheus. After the opening, we met in our 34th Street office where Danny reported that "Brooklyn is a different world. Orpheus is a 'white elephant' because guests expect the bar to be open all night. Some patrons get angry when we announce 'last call.'" Danny went on to say, "The neighborhood around Orpheus is not policed at all so there are many after hour clubs that we're competing against. This is not the best situation — we need to figure out how to make the most of it."

We wanted to have a club in Brooklyn because of the large African American population there. We knew Brooklyn was a lot different than Queens and Manhattan and we were about to find out just how different. Tony and Danny found a building on Washington Avenue, across the street from the Brooklyn Botanical Gardens and down the street from the old Ebbets Field, Orpheus had been an Italian catering hall with a capacity of 400. By the time Mr. Cooper was done building it out, it looked beautiful. He used the same physical guidelines and standards as our other clubs.

Leviticus and Justine's were a bit of an anomaly in midtown because there was nothing like them anywhere in the area but Orpheus was one of many clubs in Brooklyn that black folks could go to. What made Orpheus stand out was how beautiful the room was. We got lots of compliments about its appearance. Many customers would arrive at Orpheus late, like around 2 am, and get pissed off when we closed at 4 am. They assumed we would be open until at least 6 am or later since that was how other clubs operated. Orpheus was only a moderate success compared to Leviticus and Othello because our business model was not an ideal fit for Brooklyn.

In 1979, music promoter Russell Simmons came by Leviticus on several occasions to try to convince us to play his hip-hop records. We refused primarily because hip-hop was not as danceable as other options, but also, we were concerned about the element that hip-hop music would attract. We did play some rap songs such as "Rapper's Delight" because it had the highly danceable track from "Good Times" that was created by Nile Rodgers. But in terms of hip-hop music in general, we had concerns. We had a strong following of upscale men and women, and it was a crowd we knew. One patron of Leviticus described the club this way, "This was one of the best clubs in the city at that time."[42] That's an accurate description of Leviticus. We believed that the reason why our clubs were virtually trouble-free was because of our dress and behavior policies, along with the relationship we had with our following. We felt it would be risky to reach out to a new crowd that we didn't know. The hip-hop crowd was younger than us, dressed in casual clothes, and often wore hats. Plus, the lyrics of many hip-hop songs were raw and aggres-

---

[42] Quotation by M. Watson Martin, as reported by Jefferson Grubbs on Bustle.com in " 'Empire' Club Leviticus May Have Biblical Origins" February 15, 2015

sive. All of that could create problems at the door and inside the club. We were not alone in that assessment.

Around that time, all the radio stations also refused to play hip-hop records. As for Russell Simmons, he was able to get enough clubs to play his records. When radio stations started getting phone calls asking them to play Russell's hip hop record, they responded. As Russell continued to persist and the culture began to shift, he cashed in big as radio station doors finally opened. Interestingly, hip-hop continues to heavily sample music from the disco library. And Russell Simmons, who grew up with little money like the rest of us in the neighborhood, achieved enormous wealth. Simmons' story is amazing and inspiring. He's written several books — all worth reading.

We had difficulty attracting guests to Orpheus early in the week, so we operated just on Thursday, Friday, and Saturday nights. To increase our profits, we rented out Sunday nights to promoters who brought in a Haitian crowd. Sunday nights turned out to be extremely successful with a huge crowd — bigger than our Saturday night crowd. The promoters took the door and we took the bar, so it was a beneficial arrangement for us, too. We made money at Orpheus but nowhere near what we were bringing in at Leviticus or Othello.

Steve Rubell, one of the creators of Studio 54, stopped by Leviticus on at least two occasions to ask how we got started; how we created the club, promoted it, what our admission policies were, dress code, and so on. He was full of questions. We were open with Steve because we knew his club would not compete with ours. We explained how Tony's father had built Leviticus and that it took a long time because he worked alone. We described how we avoided using mass media because we didn't want to attract bad actors. We also detailed our dress code, admission policy, drink prices, and so on.

Rubell and his partner, Ian Schrager, developed a much different approach for building and operating their club. They hired a construction crew of over a hundred workers and completed construction in just six weeks.[43] The way they operated Studio 54 was also vastly different than our operation. In 1977,

[43] "Operators of Studio 54 In New York Indicted On Skimming Receipts". The Wall Street Journal. June 29, 1979. p. 22.

we charged $7 admission, and guests had to comply with our dress code. Rubell and Schrager charged different amounts on different nights, but $20 was common. Guests wearing unusual, outlandish, or exciting outfits were more likely to be allowed to enter than someone in a business suit — just the opposite of our dress code. Gay people were let in over straight people because they felt gay people tended to be more interesting than straight people. Rubell wasn't concerned about letting in troublemakers because the relatively high admission prices at Studio 54 kept most of them out. Patrons used drugs in Studio 54, and there seemed to be no effort to discourage it. In fact, there were many reports that Rubell dispensed drugs. Again, just the opposite of our clubs. We were diligent in preventing drug use in all our locations, and anyone caught using drugs was escorted out and banned for a month. At Studio 54, people danced with or without a partner. Couples danced at our clubs. Only later, as the culture shifted toward a more relaxed and casual style did patrons feel comfortable dancing as individuals without a partner.

Steve's admission policy at Studio 54 was highly subjective and controversial - the opposite end of the spectrum from ours. A host at the front door allowed people who looked "interesting" to come in. Steve himself would occasionally stand outside and decide who to let in. Many patrons waited for an hour or more trying to get into Studio 54, and some never got in, even when it wasn't crowded. These experiences generated tremendous publicity. Eventually, it created a negative backlash but that only served to generate even more publicity. Studio 54 was mentioned on TV a lot, and articles about the club were non-stop. Harry and CP knew the bouncers at the door at Studio 54, so they never had a problem getting in. Although due to our crazy schedule, the rest of us only went once or twice.

Studio 54 attracted a higher-income, primarily white clientele compared to patrons at our clubs. Our admission price was modest since African American income was lower on average. Studio 54 also attracted many people who simply wanted to people watch and see wild outfits. Guests at our clubs pri-

---

[44] "Hot Stuff" by Dr. Alice Echols, pg. 195. Dr. Echols is Barbra Streisand Chair of Contemporary Gender Studies, USC

marily came to dance.

After a while, some Studio 54 patrons got tired of getting dressed up and waiting at the entrance only to find out that they would not be admitted. It was frustrating and it turned off a growing number of customers. In contrast, the atmosphere at our clubs was like family. Many regulars enjoyed the fact that they would see a lot of friends there and celebrated special occasions at our clubs. There were handfuls of regulars at our clubs to whom we became the closest thing they had to family. It's where regulars came to hear people wish them a happy birthday or congratulate them on a new job. Studio 54 had their share of regulars also, but most people couldn't plan to meet friends there since you never knew if you would get in.

Dr. Alice Echols, a noted historian, author, professor of history at USC, wrote about discos in the '70s in a book called Hot Stuff. In it, she said, "Steve Rubell and Ian Schrager's glam palace of disco, Studio 54, was reportedly meant to be a white, Hollywood version of the fashionable black Manhattan disco Leviticus...."[44] Studio 54 certainly was glam, but it was nothing like Leviticus.

Tony and Danny didn't like the vibe when they visited Studio 54. The night Tony went, he was with the Dow Twins and a model named Romni. When they got there, they were waiting behind a small crowd, and Paul Newman was in front of them. It took awhile for them to get in and they noticed that Paul Newman paid so they knew they would have to pay also. Once inside, they walked around for a while to see the place. Tony was impressed with how the lights came down out of the ceiling, but less impressed by a large image of a person snorting from a spoon embedded in the dance floor. When Tony needed to go to the bathroom, it took him half an hour to find it. It was hard to find because it was labeled something like "Smoking Room." Inside, Tony encountered a group of people smoking and another door to the actual bathroom. There was only one urinal, and a woman was sitting on top of it with her legs wide open, one on each side of the urinal.

"Do you mind?" Tony said. "I have to go to the bathroom."

She did not respond. By now, Tony really had to go, so he zipped down his pants and urinated between her legs into the urinal.

Nick Ashford, Ray Simpson, Nile Rodgers, Valerie Simpson, and CP at Leviticus

Danny went on a different night and described it this way: "Studio 54 was a spectacle to us."

Rubell and Schrager hired a high-powered public relations person to encourage media coverage and a separate celebrity wrangler who brought in celebrities to help generate talk. They kept Studio 54 in the news and helped generate a level of media coverage that far exceeded the coverage any other club received. In contrast Leviticus did not receive anywhere near the media coverage that Studio 54 had, but within the black community the word of mouth for Leviticus was enormous. Rubell was also personally involved in celebrity wrangling and was successful in getting many A-list personalities to come to his club. The mainstream media never tired of covering Studio 54.

I was working at Ogilvy & Mather Advertising when Studio 54 was open and can remember seeing daily faxes from Studio 54 promoting the theme for the night. Some nights the theme was nurses, or flight attendants, or secretaries. I heard they had an unusually large crowd when the theme was models. Many of my friends at other companies also received faxes from Studio 54. Using faxes was inexpensive and a smart marketing move because it drove their message directly to folks working in midtown. Secretaries would typically retrieve the flyers at fax machines and quickly share them with friends and bosses. I remember hearing coworkers getting on the phone to arrange to go to Studio 54 with friends after seeing a flyer. I was not aware of any other nightclub using this technique, so with little or no competition, it had a tremendous impact. Everyone in my office environment was talking about Studio 54.

I should point out that there were important reasons why Studio 54 had a different marketing strategy than us. Not only did they cater to a different audience, but Studio 54 also opened after there was a strong demand for discos. Our clubs were opened at the very beginning of the disco era when the concept was still being formed. When Studio 54 opened, discos were in high gear. Everyone knew what it was and wanted to experience a disco. Studio 54 was right on time in providing an extraordinary experience that generated an unprecedented level of interest.

According to Nile Rodgers in his book Le Freak, Grace Jones invited Nile and Bernard Edwards of the musical group Chic, to Studio 54 one night in 1978. Chic only had one successful song at that point, "Dance, Dance, Dance," but it was a pretty big hit. Nile and Bernard were supposed to go to the stage door and say they were friends of Grace Jones to get in but, apparently, Ms. Jones forgot to tell the doorman. When Nile and Bernard arrived and mentioned Grace Jones' name, the doorman wouldn't let them in. When they persisted, the doorman got fed up, told them to "F*** off!" and slammed the door in their faces. After that insult, they gave up and went around the corner to a DJ friend's apartment.

Nile and Bernard bought a couple of bottles of vintage Dom Perignon and wrote a song called "F*** Off!" They liked the song, but when they agreed that it would never get on the radio with that language, they changed the words to "Freak Off!" That didn't sound so catchy, so eventually they changed it again to "Freak Out!" It proved to be their biggest hit. The song went triple platinum and was number one for seven weeks. So, they redeemed themselves after the embarrassing indignation at the entrance to Studio 54. (Interestingly, about 30 years later the doorman who refused Nile and Bernard entry, posted an apology to them on Facebook.)[45] Nile wound up going to Studio 54 a lot after that incident. After his success with "Freak Out," Nile was a major celebrity. Nile also came to Leviticus, not to perform, but to enjoy the club. In fact, the first time he heard "Rapper's Delight," was at Leviticus.[46] Although it was considered a hip-hop song, the beat was infectious and danceable, so it fit in nicely with a disco playlist.

Publicity about the genre of disco continued to accelerate to the point where it became overexposed and overly commercialized. Before long, there was Christmas Disco, Mickey Mouse Disco, Polka Disco, and more. Everything related to disco was selling and profit-hungry people began churning out disco music and products that were pure garbage. Studios even re-released blockbuster movies like Star Wars and Superman with disco tracks. Disco became so common and stereotyped with outlandish outfits and comical styles that the overexposure fed into an already growing backlash starting in 1978. Blacks, gays, and Hispanics were so prominent in the disco scene, many white rockers resented the genre because it displaced the amount of rock music played on radio. Black entertainers — male and female — were dominating the Billboard charts with disco songs. Rock & Roll, by comparison, was a predominantly white male environment and many popular radio stations were switching from rock to disco music. That incensed many rock fans.

Danny referred to Studio 54 as "the diamond of disco nightclubs" when

[45] Nile Rodgers, Le Freak (Great Britain: Clays Ltd. Elcograf S.p.A., 2012), pages 135-138.
[46] Wall Street Journal, January 29, 2017, "How Chic's 'Good Times' Launched Rap" by Marc Myers

it opened. But Steve Rubell was cocky and a bit of a hotshot. In 1978 he was quoted in the media as saying, "Only the mafia makes more money than the club brought in."[47] Later, Danny observed, "Steve's statement led to the demise of disco. It hurt the whole industry." A few weeks after Steve's comment was published, two dozen IRS agents raided Studio 54, confiscating drugs and financial records, and arrested Steve and his partner, Ian Schrager. They were convicted of tax evasion and other crimes and each given a sentence of three years. The night before they had to report to prison to start their sentences, they staged one of their best parties.

Many celebrities, close friends, and frequent customers attended. Steve and Ian only spent about a year behind bars. They had their sentences commuted because they cooperated with authorities and identified other clubs that they thought were hiding cash and underreporting their income. The IRS busted several of these clubs, including Bonds, Infinity, and New York, New York.[48]

IRS agents also came to Leviticus and had someone stand at the door with a clicker to count how many people paid to determine if our reported income was accurate. They came on a Saturday night and simply multiplied the number of guests they counted times seven to estimate our weekly take. Tony and Danny had to set them straight by pointing out that Saturday night is the busiest night of the week. Far fewer guests come on weeknights. We passed that inspection, but with the closure of several clubs and the "Disco Sucks" mantra that had become popular, the demise of disco was hastened.

Our clubs were popularly referred to as "discos" starting around 1974, but they were never similar to what Studio 54 became. Studio 54, and some other discos, were known for scantily clad women, drugs, sex, outlandish costumes, and wild dancing. Our clubs were much more conservative in dress and behavior, thanks to the rules that we enforced — we had a strict dress code, people danced as couples, drugs were banned, and users punished if caught. There

---

[47] NY Times, October 5, 2018, "A History of Studio 54, This Time Told by the Quiet Partner" by Alan Light
[48] NY Times, October 5, 2018, "A History of Studio 54, This Time Told by the Quiet Partner" by Alan Light

were plenty of casual and even wild discos that existed, but our strength was in attracting an upscale, conservative crowd, and our policies kept it that way.

I was always at the door collecting the entrance fee on the nights I worked, so I knew who we let in and who we turned away. Not everyone who came into the club was of means. I cashed one or two welfare checks. And on more than one occasion, someone I admitted into the club would say to me, "I have just enough cash to get in and buy one drink." Some folks were broke, but you couldn't tell because they were appropriately dressed and fit in once inside.

We added a pinball machine to the backroom of Leviticus to provide an additional activity. One night, Danny was playing pinball when a young lady came over and challenged him to a game. While they were playing, Steve Roberts, our MC at Leviticus was mouthing something to Danny every time it was the lady's turn to play, but Danny couldn't understand what he was saying. It was a bit comical to watch their facial expressions as Steve overexaggerated his silent message and Danny responded with increasingly confused looks. Only after they finished playing did Danny learn that he had been playing pinball with Pam Grier. Pam's career was riding high at the time as she had recently starred in Coffy and Foxy Brown, which were big hits in the new blaxploitation movie genre.

With the conspicuous success of TBOF, a steady stream of people approached us to invest or partner in various projects. We were by nature very cautious and turned down all requests and offers — except one. There was a request from a frequent customer that Mal knew. He had a short-haul trucking business called TNT Trucking and needed money to buy one more truck. He promised that his business would then be so profitable he would pay back the loan in short order. Tony was typically steadfast in rejecting such requests, but since Mal pushed for us to help this company, he relented. I'm not sure what was different with this request; maybe it was a desire to do something philanthropic. We were raking in some pretty big money so it didn't hurt us financially to approve the loan. We discussed loaning $25,000 but decided to start with an advancement of $5,000 to TNT Trucking. Once the check was cashed, it was difficult to get in touch with the borrower and not a dime was ever repaid. Lesson learned. That was the last loan we ever made.

Chapter 20

VAUGHN HARPER AND FRANKIE CROCKER

"You have a voice that should be on radio!"*

One evening at Leviticus, Vaughn Harper was introducing the live act and in the back of the room was Frankie Crocker, the top radio personality in New York who was enormously popular within the African American community.

Frankie interrupted Vaughn's intro and yelled out, "You have a voice that should be on radio!"

Vaughn didn't miss a beat. "Well, why don't you hire me?"[49]

Vaughn and Frankie spoke afterward, and the rest is history. Vaughn went on to host "Quiet Storm," one of the top-rated radio shows for many years in New York.[50] Vaughn's rich, velvety voice and quick humor endeared him to a vast radio audience. His show was syndicated in markets around the U.S. and

[49] Amsterdam News, July 11, 2016, "Vaughn Harper, WBLS & 'Quiet Storm' Pioneer, Dies at 71"

[50] NY Times, July 11, 2016, ""Vaughn Harper, Silky-Voiced DJ, Dies at 70" by Daniel Slotnik

even in several other countries, including Japan.

Vaughn Harper had previously been a star basketball player at Boys High and Syracuse University, and a fifth-round draft pick by the Detroit Pistons. His career in the NBA, however, didn't last long.[51] Vaughn injured his knee during training camp and, as a result, didn't make the team. For such a highly decorated NCAA player, it was a major blow for his basketball career to come to an abrupt and painful end. As with many other great college basketball players who aspire to be in the NBA but get cut due to injuries or to make room for better players, it can lead to depression.

Vaughn was understandably heartbroken and bitter when his NBA career ended. He started coming to Leviticus and befriended CP, who hired him to do a variety of tasks, including working the door. With his 6' 4" size, he was a natural. However, Vaughn's talent was so apparent, he was quickly promoted to manager. Danny noted that Vaughn's low octave, velvety smooth voice, could make him a good MC. One night when Steve Roberts, who always did a great job in announcing our performers, was not available, Vaughn gave it a shot. He was a natural. Vaughn's voice, combined with his ability to think on his feet and playfully banter with the audience, made him the perfect MC. He became our primary announcer.

Tony shared this story about Vaughn: "One night, Billy Paul was the live show. He wasn't feeling well, and we were concerned that he might not be able to perform. It was touch and go. However, after Vaughn introduced him with lots of fanfare, Paul responded. He made his way to the microphone and promptly brought the house down."

Even after he became a major radio personality, Vaughn continued to stop by Leviticus and often stepped in to MC and introduce the show for the evening. Vaughn remained close to TBOF until he passed away from health issues in 2016. Before he passed, an interviewer asked Vaughn about the old days when he spent a lot of time with TBOF. He became emotional and said, "As much as I'd like to talk about it, I can't...because it will make me cry.

---

[51] Amsterdam News, July 11, 2016, "Vaughn Harper, WBLS & 'Quiet Storm' Pioneer, Dies at 71"

Those days at Leviticus were...wonderful!" Vaughn was extremely popular in New York, and not just among those who frequented our clubs. Whenever Vaughn visited Leviticus, he brought glamour, sophistication, and an energy that made the evening even more special.

Vaughn overcame the disappointment of having an NBA career-ending injury. But many athletes aren't as fortunate. I remember Sonny Dove, who was on the bus with me to Ft. Hamilton in Brooklyn for our Army physical. The Detroit Pistons also drafted Sonny, who played in the ABA. When he retired from pro basketball a few years later, he wound up driving a taxi. Ending a pro basketball career can be tragic and calamitous for an athlete who is on the doorstep of making it big. When an athlete gets cut, they lose the camaraderie and structure of the team, the paycheck, and the glamour - all at once. Sonny lost his life one night when his taxi went over a partially open bridge and fell into the Gowanus Canal in Brooklyn. Some say it was suicide. Regardless, it was so sad to lose such a talented young man.

By 1977, attendance at Leviticus had leveled off. It seemed the interest in dancing was beginning to wane just a bit. But when the movie Saturday Night Fever was released on December 16 that year, attendance at our clubs took off again. This time, the percentage of non-black patrons increased from around 10% to approximately 15%. Saturday Night Fever had a more significant impact on our business than any other event. The movie's soundtrack was the biggest grossing album in history. In fact, it caused discos to explode around the world. Our attendance numbers never wavered when Studio 54 opened in April 1977. After all, their audience was very different than ours. While Saturday Night Fever gave us a shot in the arm, it was also a shot in the foot. After the initial surge of interest that the movie created in disco, overexposure and the abundance of corny and tasteless disco associations, hastened its decline.

The memorable dance moves that John Travolta performed in Saturday Night Fever were taught to him by two choreographers, Deney Terrio and Lester Wilson. Deney Terrio took Travolta to several discos and showed him a series of basic moves. Lester Wilson refined those moves and prepared Travolta to move with rhythm for the film.[52] Lester Wilson grew up in Hollis, right around the corner from where my wife Gwen grew up. Lester's mom and Gwen's mom were best friends.

That same year, 1977, we refreshed the appearance of Leviticus and changed the name to "Leviticus International" and referred to it as an entertainment complex. We complemented the dancing sets with live music by featuring nationally known acts to broaden the appeal of the club. The surge in business from Saturday Night Fever only lasted a year or so. Besides, many of the new customers that came as a result of the movie were more into watching than dancing.

CP booked lots of exciting live acts, and it kept Leviticus jumping. Unlike other venues that booked acts, CP rarely went through booking agents. Instead, he used his relationships with record company executives and dealt directly with the performers. He became personal friends with many of the performers and built a reputation for being trustworthy and reliable. As a result, he was very successful in booking the hottest acts. When Taste of Honey was at their peak in 1978 with "Boogie Oogie Oogie," CP brought them to Leviticus. They were out of Los Angeles and this was their first time performing in New York. When the show was announced, the line at Leviticus was down the block and the phone never stopped ringing. Dick Clark's office called CP to find out how he was able to get Taste of Honey, and other acts, before anyone else. It was mainly because of CP's close relationship with record company execs.

Dick Griffey, founder and president of SOLAR Records in Los Angeles was a frequent guest at Leviticus. Dick was known as the "Kingpin of Soul Promoters." SOLAR records produced top acts such as The Whispers, Shalamar, and Deele, which featured Babyface. Stevie Wonder credits Dick Griffey by saying, "Professionally, I could not talk about my life without there being a chapter on how Dick Griffey, as a promoter, helped to build my career."[53] It

[52] Oxford's Handbook Online, August 2016, "Behind the Screens: Race, Space and Place in *Saturday Night Fever* by Sima Belmar
[53] Hevesi, Dennis. "Dick Griffey, Founder of Solar Records, Is Dead at 71", *The New York Times*, October 4, 2010

Taste of Honey at Leviticus

was through Dick Griffey that Tony and CP were able to get the Whispers to perform at Leviticus. The Whispers performed there often and always wowed the crowd. Then they came out with a huge hit song "And the Beat Goes On," which catapulted them to performances at Madison Square Garden. After that, their shows were too big for Leviticus. But Dick always had after-parties for the Whispers at Leviticus. Through that interaction, Tony and CP got to know Dick very well and in October 1982 created a record label called Leviticus International Records (LIR) to emulate SOLAR. As it turned out, LIR discovered how difficult it was to get new records played on the radio. Lots of competition and lots of personal relationships stand in the way.

One night, Dick Griffey challenged Tony to a drinking contest. Dick won. He turned to Tony and said, "You thought I was a California boy. No! I grew up in Tennessee where I learned to drink moonshine!" They had a good laugh.

But they had several more drinking contests after that and Dick usually won. Tony was at the club all night and typically already had a few before Dick arrived so Tony was at a disadvantage. Getting wasted together strengthened their friendship. When Tony and CP were on the west coast to meet with a technology company, they visited Dick Griffey at his horse ranch outside of Los Angeles, where they spent a few days. In 2010, Dick had a coronary artery bypass operation. During his rehabilitation, the fun-loving Dick Griffey passed away at much too young an age.

Another frequent guest at Leviticus was Ray Harris, who worked for Dick for many years. Before joining SOLAR, Ray ran the black music division for RCA records and was very successful in the industry. Ray worked with Nina Simone, Diana Ross, the Main Ingredient, Hall & Oates, and many, many others. Ray came by Leviticus often and got to know all of us TBOF partners. He still stays in touch from time to time. Many other record company executives like Neil Bogart and Cecil Holmes, both of Casablanca Records; Jheryl Busby, Motown Records; Sharon Heywood, RCA Records; Sylvia Rhone, Epic Records, and many others, frequented Leviticus and became good friends with many TBOF partners, but mainly CP.

Leviticus became such a hot showplace for entertainers that many acts approached CP to perform there. But CP only booked talent with a sound that meshed with the vibe at Leviticus. He knew what would draw a crowd and what wouldn't. CP once turned down Prince who stopped by Leviticus with his little sister Tyka to ask if they could perform at Leviticus. CP said, "They were unknown kids and I wasn't sure how the crowd would react to their music." This was around 1978, well before Prince's talent emerged so comprehensively. Does CP regret turning down one of the biggest stars in the history of music? "No," CP said. "At the time, they would not have been a draw." CP knew our crowd and the music they liked and if he felt it wasn't a good fit, it wasn't. About a year later, Prince hit it big with the album entitled Prince, the first of many platinum albums. During his shortened career Prince went on to sell over 100 million records worldwide. While we couldn't afford Prince after he became a mega-star, his recordings were a big hit on our dance floors.

l-r kneeling Michael Glenn (NY Knicks), Vaughn Harper, Frankie Crocker, Ken "Spider" Webb (WBLS Radio DJs), standing in the rear l-r Geoff Huston, Hollis Copeland, Cal Ramsey, Earl Monroe, Ray Williams, Michael "Sugar Ray" Richardson, Melba Tolliver, Bob McAdoo, Norman Dow, Paulette LaMelle, Harold Dow

Frankie Crocker, the person who gave Vaughn Harper his big break, was also a frequent guest at Leviticus. With his full-length mink coat, matching mink hat, and Rolls Royce, he brought generous amounts of glamour, charisma, and energy to the club. Frankie got our word-of–mouth marketing machine revved up because guests were quick to tell their friends, "Frankie Crocker was there!"

Frankie had a rare gift. He was, by almost any measure, pompous and braggadocios, yet somehow, he managed to remain accessible and admired.

Frankie Crocker at Leviticus

An essential part of Frankie's genius was that he could brag boldly but make the listener feel included. Listeners felt Frankie's glamour enveloped them too. However, those who were around Frankie in person for any length of time, saw a different side. Many felt that Frankie thought he was God's gift. He was obnoxious and dishonest. Payola was illegal, but Frankie accepted $1,500 with a promise to play a record by a group we were managing called Lamelle. He never played the record and he never returned the money.

A man named Luke Bolden had a similar experience with Frankie Crocker. Luke was a major drug trafficker who inherited control of the heroin trade in Harlem when Nicky Barnes was sent to prison. Like many hustlers, Bolden wanted to engage in a legitimate business to go along with his lucrative drug trafficking.

Most of these characters got involved in various aspects of the entertainment industry. Luke had a couple of groups he was promoting, and paid Frankie Crocker to play their music on WBLS in what was called a "heavy rotation." A heavy rotation meant lots of air time and a greater likelihood that the record would go Gold. But when Luke got stiffed by Frankie, his reaction was a lot different than ours.

Luke decided he was going to make an example of Frankie Crocker. He arranged to have a meeting with Tony in the TBOF offices on the second floor of Leviticus and invited several gang members including the Flewellyn Brothers from uptown and a big-time mobster from Brooklyn. The Flewellyn Brothers sent an underling, which pissed off Luke because, in those days, bosses dealt with bosses, and underlings dealt with underlings. This was an insult to Luke, and he reacted to it by ranting and cursing.

Luke wanted Tony involved because he knew Tony had also been stiffed by Frankie Crocker. Norman Dow was invited because Justine's featured lots of entertainers as well. Almost all program directors demanded pay to play any record with a heavy rotation, so what we were doing, while technically illegal, was routine at the time.

Luke explained to Tony and Norman: "I know you guys got stiffed by Frankie too, so that's why I wanted you to be a part of this. I'm going to get rid of Frankie to make sure this never happens again."

Tony was shocked. "What!" he cried out.

This was a chilling idea that caused extreme concern in Tony. Tony had to think quickly because he wanted no part of it, and certainly did not want any of us or our office implicated. "If you bump off Frankie, we don't know what we're going to get. It will also lead to an investigation, which would be bad for everyone. Why not just scare him?"

Luke went silent as he stared into space. A few moments later, he turned back to Tony, and simply said, "Okay." The next time Frankie appeared in public, he had a cast.

Luke was quick to solve problems by killing people. He'd killed before, and he would kill again. In 1983, several years after that meeting, Bolden was put on trial and convicted of murder, criminal conspiracy, and drug trafficking. He was sentenced to life in prison with no chance of parole. Luke's former mentor and rival, Nicky Barnes, turned informant on him because Luke was having an affair with Nicky's girlfriend and redirecting funds that were supposed to go toward Barnes' legal fees. As you may recall, Nicky's testimony earned him admission into the witness protection program, so he got out of what would have been a very long sentence.

Meanwhile, Frankie Crocker continued his career on radio where his show catapulted WBLS to the number one slot among 18-34 year-olds in New York, a position it occupied for years.[54] Although his audience was mostly African American, he played a wide array of music. Hal Jackson, a black pioneer in radio as a sportscaster and disc jockey[55], said that Frankie Crocker plays everything "from James Brown to Dinah Shore."[56] He might play "Come Fly With Me" by Frank Sinatra and back it up with the Temptations' "You're My Everything." What Frankie heard at our clubs was also a diverse mix of music, but all music at our clubs had one outstanding feature — it kept people on the dance floor. It didn't matter who performed it. In 1985, Frankie ended his brilliant radio career and transitioned to MTV as a VJ. And in 2000, while living on the west coast, he succumbed to pancreatic cancer.

In 1978, as part of the transformation from Leviticus to Leviticus International, we added the second floor of Leviticus to our lease, where CP created an art gallery and a reception area for jazz concerts, art shows, and weddings. Many up-and-coming artists were very appreciative because they were able to sell their paintings there. Tuesday was jazz night hosted by Wayne Cobham and Cobham's Coalition. Jazz performers included many of the biggest names of the day, such as Gary Bartz, Cedar Walton, Wynton Marsalis, Leon Thomas, Reggie Workman, Chico Hamilton, Ray Rivera, and Oscar Brown, Jr., to

[54] NY Times, October 24, 2000, "Frankie Crocker, A Champion of Black-Format Radio, Dies" by Monte Williams
[55] NY Daily News, May 23, 2012, "Hal Jackson, Pioneer On Black Radio, Dies at 96" by David Hinckley
[56] NY Times, October 24, 2000, "Frankie Crocker, A Champion of Black-Format Radio, Dies" by Monte Williams

Earl "The Pearl" Monroe and Walt
"Clyde" Frazier

Cuba Gooding, Sr. at
Leviticus

Pointer Sisters dancing at
Leviticus

name a few. The art gallery and jazz concerts brought in a different crowd than the discotheques, so it was successful in expanding our reach. CP was so successful in promoting jazz that NYC Mayor Ed Koch chose Leviticus International to present a proclamation declaring June as Jazz Month.

Our clubs became popular places for uptown politicians to host fundraising parties and rallies. Years later, former Congressman Charlie Rangel, told me that the success of our discotheques in midtown closed down many nightclubs in Harlem. I never thought about that because our crowd was quite a bit younger than the uptown crowds I saw in the famous Harlem clubs of the day. However, I'm sure we had an impact. After all, we attracted over a thousand people, mostly black, to midtown on many nights every week. Plus, our clubs introduced blacks to midtown Manhattan in a broad way (no pun intended). From talking to guests as they paid the entrance fee at Leviticus, I learned that

*Congresswoman Shirley
Chisholm campaigning for
re-election at Leviticus*

they were frequenting restaurants in the area, shopped after work until we opened, and generally spent more time in midtown than before.

In 1981, we took over an existing disco on East 48th Street and 2nd Avenue called Bogard's. The deal was that we would assume their debt with no exchange of cash. We knew we could bring in a steady crowd, so we took the deal and enjoyed excellent success for several years. Bogard's had a metal dance floor and a capacity of about 200 people. Our clubs were hitting on all cylinders and reaching an array of audiences across the metro area and beyond. At our peak, the overall operation had more than 100 employees, and with each club open seven days a week, we entertained several thousand guests each week or over 400,000 people a year. There were big spikes in attendance when there was a holiday. Attendance was typically stronger on Thursday through Sunday nights. Here is a conservative breakdown for an overall weekly average:

- *Leviticus (midtown west) — 3,500/week*
- *Justine's (midtown west) — 2,800/week*
- *Brandi's (Brooklyn) — 700/week*
- *Bogard's (midtown east) — 600/week*
- *Lucifer's (Queens) — 400/week*

Congressman Charlie Rangel, who was very close to Mal, commented: "You get more people on a weekend than I can get to come out to vote for me every two years! If you ever decide to run for office, be sure to let me know."

Stevie Wonder came by Othello (later Justine's) on his birthday every year for several years to celebrate and, without being paid, sang and played the piano to the delight of the audience, often for over an hour. In 1976, Stevie decided to celebrate his birthday at Leviticus. He played songs from a new album he had just recorded. That album was "Songs in the Key of Life." He sang every song on the album before it dropped! For those who were there to hear "Isn't She Lovely," "As," "Sir Duke," and all the others, it was a night to remember. I believe Stevie debuted his new album at our club because he appreciated the audience's enthusiastic support, and he wanted to give them a gift. He also

Norman Dow with Stevie Wonder at Bogard's

knew who owned the club and may have been proud to know that it was black owned. Justine's was our second discotheque in midtown Manhattan.

On another night, Stevie came by Bogard's and played for about an hour on the white baby grand piano that was next to the bar. Again, Stevie did this because he wanted to, he wasn't paid. We had a regular piano player who was there that night. Unbeknownst to anyone, he taped Stevie's set and afterward tried to sell it. When we got wind of what was happening, TBOF staff made it clear that he would never be able to perform for TBOF again and that other venues would find out about his indiscretion also. Fortunately for the piano player, he gave up the tape and that was the end of it.

In 1978 we got an offer to buy the building that housed Leviticus, which was owned by Keyser-Roth, the old legwear company. The building was five stories, and we were already occupying the ground floor, 2nd floor, and basement. The offer was attractive: Buy the building for $250,000 and take on a mortgage that would be similar to the rent we were paying, or about $5,000 per month. If we only rented out one floor, we would be ahead of the game. It was a good deal, but not necessarily a slam-dunk. We were cautious because the city was losing population and in dire straits financially. No one knew if the city would bounce back or continue on a downward spiral. We were optimistic and decided to move forward with the acquisition. Tony successfully negotiated with the landlord and reached a verbal agreement with Keyser-Roth to buy the building.

We were excited about the idea of TBOF becoming a landlord and felt confident it would be a good financial deal. Tony moved quickly — but not quickly enough. The verbal agreement was reached on a Thursday and the following Monday, Gulf + Western purchased Keyser-Roth. Gulf + Western only honored contracts that were signed before the acquisition date and ours was not. We were extremely disappointed. Acquiring that building would have been a game-changer. Today, the building is probably worth north of $75 million.

To me, this moment felt like a crossroads. Do we continue to focus exclusively on the nightclubs? Or do we segue into something else?

Chapter 21
"DISCO SUCKS"

"*D*ress up? No. Dance lessons? Hell, no.*"*
Steve Dahl, the die-hard rocker and popular Chicago radio DJ, summarized his dislike for disco by writing: "Dress up? No. Dance lessons? Hell, no. Cover charge? No. There was a lot of intimidation and disenfranchisement, especially if you were a male."[57] Steve spoke for a lot of rockers who weren't crazy about dancing and certainly didn't want to have to dance to get a girl. This attitude reflects the stark difference between rockers and our followers. Black middle-class folks enjoyed getting dressed up — we wanted to be fashionable. No one took dance lessons, we learned by watching and doing our own thing. And with the popularity of dancing separately, there was no longer a need to match your partner's steps closely. Regarding the admission charge, it made our patrons feel comfortable and safe because it helped keep the riffraff out. Even those who struggled to come up with the admission fee felt it was worth it to feel special and equal to everyone else

[57] *Timeline*, February 15, 2018, "When a loudmouthed DJ tried to kill disco, the homophobic and racist implications were impossible to ignore"

once inside the club.

As disco became overexposed and commercialized with a stream of corny associations, the appeal of the concept began to fade. Separately, many white rockers grew to hate disco, and a negative backlash began to grow. The backlash came to a head at the high profile burning of disco records at Comiskey Park in Chicago on July 12, 1979, between games of a twilight doubleheader. The event is often referred to as "the night disco died." No one hated disco more than Steve Dahl. As a publicity stunt, Dahl, along with Chicago White Sox owner, Bill Veeck and his son, Mike, turned the break between a doubleheader at Comiskey Park into "Disco Demolition Night." For 99 cents, fans would get a ticket to the game if they brought a record to blow up between games. Dahl hyped the event on his radio show, along with his rhetoric about the horrors of disco music. The security staff at Comiskey Field was overwhelmed when fifty thousand fans showed up — more than twice what was expected."[58]

A crate filled with disco records was hauled out onto the field where it was exploded and burned, and hundreds of fans went wild and ran out onto the infield. Fans tore up the grass and caused the White Sox to forfeit the second game to the Detroit Tigers.[59]

According to NPR Music, there was an usher at the game who hoped to gather up a few of the discarded disco records since he was an aspiring musician saving up for a synthesizer. "…he was one of the few African Americans there that night. Soon he began to notice something about the records some people were bringing. 'Tyrone Davis records, friggin' Curtis Mayfield records, and Otis Clay records,' he recalls. Records that were clearly not disco, but that were by black artists." The usher went on to say, "I was faced with some guy rushing up to me, snapping a record in half in my face and going, 'Disco sucks! Ya see that?' Like an overt statement to me like I was inherently disco."[60]

[58] Noisey Music by Vice, July 12, 2019, "'Disco Demolition Night' Was a Disgrace, and Celebrating It Is Worse", by Josh Terry
[59] Chicago Tribune, June 12, 2019, "Disco Demolition at 40: 2 Views of an Explosive Promotion that Caught Fire at Comiskey Park in 1979" by Paul Sullivan and Phil Rosenthal
[60] NPR Music, "July 12, 1979: 'The Night Disco Died' Or Didn't", by Derek John, July 16, 2016

Although black folks never hated disco music — not even close — the tremendous overexposure and negative publicity were so pervasive, it created concern about the use of the word "disco." Straight white males were the ones who primarily hated disco. They perceived disco to be too closely aligned with blacks, Latinos, and gays.[61] After the "night disco died," disco was never the same. It's hard to imagine that a form of music could generate such a strong negative response. The event at Comiskey Park further reinforces the thought that the backlash was not just about the music, but what it stood for. Danny pointed out that "The majority of top disco records were by black artists. Some whites didn't like that."

An article by Timeline expressed the reaction to Disco Demolition Night this way: "'Disco' was suddenly a bad word, and the record industry reacted swiftly. In just over eight weeks, the number of disco songs on the Billboard Top 10 went from six to zero." Nile Rodgers, the guitarist for the hit disco band Chic, found himself blacklisted. "People weren't answering our phone calls…And then the 'Disco Sucks' thing became very real. It was scary," Rodgers recounted in Disco Demolition: The Night Disco Died, by Steve Dahl and Dave Hoekstra.[62] During an interview with The Guardian, Rodgers added, "The Disco Sucks movement, where they held big events and burned our records, was racism. It wasn't about them not liking the music; they were scared of the societal change that disco was bringing about."[63] The Bee Gees, who had a portfolio of huge number one disco hits, also became a target among disco haters. The Bee Gees had FBI protection wherever their plane landed in the U.S. because they received many serious death threats.

Ironically, a year after rockers burned disco records at Comiskey Park in Chicago, the Pittsburgh Pirates won the World Series and celebrated their win by playing the disco song "We Are Family" in the same stadium. The

[61] Noisey Music by Vice, February 10, 2016, "Why Did 70s Rock Music Hate Disco So Much?" by Eve Barlow
[62] Timeline, February 15, 2018, "When a loudmouthed DJ tried to kill disco, the homophobic and racist implications were impossible to ignore"
[63] Theguarding.com, July 13, 2019, "Interview, Nile Rodgers: 'I'd Always Talk About Strange Jazz with David Bowie'" by James McMahon

hit song became even more popular across the country after the Pirates' victory and was featured on wearables and various promotional merchandise. "We Are Family" was written by Nile Rodgers and Bernard Edwards and performed by Sister Sledge.[64]

Among our followers, the level of interest in disco dancing that was experienced in the early and mid-70s faded but only slightly. Along with our clubs, many other successful discotheques opened and thrived well into the '80s and beyond, such as Bentley's, The Garage, Palladium, Red Parrot, and the Tunnel. Even La Martinique continued as a successful discotheque under the name Ice Palace 57 then renamed the Silver Shadow in 1985. As for disco music, it lived on, just in a slightly different form. In December 2002, Kurt Reighley, a well-known writer, DJ, and entertainer, wrote that "The warmest, fuzziest, and most obvious of disco's successors is house music. Ironically, the style was born in Chicago, the same city that served as the epicenter of the 'Disco Sucks' movement by hosting the record-burning rally in 1979."[65]

Reighley goes on to note that house aficionado DJs "Pared down and refined the sound, the relentless beat of a kick drum became synonymous with the new form." Reighley points out that hip-hop and disco music emerged around the same time and that many early hip-hop recordings have a DJ rapping over the rhythm of dance floor hits. He gives these examples: Chic's "Good Times" rhythm track-inspired Sugarhill Gang's "Rapper's Delight" as well as Grandmaster Flash's "Adventures on the Wheels of Steel." Diana Ross's "I'm Coming Out" is the foundation of Notorious B.I.G.'s "Mo Money, Mo Problems." "I Did it For Love" by the Love Unlimited Orchestra is the rhythm arrangement for "It's All About the Benjamins" and Unlimited Touch's "I Hear Music in the Streets" provides the track for Faith Evans's "All Night Long."[66]

DJ Danny Krivit of NYC's now-defunct house party Body & Soul observed, "Young [drummer Earl Young] did a simple, four-on-the-floor beat.

[64] People, November 5, 1979, "When the Pirates Hustled to Sister Sledge's 'We Are Family,' the Steel City Went Platinum" by Richard Rein
[65] Time Out, December 2002
[66] Time Out, December 2002

Ribbon cutting ceremony for Leviticus International

And house music was [built from] that beat. Most of today's dance music is based on it."[67] In the same 2002 article, Giorgio Morodor, the famous DJ and record producer, was quoted as saying, "It's interesting to hear not just the sounds but the exact notes and rhythms I used on my albums, used now as they were 25 years ago."[68]

CP took the lead in transforming Leviticus. The new name, "Leviticus

[67] Danny Krivit Biography, August 12, 2019, "Dekmantel and Grolsch Present: Selectors – Danny Krivit
[68] Time Out, December 2002

International," reflected the large international audience we were getting from Africa, Europe, and the Caribbean. Importantly, we began to bring in live R&B acts to perform, such as Cuba Gooding & The Main Ingredient, Blue Magic, the Originals, the Pointer Sisters, Curtis Mayfield, Mtume, the Dells, Phyllis Hyman, Bootsy Collins and the Rubber Band, Gladys Knight and the Pips, Stevie Wonder, Leon Thomas, Archie Bell & the Drells, and many others. There weren't many venues that featured live acts as frequently as Leviticus so it was on the radar for many entertainers.

We had a host of celebrities come through our clubs: Fashion model Iman, Reverend Ike, Don Cornelius from Soul Train, Presidential candidate Shirley Chisholm, Chico Hamilton, Grace Jones, Nick Ashford and Valerie Simpson, Rick James, Elizabeth Taylor, Andy Warhol, Jim Brown, Lola Falana, Esther Phillips, Dallas Cowboy great Ed "Too Tall" Jones, Valentino, Nick Nolte, Janet Jackson, Pam Grier, the Negro Ensemble Company Director Douglas Turner Ward, Yolanda King, Nile Rodgers, Madonna, Arthur Ashe, and many more. Reverend Ike pulled up to Leviticus one night in a green Rolls-Royce. Some will recall that he made a fortune selling prayer clothes for a dollar each.

Iman was relatively new to the United States and New York City when she first started coming to Leviticus. While she was a major fashion model, she seemed a bit shy and didn't know many people, so we always took good care of her. CP typically took the lead in dealing with celebs, and he got to know Iman fairly well. He first met Iman when Johnny Seka brought her to La Martinique, which was her first, or one of her first, trips to New York City. Iman was from Somalia and went to boarding school in Egypt. A couple of years later, when she came to Leviticus, CP sat her in the VIP area up on the platform and made her feel welcome. This was before superstar Spencer Haywood of the New York Knicks started dating her. Eventually, she married Haywood. About 30 years later, when she was married to music legend David Bowie, CP went to a reception for a non-profit at a popular restaurant called the Shark Bar in New York City. A group of people surrounded Iman and were vying for her attention. After all, she was a big celebrity by then. CP

*Negro Ensemble Company at Leviticus; (l-r)
Adolph Caeser (leaning), Douglas Turner Ward,
Samuel L. Jackson, and (far right) Charles Fuller*

*Attallah Shabazz, Coretta
Scott King, CP at Leviticus*

*Johnny Allen, Phyllis
Hyman, Vaughn Harper at
Leviticus*

*Music industry execs and performers:
Merald "Bubba" Knight, Ruben Rodriquez,
CP, TK Kirkland, unk, Cecil Holmes*

CP, La Toya Jackson at Leviticus

Andre, Bobby "Count" Simms, Harry, CP, Danny, Steve

Curtis Mayfield performing at Leviticus

walked over and re-introduced himself. He had not seen her during those 30 odd years.

When Iman realized who he was, she got up and walked with CP to a table in a far corner. CP filled her in on what TBOF had been up to then they reminisced about her visits to La Martinique and Leviticus many years ago. It was clear to CP that those occasions were very important to Iman. While they were reminiscing, several people came over to their table and tried to interrupt the conversation. Iman held up her hand, palm out, and said, "Sorry, I'm talking to CP and I want to hear every word!" CP was genuine in all his relationships. I don't know if it was because of his helpful attitude or his natural bonhomie, but he was especially effective in dealing with celebrities. They all liked CP and trusted him completely.

Harry was working one night at Leviticus when Rick James and Nick Nolte walked in. Who would have thought these two would hang out together? Harry could tell they had been drinking and that this was not their first stop. They made their way to the bar, sat down, and ordered drinks. Harry and CP walked over to chat with them. After an hour or so, they decided to get something to eat. They asked Harry and CP where they could grab a bite and said, "Join us." The four went to a restaurant in the Village and, afterward, stopped by the Garage then another club. Harry and CP ended the evening after that but Nick and Rick continued to hang out. Harry remarked "It was interesting to see how well they got along together. All they wanted to do was get drunk and find women."

The upper west side in the 1960s and 1970s had a cluster of popular jazz clubs that attracted folks from all over the city. Black folks felt comfortable hanging out at these clubs, including Vic & Terry's (renamed Mikell's), Under the Stairs, the Cellar, and Rust Brown's. Rust Brown's was owned by two impressive men, popular sportscaster Art Rust Jr., who was considered by many to be the godfather of sports radio, and Roscoe Brown Jr., a highly regarded Tuskegee airman who would later become President of Bronx Community College. Art and Roscoe were super bright and savvy. During WWII, when a German jet attacked Roscoe's propeller-driven P-51 Mustang, the German pilot didn't have a chance. Roscoe told me that he faked out the German by

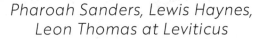

Pharoah Sanders, Lewis Haynes, Leon Thomas at Leviticus *Bootsy Collins at Leviticus*

dropping down low and pretending to run away. Then he turned his plane around, got behind the German jet and shot it down. Quite a feat.

It was at Rust Brown's where Danny heard Phyllis Hyman before anyone knew of her. Danny was immediately impressed. CP, who lived on the upper west side, heard her next and arranged for her to perform at Leviticus, which was her first appearance in midtown. CP called all of us TBOF partners to ensure we came to the club that night to hear Phyllis. She was mesmerizing and you didn't have to be a music industry expert to recognize that she was going to be become a huge hit, and she did.

Unfortunately, Phyllis developed health issues, got involved in drugs and, in certain circles, developed a reputation for being unreliable and coming late to appointments. I remember talking to producers at Ogilvy & Mather Advertising where I was working, who indicated that they would be reluctant to hire Hyman for a commercial for fear she would come late or not show up.

Despite her problems, CP and Phyllis became good friends. Some people felt Phyllis was stuck up, but CP said the opposite was true: "She was down to earth and would step in if you needed help." He went on to say that "When I was marketing Lawless (a ladies fragrance) at trade shows in New Jersey,

Percy Sutton and Mal arriving at Leviticus

she would show up at my booth to help promote it. Plus, she bought several cases of Lawless and gifted it to friends as a way to help spread the word." Phyllis and CP had a special relationship that lasted until her untimely death. Her passing was a blow to the entire music industry and her many fans, but especially to CP. At her funeral at Lutheran church on the east side of Manhattan, one of Phyllis' friends blamed the music industry for her death. Phyllis was "good people" as CP would often say. But the music industry is a tough environment with a unique type of pressure — even when you're successful. Maybe more so when you're as sensational as Phyllis Hyman.

CP created Sunday afternoon jazz concerts and other events, such as weddings, both in the upstairs art gallery and on the main floor of Leviticus. CP, Tony, and Danny were always at the clubs, and, more than the rest of us, they were the faces of our organization. By this time, we welcomed publicity.

Percy Sutton campaigning with his son Pierre "Pepe" Sutton at Leviticus (photo via Copper Cunningham)

However, it happened on its own because we weren't savvy in creating publicity and didn't hire a PR person until sometime later.

Mal introduced political fundraising events to the mix. The so-called "Gang of Four," comprised of Mayor David Dinkins, Congressman Charlie Rangel, Manhattan Borough President Percy Sutton, and Secretary of State of New York Basil Paterson, along with many other Harlem politicians, had fundraisers at Leviticus and Justine's. These events were the first fundraisers for black politicians in midtown Manhattan, which enabled them to tap into a broader swath of donors. Those running for office were very pleased and appreciated the opportunity. We also had a fundraiser hosted by Shirley Chisholm, the first black woman in Congress. She was elected in1968 and four years later became the first black female candidate for President of the United States. Shirley Chisholm was the real deal, an impressive personality, and speaker; she is revered to this day by those who know her story.

Mal also connected with a score of African diplomats at the UN, many of whom became regulars at Leviticus. Among them was Mamadou Johnny Seka, a Senegalese promoter who was one of the best-known personalities across West Africa. Johnny was outgoing and became quick friends with all of us. He not only attended Leviticus several times a week; he would stop by during the afternoon to spend time with CP, Mal, and the other partners. Johnny went out of his way to arrange to take Gwen and me out to a wonderful dinner. There was no special occasion, he was just generous like that.

In 1974, Johnny helped bring the Jackson 5 to Senegal, which made him even more popular among Africans in the New York area and across West Africa. He genuinely liked all of us in TBOF and used his popularity to introduce many African diplomats to Leviticus. Quite a few became regulars. Sadly, in the late '80s, while Johnny was still a young man, he succumbed to cancer. About 35 years later, Mal was in a restaurant in Harlem that had a kitchen and waitstaff from West Africa. Mal asked if they had ever heard of Johnny Seka. They got excited, came out of the kitchen, and talked about Johnny with great reverence. They viewed him as a hero who was an inspiration to them.

Another impressive African who often came to Leviticus was diplomat Dr.

First convention of the World Association of Black Club Owners; l-r, Mal, Wayne, Norman Dow, CP, Steve Roberts, Harry, Tony

TBOF Phily, James "Bond" Peters, Judge Jimmy De Leon, James Peters' wife, band member, Mal, George Carey, Arnold Randolph, Paul Hill, Mrs. Hill

Joseph Wayas. He was the third President of the Nigerian Senate from 1979-1983. Dr. Wayas was a wealthy man, and he loved Leviticus. So, when Tony mentioned that we were going to undergo a major renovation, Dr. Wayas said, "I want to make a gift to help with the renovation. I love this club and want to see it thrive." He then wrote a check for $35,000. Dr. Wayas wanted nothing in return, but Tony and the other TBOF partners wanted to do something special for him. As it turns out, Dr. Wayas was partners in a travel agency with Lloyd Price (of "Stagger Lee" and "Personality" fame.) Tony decided to throw a party for the travel agency and all its employees with a full open bar. This was a token gesture to thank Dr. Wayas for his generous gift. It was held at Leviticus, of course, and was a beautiful affair. Later that year, Tony had the club renovated to refresh Leviticus. That is when we changed the name to Leviticus International. We had to renovate all the clubs periodically because, with thousands of people coming through each month, the wear and tear was significant. As usual, Harry supervised the contractors during the renovation.

Mal was the outreach man. He founded the Association of Black Club Owners (ABCO), which had 125 members stretching from the Caribbean and Bermuda to California. The purpose of the ABCO was to breathe more life into clubs at a time when dancing was fading in popularity, and "disco" was a bad word. This arrangement helped create word of mouth and brought more business to member clubs. To build membership in ABCO, Mal would ask the many out-of-towners who came through our clubs about the best discotheques or dance clubs in their home towns. Then he reached out to those clubs and, given that the discotheque era was softening, encouraged them to join the ABCO as a way to increase traffic in their clubs.

A benefit of joining was that owners of the other member clubs received free access. This translated into more big spenders coming through member clubs on occasion. This strategy proved to be successful for several years. Some of the more active member locations and club names were: Philadelphia's La Ferry, Erlanger, and Juice; Detroit's My Fair Lady; Cleveland's Vel's Red Cocktail Lounge; Washington, DC's Foxxtrappe Town Club, Rafael's, La Café, and Mingles; Atlanta's Mr. V's One and Two; Chicago's Godfather One, Two and Three, Copper Box One and Two, and Ivey's; Berkeley's Dock of the Bay; and in NYC, our five clubs, Leviticus, Justine's, Bogard's, Brandi's, and Lucifer's.

Mal organized international conventions for the membership, the first one was at Leviticus and the second in Bermuda. Danny and Tony had such a good time in Bermuda with the club owners down there that they went back every year for the next ten years. Danny said, "The best time I ever had on vacation was on those trips to Bermuda."

Another strategy that Mal pursued was to tap into black organizations that were planning a convention in NYC. These were primarily civil rights, education, social services, and trade organizations. Mal approached each organization's national office and suggested they include our clubs on their list of activities for specific nights. This effort helped bring in guests on nights that might otherwise be slow.

We could all see that club culture was beginning to change. Our original business model with dancing in a pure discotheque environment as the centerpiece was no longer as magical as it had been in previous years. Could live music replace that appeal? We were about to find out.

Chapter 22
CULTURE SHIFT

"*There was no life.*"

One night, Jeff, the manager of Brandi's, needed to run an errand but was blocked in by Tony's car in the parking lot next door. Instead of moving his car, Tony simply said, "Take my car," and passed his key to Jeff. Jeff left and about 15 minutes later, staggered back in through the front door and collapsed. Harry was there that night and said afterward: "When I saw his face, he looked dead. There was no life."

Harry was right. Jeff was rushed to the hospital and pronounced dead on arrival. He had five bullet holes in his chest. Someone shot Jeff as he was about to enter Tony's car. Initially, some thought it was a robbery attempt or that Tony was the intended target and the assailant mistook Jeff for Tony. However, we know that Jeff had family members who were known gangsters, so it's possible he was the target. Regardless, we didn't think that the shooting was random, and neither did the police. We knew the detective who led the investigation to find the shooter. But ultimately, no one was ever arrested or charged with the crime.

We changed the name of Orpheus to Brandi's as a way to add newness and freshness to the club. Even though Brandi's was nowhere near the success of our Manhattan businesses, we knew it took significant business away from many of the area bars and clubs. We had the largest venue and attracted the most patrons, so we were sensitive to that dynamic and what it meant from a security standpoint.

The shooting rattled everyone, especially Tony since it was not clear — and still isn't — who the intended target was. After that incident, Tony took a step back in terms of visibility and was no longer the day-to-day face of Brandi's. We operated Brandi's just on weekends and rented it out on Sunday nights to a group of Haitians. They attracted a huge crowd and enabled TBOF to take a back seat on those nights. The Haitians took the door and we took the bar. About two years later, we sold Brandi's.

A Jamaican man named Winston Dyer bought Brandi's, changed the name to Love People, and catered to a Jamaican audience. Unlike us, Winston operated Love People as an after-hours club and achieved enormous success. Love People became the number one Caribbean club in the country, and we were told by the Schieffelin sales rep, the number one account for Moet sales in the country. The reason why Moet sales were so strong was that many Jamaican gang members, known as "posses," hung out at Love People, and most drank Moet almost exclusively. Some posse members would buy six, seven, or even eight bottles at a time. Moet was served in a large bowl with bottles laid down in a circle as if it was a large flower. When it ran out, they'd order another large bowl. Interestingly, gang bosses drank together but their staff never drank with them. That was forbidden. Staff members would typically go to the bar, order 6 or 12 splits of Moet in a cardboard carrying case, and bring it back to their table.

Rival gang members put their differences aside when they were at Love People because it was considered neutral territory. Unfortunately, it was no longer neutral when you stepped outside. As soon as you went around the corner there was plenty of violence. There were many killings outside the club and that went on for several years because the area was not policed.

Before buying Brandi's, Winston spent a lot of time at Leviticus and dropped a fair amount of money there. So, when Winston invited TBOF to come to Love People, Tony and Danny knew they had to reciprocate. They would typically go on a night when there was a birthday celebration. Tony and Danny would take a few staff members who felt like hanging out and head over to Love People after closing down our clubs. Tony would leave from Leviticus and Danny from Lucifer's in Queens. On those occasions, they would arrive at Love People around 6 am.

Violence in the streets of NYC was extremely high during the '70s and still on the rise into the '80s.[69] For example, in 1990 there were 2,225 murders[70] compared to only 289 in 2018.[71] Policing didn't improve until 1990 when Mayor Dinkins was elected. Mayor Dinkins added more cops on the street and dramatically increased the number of cadets who became police officers after he left office.[72] The work Mayor Dinkins started led to a marked decline in crime that lasted through Mayor Giuliani's tenure.[73] Some of the credit that Giuliani received for reducing crime in New York City should have gone to Mayor Dinkins and the foundation he set.

One Saturday night, Mal and CP were working at Lucifer's. By this time, we had dropped the dress code during the week, but we did not allow jeans on Saturday nights. Tony had worked Lucifer's for 38 straight days and took a much-needed night off. So Mal and CP filled in for Tony and sat at the closest table to the front door so they could monitor folks as they came in. Mal and CP alternated which one would speak to guests who were improperly dressed. What happened next was another incident of violence that made us all wonder if what we were doing was worth the risk.

A man came in wearing jeans, and it was CPs turn to talk to him. CP followed the man who was walking toward the rear room, got his attention,

[69] Disastercenter.com, "New York City Crime Rates 1960-2016

[70] *The New York Times*, "New York Killings Set a Record, While Other Crimes Fell in 1990," April 23, 1991 by George James

[71] https://abc7ny.com/nyc-sees-record-low-homicides-in-2018-based-on-preliminary-data/5000622/

[72] NY Times, September 20, 1992, "Dinkins and the Police: A Campaign Issue" by Sam Roberts

[73] Disastercenter.com, "New York City Crime Rates 1960-2016

and politely said, "Sorry, mister, but we don't allow jeans on Saturday nights. You're welcome to come back another night, and we'll be happy to give you a drink on the house."

The man didn't want to leave, but CP was insistent. After arguing his point again and realizing that CP was not going to let him stay, the man reached into the front of his pants, fumbled a bit, and pulled out a gun. Instinctively, CP grabbed the man's gun arm and tried to knock the gun out of his hand. As the two wrestled the gun went off and a bullet grazed CP in the arm. Guests screamed when they heard the gun blast and chaos ensued on the dance floor. The gunman pushed CP aside, turned toward Mal who was rapidly approaching, and pointed the gun directly at Mal's head. The bar was a step down from the main level, and when Mal saw the gun, he took one step back toward the bar and slipped down the one step — just in time to miss a bullet that whizzed over his head. The gunman turned and fled out the side door of the club. "I thought I was dead! I saw the gun, took a step back and, if it wasn't for the step down to the bar area, it would have been all over for me. I could hear the bullet going past my head!" said Mal.

After the incident, CP said he wasn't scared. "I didn't have time to be scared. I saw the gun and tried to slap it out of his hand. Then it went off. I was operating on instinct." CP was patched up and recovered fully, but the incident shook everyone. CP continued to stop by Lucifer's to check up on it, but far less frequently. Mr. Cooper, Tony's dad, had applied a rough stucco on the walls in Lucifer's with small, fairly sharp peaks of plaster. When the shots were fired, several patrons cut their arms and tore their clothes when they pushed up against the walls in their rush to get to the back of the room. The adrenaline must have been flowing because some folks didn't even realize they were bleeding until well after everything calmed down.

We all knew that there was a degree of danger that came with being in the nightclub business, in part because that business attracted more than its fair share of unsavory characters. The members of TBOF were getting older, more mature, and we had families of our own. So, when the danger hit close to home, it shook us to the core. Sadly, this wasn't the last time TBOF had to deal with a violent crime in one of the clubs.

On another occasion, five armed men held up Lucifer's. They came appropriately dressed in jackets and blended in with other customers, so they were not noticed. When they announced it was a stickup, they had the front and side doors covered and robbed everyone. They even made a few people strip down. Shortly after the robbery, the men were caught, convicted, and sent upstate to the Green Haven Correctional Facility in upstate New York. We know they were there because Danny had a relative who was part of the warden's administration at Green Haven, and he saw them there. Danny's relative made sure the robbers paid the price for their deed and that everyone knew that it was a bad idea to target Lucifer's. Despite the fact that bar robberies were prevalent, Lucifer's was never robbed again. Right after the robbery, we remodeled Lucifer's and gave it a new name, Trixx. Once again, Mr. Cooper did the remodeling, and this time he made the walls smoother.

Considering the number of years that TBOF operated clubs — from 1971 to 1986 — and the fact that hundreds of thousands of people came through our clubs each year, robberies and incidents were extremely low, especially given the low police presence and the high crime rate in the city. A significant reason for the long-term success of our clubs was the strategies we put together to market and manage the clubs. We exercised a high level of control, knew who the troublemakers were, and generally kept them out, or in check. Men and women felt safe coming to our clubs, whether in small groups or by themselves.

I give credit primarily to Tony for getting the drug dealers and other gangsters to respect our establishments. Tony never acted like he was better than them and, by doing so, set the tone for how other partners needed to relate to these guests. "Most straight [law abiding in this context] guys don't show respect to gangsters. In fact, they look down on them." Tony noted. In contrast, Tony treated them like gentlemen while always maintaining a reasonable distance. The result was that gangsters viewed Tony as a friend, trusted him, and showed their respect.

While we were enjoying an impressive on-going success with our clubs, there was a culture shift in the works. Folks didn't go out dancing as much as they used to and attitudes about fashion and music were rapidly evolving as the rise of hip-hop represented the dawn of a new decade and, along with it, a more casual lifestyle.

Dancing was on a decline in general but much less so among our followers who were mostly African American. Dancing was at its peak when people danced specific dances to specific songs. Dances that involved holding hands required practice because you had to perform the steps correctly, or it would confuse your partner. "The Hustle," with all its permutations ("New York Hustle", "Philly Hustle", "Latin Hustle", etc.), was the most popular dance where you held hands. When you are well-rehearsed, you look forward to showcasing what you can do. However, when people started dancing separately, the need to practice disappeared.

The fragmentation of media, especially TV, also contributed to the demise of dancing by pulling people's social lives in many different directions. In the '70s, most folks watched the same handful of TV shows. That began to change in the '80s and, with the mushrooming of cable TV in the '90s, it was a different world. Today, it would be uncommon to get a date by saying, "Let's go dancing." Most people wouldn't even know where to go because venues that feature dancing are rare. However, the freedom to create moves spontaneously and to dance independently was liberating and, for a short time, took dancing to a high level. Interestingly, people in our cohort, never stopped dancing. One of the common occasions where we dance are celebrations, special events, and parties hosted by social organizations.

Realizing that the disco concept would not last long, CP was on point when he emphasized live music and other entertainment features at Leviticus. We already had a back room with lounge chairs and sofas along with video and board games. By billing Leviticus as "Leviticus International, an Entertainment Complex," we repositioned the club from what was a pure discotheque into a club that gave people more variety. Live music became a larger part of the offering and was supplemented by the upstairs jazz club and art gallery.

Some of my partners were so pleased with the operation at Leviticus and

Noel at Ogilvy & Mather Advertising

the steady, predictable stream of nightly guests, they believed our clubs would last for the long haul – even though the popularity of dancing was crumbling in the larger society. The vision these partners had was to be nightclub owners as a final destination. Some of us viewed the nightclubs as a steppingstone or springboard that could take us to other, more sustainable enterprises. This difference in vision widened the schism within TBOF.

For me, working the door became increasingly difficult as my day job and family responsibilities grew. Even with a scaled back schedule, working the door created a growing stress when I had to work the next day. I was already in my early 30s and those late nights became increasingly difficult to handle. When my second daughter was born in September 1978, the schedule became even more challenging. When I got home early, it was around 7 pm, and I was already exhausted. My daughters were ready for bed at 8 pm, so I didn't see much of them nor was I much help to Gwen. She complained about my absence and often reminded me, "You're missing the experience of watching the girls grow up!"

On the nights I worked the door, I would stay in the office until around 8 pm, pick up a sandwich, and head to Leviticus. I often went to a famous Jewish deli called Sarge's for a corned beef or pastrami sandwich. Sometimes, I would eat at the door before the crowd showed up. At the end of the night, we shut the bar down around 3:30 am so that guests could finish their drinks by 4 am. We turned the lights up and locked the door after the last guests left. Then it took another 45 minutes to cash out the bartenders and wait staff and secure the money. Sometimes we put the cash in a safe in the basement and other times one of us took the money home. We mixed up the routine deliberately. Everyone had to wait around so we could walk out together. That meant I got home around 5:15 am., and after about an hour of sleep, it was time to get up and head to the office. I tried hard to get there by 9 am. but usually arrived around 9:30 am.

In 1978 I made a big decision; I resigned from TBOF. I didn't want the nightclubs to jeopardize my marriage or my career in advertising and I felt it had been doing both. Andre had the same issues I had and resigned a few months after me. Andre joined Foote, Cone & Belding, a large ad agency. I also went back to Madison Avenue and joined Ogilvy & Mather.

With Wayne, Andre, and myself gone, TBOF was down to five members. Tony and Danny split the responsibilities into regions — Tony managed the Manhattan clubs and Danny took care of Brooklyn and Queens. That allocation of tasks worked well and lasted until each club ran its course.

I always felt the talent we had within TBOF could be applied to other businesses. We tried a few ideas, but the result was nowhere near as rewarding as the impressive cash flow from the night clubs. Looking back, Tony believes we should have segued into the music business. An effort to do this was made, but we never turned the corner. We came close to investing in real estate and that would have taken us to another level. Another option was to invest in fast food franchises, which probably would have given us stability and led to real estate investment opportunities. However, in the early and mid-70s, even at a cost of only $25,000, a McDonald's franchise seemed like a long shot to us. The city was in a downward spiral and no one knew if it would recover. This is where our tendency to be cautious and conservative held us back from taking that next step.

Chapter 23
FADE OUT

"*When I'm dancing, I feel good.*"

As leases expired for TBOF clubs, they were closed down. Brandi's in Brooklyn was the first to close. The original building isn't there anymore. In its place is the Gospel Truth Church of God. Bogard's had been doing well with a steady, reliable crowd. The problem was noise complaints from residents in the high-end co-ops in the high rise above the club and in nearby buildings. The noise didn't come from music inside the club because Bogard's was well insulated. However, when patrons left at two and three in the morning, they would occasionally shout to one another from down the block. Folks were looking for a ride or making plans for breakfast, and so on. Voices carry far in the still of the night and all those complaints doomed us. Today, the space Bogard's was in is now a karaoke club with rows of small sound rooms.

Trixx closed in 1985, and where it once stood is now a restaurant. Within a year of Trixx' closing, Tony and Danny partnered with the Dow Twins, and a manager from Justine's named Justice Vasquez, to open Manhattan Proper, a neighborhood club similar to Trixx but twice its size and located directly across the street from where Trixx had been. Manhattan Proper, subsequently renamed the Proper Café, was an immediate hit on Linden Boulevard. The Proper Café featured an array of special events conceived and executed by The Dow Twins, which kept the crowds coming. In the fall of 2017, after a 30-year run, The Proper Café closed when Tony and Danny retired.

Leviticus, our flagship club with a broad, national reputation, closed on October 18, 1986 after a 12-year run. The landlord raised the rent from $6,000 to $30,000 per month and on top of that TBOF would lose the second floor. This extraordinary rent increase was not unusual in Manhattan during the late '80s. Rents were dramatically increasing everywhere due to a major reduction in crime and an improving financial situation for the city. Today, a series of small retail stores occupy the space where so many people got up to boogie and many memories were made.

Justine's was the last club to close. The final night was in 1987. Tony asked the Dow Twins what they thought of extending the lease and renaming the club Metro West. But with an astronomical increase in rent, they decided to shut it down. Today, there is a Staples, Taco Bell, and other retail stores occupying the same space.

We created our clubs during a difficult transitional time in New York City. We took a significant risk by investing millions to build five nightclubs in a city that some believed would never recover from financial and political setbacks. The exodus of white-collar taxpayers created an enormous financial crisis with no easy solution in sight. President Ford's decision not to bail out the city was like a death knell. With the escalating rate of violent crimes and robberies, some thought New York would become a second-rate city. But despite this gloomy picture, it was an exciting time for many in my network. During the height of the civil rights struggles and demonstrations, a generation of blacks entered college, and as they graduated, they formed an emerging black middle class.

For the first time, we enjoyed midtown Manhattan in a way that made us feel accepted and comfortable. The disco vibe was also a new and energizing phenomenon. The sound of disco swept across the country and beyond. The

---

THE MILLION DOLLAR PARTY

The Best of Friends: Perry, Berry, Woolfolk, Felder, & Cooper

Who would have thought that a group of guys who gave college parties would end up owning five of the hottest dance clubs in New York

O ver a Chinese lunch on a rainy windswept Manhattan afternoon, the five owners of the Leviticus International Entertainment Complex reminisce about old times, going back a decade to when they called themselves things like the Raunchy Five and the Lowlife Limited. Someone strikes a familiar memory chord, and the five become a harmony, each supplying a different note of the anecdote. In moments it is clear that these fellows, no matter what they've called themselves, are and always will be The Best of Friends.

"Even after 10 years," says Tony Cooper, the group's softspoken, 34-year-old president, "we're all putting in 10- to 12-hour days, but we're still having fun. The five of us are still close today and people meeting us for the first time have to learn to accept that."

TBOF (the acronym by which they are known) own and operate four nightclubs and a bar in New York City. Headquarters is what they proudly call their "flagship," Leviticus International, in the heart of midtown Manhattan; Bogard's is an elegant bistro on

Manhattan's posh East Side; Justine's, just below Times Square, is where younger dancers like to check out the latest steps; Brandi's, in Brooklyn, is also a dancing club; and the venerable Trixx, a neighborhood bar in Queens, is where TBOF first taught themselves the nuances of the liquor business.

Last year TBOF grossed $2.2 million from the clubs and they are hoping the lights stay on for the black entertainment industry in the 1980s. "It's been a very good year," says Cooper, "and I only see the business getting stronger. Eighty was not a record year—our best was '78, when we grossed $1.8 million through four clubs. But '81 looks like a record-breaker. We've learned every lesson there is to be learned and we've done every job: manager, bartender, bouncer, janitor, and waiter. And now we're an institution among the handful of black clubs in midtown just because of our longevity."

TBOF may well have started their business just in time. Real estate prices in Manhattan have become so prohibitive that only the best-heeled entrepreneurs can afford the kind of investment necessary to start a first-class bar or club. Even established club owners are feeling the pinch of higher prices and tight money, with small discos closing and big exclusive ones like Xenon's and Studio 54

By Stephen Gayle

music we listened to — urban contemporary, funk, and up-tempo R&B — was enjoyed by millions of people around the world. Disco would not have been disco without fashion. The styles of the day were colorful and unique. Afros and other big hairstyles were popular, glamorous, and a symbol of black pride. Dancing, as a visual spectacle, was at its pinnacle as a pastime. Hundreds of people doing the same dance on the floor with mirrored ball and strobe lights…those are scenes that live on with a certain amount of emotion that only those who were there can fully appreciate.

Disco dancing brought together people whose paths would not have crossed otherwise. And it did so with grace and authenticity. Everyone could be themselves, and everyone was accepted. The common enjoyment of the music and dance broke down all types of barriers and attracted an unprecedented level of diversity. When folks hit the dance floor, all were equal, and everyone admired those who could dance well without reservation. This dynamic was unique and organic and has not been repeated since. As Nile Rodgers put it, "[Disco] music reached across all social, racial, and political boundaries."[74]

People are transformed into a happy, carefree state when they dance. It is euphoric. They reveal a dimension of themselves that is otherwise invisible, yet always compelling to both the dancer and observer. Dancing breaks down barriers. For some people, dancing is a form of escape. Back in the day, Rochelle Adams of New York said in an Ebony magazine article, "I go to escape. I go to escape my job and my bills and everything else. When I'm dancing, I feel good. Nothing else matters."[75]

[74] "Nile Rodgers, Le Freak" by Nile Rodgers, published by Sphere, an imprint of Little Brown Book Group, 2011, pg. 153.
[75] Ebony February 1977, *Discomaniacs get down, style and profile from coast to coast*, by Herschel Johnson

Chapter 24
LESSONS LEARNED

"Success is measured not only in achievements, but by lessons learned, lives touched and moments shared along the way."

Nishan Panwar

All of us in TBOF were changed in profound ways by our experience in building and managing discotheques. We were fully immersed in a social environment that taught us a lot about how to relate to many different types of people, and the importance of treating everyone with respect. The level of diversity in our midtown clubs was unusually high. With patrons ranging from CEOs to mail room workers, from Rick James to Elizabeth Taylor, and from big time mobsters to FBI agents, it's difficult to imagine such a diverse gathering at any other purely social function.

Every member of TBOF was informed by this experience in a way that enabled each of us to perform at a higher level in our subsequent endeavors. Tony, Danny, and the Dow Twins made the Proper Café an impressive success that lasted 30 years. The Proper Café dominated the social scene in south Queens and it was a destination during the entire time it was open.

Harry focused on managing the renovations of our discotheques as well as construction of various projects such as building out the second floor of Leviticus with offices and a reception area for jazz concerts, art gallery, weddings, and other social events. When TBOF was dissolved, Harry leveraged his experience by working for the NYC Board of Education to assess its brick and mortar needs and supervising various construction projects throughout the city.

Andre and I went back to work in the advertising industry. After several years at Foote, Cone, Belding, Andre and one of his business associates formed FraserSmith, a management consulting firm. Andre's experience gave him a great appreciation for the importance of respecting the consumer and insuring that all programs were specifically relevant to the target audience. He developed marketing plans for prestigious clients such as Miller Brewing Company and Moet Hennessy USA. In all cases, his plans started with a laser-like focus on the consumer. Of course, focusing on the consumer is Marketing 101 but for Andre and the rest of us, the discotheque experience provided an unusually deep appreciation for this dynamic.

Wayne, who resigned from TBOF in 1977, was sworn in as a criminal court judge in Queens by Mayor Ed Koch. Sadly, after several years on the bench, Wayne developed a cerebral aneurism and passed away just as his career as a judge seemed destined to take him to a higher level.

CP took over the liquor concession at the Apollo Theater, which he managed for a number of years until he retired. While at the Apollo, CP continued to stay in touch with his many friends in the entertainment industry, including many nationally known performers, producers, and various executives.

Mal went to work for WBLS in sales. Mal's strength was connecting with people with tremendous focus – perfect for sales. When the radio station was sold, Mal and a partner formed a company that specialized in financial services.

After resigning from TBOF, I joined Ogilvy & Mather Advertising where

I helped develop an exciting new campaign for Schaefer beer. The folks at Miller Brewing took notice and hired me to run their Miller Lite business. At Miller, I recognized the need to build an emotional connection with African American consumers, which led to the creation of the Thurgood Marshall College Fund. I originally conceived it as a Miller Lite program but recognizing the magnitude of the opportunity, established it as an independent, non-profit organization. As of this writing, the Fund has raised $300 million and helped 260,000 students by providing scholarships and leadership training.

After eight years at Miller Brewing, I joined Moet Hennessy USA (nee Schieffelin & Somerset) where some of the brands like Hennessy cognac and Moet & Chandon champagne, were missing an opportunity with African American and Hispanic consumers. Brand managers were so busy, they couldn't spend much time in black and Hispanic neighborhoods to learn about these consumers. Also, some were uncomfortable going into these ethnic neighborhoods at night, which was unfortunate because that's when consumption takes place.

I addressed this problem by instituting an annual two-day multicultural conference where brand managers presented their plans to street-level distributor sales reps. Every day, sales reps see and hear consumer and store manager reactions to our brand programs as well as those of competitors so what they know, they know better than anyone else. After each brand presentation, the sales reps would render their opinions. Based on their comments, brand plans were changed, timing adjusted, etc. to create stronger, more relevant programs. The result was elevated sales. I started the multicultural conference at Moet Hennessy USA in 1998. As of 2020, it was still an important part of the brand planning process.

Today, although all the TBOF discotheques have been closed for over 30 years and most TBOF members have ventured into different directions, there are thousands of people who enthusiastically reminisce when they hear names of clubs like Leviticus, Justine's, and Bogard's. For some, certain songs like "You and I" by Rick James or "Ladies' Night" by Kool and the Gang, trigger joyous and nostalgic memories. I asked CP how he felt when he was spinning records and had the crowd in the palm of his hand, driving them to a state of euphoria. He said, "I was just doing my job. I didn't have time to focus on anything else."

Tony summed up how I believe all my TBOF partners felt when he said, "We learned a lot about the social phenomenon that was happening. We went through cycles and learned about people and the music industry, which can be unscrupulous. But the experience was a lot of fun. We got to know a great many people from all walks of life, and that's what made it so special." The hit TV drama series Empire features a swanky nightclub called Leviticus. The TV version has a large dance floor, plush couches, and never-ending bottle service — just like our own Leviticus. Is the nightclub name in Empire inspired by our Leviticus? Some say yes, some say no. What we do know is that just about all African Americans in New York who were of age during the '70s and '80s knew about our Leviticus.

Despite the economic, health, and safety issues facing New Yorkers back in the '70s and '80s, most of our patrons enjoyed the ride. I suspect many would rank this period as one of the happiest in their lives. And when they bump into folks they remember from our discos, it brings a smile to their faces. As I write this, my former partners and I, and many of our former patrons, are in our 70s but we're still dancing.

Epilogue

Most disco establishments died out in the '80s, but the music itself never died. In fact, it remained strong all through the years, right up until today. The word "disco" lost its glamour due to over-commercialization, but thousands of DJs emerged after the disco era with access to sophisticated sound system technology featuring monitor speakers, headphones, mixing boards, laptop computers, and special DJ software. Technology has taken the disco sound and mindset to a whole new level and for a whole new audience.

Many DJs remix records from existing songs and achieve remarkable sales success. Although most don't play an instrument, they absolutely have musical skills — they are just unconventional. DJs are effective in creating new experiences by matching lyrical and instrumental content, just like our DJs did in the '70s. Good DJs know what turns on their audience and are effective in creating a memorable journey. It's an art that generates billions of dollars in revenue and has captivated the interest and engagement of a large portion of today's youth. The DJ and remix industries would not exist if it were not for groundwork laid in the disco era.

The post-disco DJ phenomenon started in New York City, Chicago, and Detroit. Today's DJs work their magic at events that resemble discos but without the pretentiousness and wild outfits that seemed iconic to the genre in the '70s. The new style is more down-to-earth, but the sounds are just as embracing and transporting.

One of the most popular clubs in the country right after the disco era was the Warehouse in Chicago, where an extraordinarily talented DJ named Frankie Knuckles routinely transported dancers to surreal dimensions, just as Danny and CP had done starting in early 1971 at the Ginza. Frankie Knuckles was born in the Bronx in 1955 but built his reputation in Chicago at the Warehouse. Here's how writer Frank Brewster described Knuckles' impact: "... here you could forget your earthly troubles and escape to a better place. Like church, it promised freedom, and not even in the next life. In this club, Frankie Knuckles took his congregation on journeys of redemption and discovery."[76] The Warehouse had a capacity of 600, but many more passed through its walls during the course of a good night. And just as with our TBOF clubs, the focus at the Warehouse was dancing. That's how people were transported to a better place. Because Frankie Knuckles was so dominant during that period, he became known as "The Godfather of House Music."

Patrons had such a good time at the Warehouse that people started referring to good things as "house." An event could be "house," food could be "house," even a person could be "house." According to Frank Brewster, the Warehouse is where the term "house music" originated. There were many other influential clubs and DJs, but the term "house music" stuck and is still used today. Clubs like the Limelight, Roxy, Palladium, Danceteria, and the Paradise Garage all focused on dancing and all played house music. Another legacy of the disco era is its inclusiveness. Disco was always marked by social liberation. Today, house music continues to carry that banner. All are welcome and it continues to be a liberating force.

In addition to Frankie Knuckles, some of the outstanding DJs of the '80s and '90s were Larry Levan, Tony Humphries, Ron Hardy, Danny Krivit, DJ

---

[76] "Last Night a DJ Saved My Life" by Frank Brewster and Bill Broughton, May 2006

Huggy Bear, Derrick Carter, Carl Cox, Danny Tenaglia, Terrence Parker, Irwin Larry Eberhardt II aka "Chip E," and Tom Moulton. Today, there are many hot DJs that know all about the sounds of the '70s and still play much of that music. Some of the most prominent DJs today are Doug E. Fresh, Rich Medina, Tony Touch, and D-Nice. There are hundreds of DJs today who are not as well-known as the ones I mentioned but who also focus on music from the '70s disco era. All of these DJs use equipment that is far more sophisticated than what was available to Danny and CP. As a result, these new DJs are more like musicians since they add drum lines, bass hits, and sound effects to reconstruct existing music and create unique experiences.

Although the top DJs starting of the '80s, '90s and beyond had more advanced equipment than my DJ partners, they are nevertheless standing on the shoulders of Danny, CP, and a handful of other giants like Gary Brodis and Frances Grasso, who pioneered beat matching. Grandmaster Flash, one of the top DJs in the world and acknowledged pioneer of hip-hop DJing and beat looping has been vocal about the importance of '70s music: "People need to understand that the '70s is where the whole hip-hop culture really started." He goes on to say, "Some of the biggest hip-hop artists dig into the '70s pie."[77]

Today, while the term "disco" is pretty much dead, there are signs of renewed interest in the essence of the genre. The term "Nu Disco" popped up in the '90s, and mirrored balls are still in use at throw-back special events. 1970s disco music not only lives on, but much of it also appeals to millennials. In the early '70s, discos primarily played Motown, Gamble & Huff, James Brown, and other soul, funk, and up-tempo R&B. By the late '70s, disco sounds became more electronic, and lyrics were minimized or even eliminated. Songs featured a repetitive 4/4 beat. In the '80s, the sounds of disco lived on as electronic dance music or house music. As DJs became more sophisticated, many developed a strong following that is comprised almost exclusively of young adults.

An important social phenomenon that occurred during the '80s were

---

[77] YouTube - "Grandmaster Flash talks 'The Theory' Of Being A Hip Hop DJ And The Beginnings Of Hip Hop!!"

raves. Raves were made possible by social media and attracted tens of thousands of fans, who were given the address at the last minute. Organizers held many of these events in public spaces such as piers or parks, or even on privately owned farmland without permission or permits. Raves featured DJs playing music from a stage with massive sound systems and lights — just like a large disco. They were occurring around the globe and had many of the same features as '70s discos, albeit in a pop-up, temporary setting. Attendees danced in place to beats that would have filled the dance floor during disco's heyday. Sounds and lights exhilarated guests who felt a sense of freedom and escape that they shared with everyone around them. You didn't need a partner — you danced as part of a group. Attendees were diverse but primarily in their teens, 20s, and 30s. Everyone felt welcome, just as they did in disco environments. The energy and vibe were tribal, drug-laden, and euphoric. Some DJs emerged as superstars and developed an extensive following. Some remixed records that hit the top 40 charts. And, as you might expect, compensation for these DJs was far more than the DJs at '70s discos.

However, legal problems and community complaints ended raves, so there was a transition to events at licensed venues such as arenas, amphitheaters, and, with a permit, parks. The emotion is similar to raves, but the environments are better controlled. DJs continue to be the center of attraction with massive sound systems and light shows. Some of the events are annual or similar to concert tours that hit dozens of cities with the same, or similar, show.

These events attract a younger generation that is far too young to have experienced the disco era. However, the attraction is pretty much the same, and the response to these events is extremely enthusiastic, which is reminiscent of discos. In most cases, these disco-style concerts attract tens of thousands of attendees. In some cases, such as Sasha in a London suburb or Space in Ibiza, Spain, 50,000 attendees are frequent. As a result, many DJs are international superstars, earn millions of dollars a year, and travel by private jet and limousine. They perform at events such as Sensation, an international event that has entertained millions of people in 20 countries.

Today, top DJs occasionally partner with live entertainers for concert tours, often hitting dozens of cities in different parts of the world. In 2017 the global DJ industry was estimated to be worth $7.1 billion. It's important to note that the current DJ industry developed as a direct result of the disco era when, for the first time, DJs learned to manipulate records to create a new musical experience. The highest-paid DJs are mostly from Europe, and, thanks to the internet, they perform everywhere, from Russia to Mexico and from the U.S. to Australia. In 2017, the top-grossing DJs in terms of annual income were Garrix with $17M, SKRillex with $24M, Steve Aoki with $24M, Tiesto with $37M, David Guetta with $37M, and Calvin Harris with $66M. Martin Garrix was the headliner on the main stage of the Ultra Music Festival in Miami, Florida, with 165,000 attendees, when he was only 17! [78]

So, while classic discos are dead, the experience they created continues to thrive and are embraced by vast numbers of young adults all around the world. When you think about it, thousands of years ago, in pursuit of primal desires, humans gathered around a fire, beat crude, rhythmic instruments, and danced into the night. Today, a similar event occurs whenever people gather at a DJ concert, such as the Electric Daisy Carnival or Ultra Worldwide. Attendees dance in front of a light show while listening to electronic or house music, just as our ancestors did.

There has never been a civilization void of music. It is a human need, and the disco era demonstrated how powerful a force it can be. If you believe in the cyclical nature of life, it seems reasonable to believe that a more structured form of dancing will become popular again at some point in the future. When it does, the music of the '70s will likely be the inspiration.

[78] "What We Started", documentary by Bert Marcus and Cyrus Saidi, 2017

"Music is a moral law. It gives soul to the universe, wings to the mind, flight to the imagination, a charm to sadness and life to everything; It is the essence of order and lends to all that is good, just, and beautiful."

Plato

Where We Are Now
CATCHING UP WITH THE BEST OF FRIENDS

Danny Berry and **Tony Cooper** made their living entirely from nightclubs, aside from the three years they worked as teachers right after college. When Leviticus and Justine's closed, they partnered with the Dow Twins and Justice Vasquez, a manager from Justine's, to open the Proper Café, which was very successful until Danny and Tony retired in 2016. Today, Danny lives in Rochdale Village with his wife. They have a son who lives in Atlanta. Tony lives in St. Albans, Queens with his wife. Their daughter is a medical doctor residing in Westchester County, New York.

Charles "CP" Perry married a childhood acquaintance who grew up on the same block, just a few doors away in Queens. They moved to Manhattan's Upper West Side and, after Leviticus closed, CP took over the liquor concession at the Apollo Theater. His wife operated a bike shop in Brooklyn. CP is retired now and still living on the Upper West Side.

Wayne Scarbrough resigned from TBOF due to a conflict of interest when he was appointed Deputy Bureau Chief in the Bronx District Attorney's office. Wayne was married twice and had two children with each wife.

Mayor Edward Koch appointed Wayne to criminal court judge in Queens. Sadly, he developed a cerebral aneurism and passed away just as his career as a judge seemed destined to take him to a higher level.

Andre Smith left Young & Rubicam to join Foote, Cone & Belding Advertising for a few years before forming his own firm in 1978. He resigned from TBOF and partnered with Terry Fraser to form FraserSmith, which provided management consulting and strategic planning for Fortune 500 clients, including Miller Brewing Company and Moet Hennessy USA. FraserSmith closed down when Andre retired after a 30-year run. Andre and his wife live in Brooklyn.

Mal Woolfolk was part owner of WBLS radio in New York City. After TBOF, Mal worked for WBLS for 15 years until the station was sold. He then became a partner in a financial services company where he still works. He and his wife live on the New Jersey shore along with his wife's two daughters.

Harry Felder lives in Queens, got married to Shelly whom he met at the Ginza. They have two grown children. Harry worked as a construction manager for the NYC Board of Education and is semi-retired. He takes on a project on occasion when he feels like working.

Noel Hankin left TBOF in 1978 to continue his career in advertising. He joined Miller Brewing Company and then Moet Hennessy USA (nee Schieffelin & Somerset) and retired in 2017. He lives with his wife, Gwen, in East Hampton, NY. They have two married daughters, one lives in New York and the other in Los Angeles.

The Dow Twins continued to promote special events to their large, loyal following. Norman died in 2005 due to a medical condition, but Harold has preserved the legacy of the Dow Twins by continuing to promote events under the Dow Twins banner. He also created the Norman Dow Fund to memorialize his twin's name through philanthropy. Harold lives in Rochdale Village, Queens.

Ricky Mangum became Deputy District Attorney in the Bronx under Robert Johnson and was highly regarded by all who knew him. He passed away in 2014, five years after a botched medical procedure. Ricky's passing was a tremendous loss and devastating to his family and many friends. His wife Karole lives in Queens. They had two sons — one lives in Queens and the other in Philadelphia.

The Best of Friends Chronology

1960s	Kingsmen members give successful parties in Queens in a club house called The Kingdom
1965	Kappa Alpha Psi members learn how to produce and promote dances
1966	1967 – The Raunchy Five and Low Life Limited formed to give parties in Queens
1968	Citywide Associates created to promote dances; Manhattan contingent was dishonest
1968	Twelve friends form The Best of Friends (TBOF); trust is basis for the organization
1969	TBOF promoted several dances per year; TBOF membership is reduced to eight
1970	The concept for a midtown discotheque is developed
1971	TBOF launches an after-work discotheque at the Ginza
1971-1972	TBOF expanded to 7 events per week at four different venues

1973	TBOF opened their first club, which was called Lucifer's, in Queens
1974	Leviticus debuted on Thursday, November 14
1975	TBOF opens Othello and hires the Dow Twins to manage and promote the new club
1976	TBOF launches Hankin & Smith, an executive search firm, and a Travel Club
1976	Orpheus opened in Brooklyn; TBOF launches Leviticus International Records (LIR)
1977	Wayne appointed Deputy Bureau Chief by the Bronx District Attorney and resigns
1978	Leviticus, Othello, Orpheus, and Lucifer's were renamed Leviticus International, Justine's, Brandi's and Trixx respectively
1978	Association of Black Club Owners, Leviticus International Records, and an art gallery on the second floor are launched
1978	Noel and Andre resign from TBOF
1981	TBOF buys Bogard's, an existing discotheque; it closed in 1985
1982	Brandi's closed
1985	Trixx closed
1986	Leviticus closed
1986	Tony, Danny, Dow Twins, and Justice open Manhattan Proper, which was subsequently renamed the Proper Cafe
1987	Justine's closed, the last remaining TBOF business

APPENDIX I

National African American Fraternal & Social Organizations (partial list):

- Alpha Kappa Alpha Sorority
- Alpha Phi Alpha Fraternity
- Cup & Saucer
- Delta Sigma Theta Sorority
- Girlfriends
- Jack & Jill of America
- Kappa Alpha Psi Fraternity
- Omega Psi Phi Fraternity
- Phi Beta Sigma Fraternity
- Red Hat Society
- Sigma Gamma Rho Sorority
- Sigma Pi Phi Fraternity (also known as the Boulé)
- Smart Set

- The Carroussels
- The Guardsmen
- The Links
- Zeta Phi Beta Sorority

Local African American Social Organizations (partial list)

- Comus
- Englewood Social Club
- Reveille Club
- The Doers of Mashpee
- The Fellas
- The Hillbillies
- The Monday Club
- Vagabonds
- Westchester Clubmen
- What Are We Good For?

APPENDIX II

Promotional Flyers

OUR MOVE...

- Our 5th Annual Christmas Dance will be held on Saturday, December 23, 1972 in the Grand Ballroom, Concourse Plaza Hotel. 161st Street and the Grand Concourse, Bronx.

- The hours are 9 pm to 4 am.

- We're spotlighting our own band, that young, talented, in-demand group called

- Also featured will be Glass and a Guest Celebrity.

- Tables are free with reservations.

YOUR MOVE...

COME.
and bring a friend.

Admission: $5.00 in advance
$6.00 at the door

For reservations call 464-3600-1

or write: The Best of Friends
P.O. Box 49
Rochdale Village Station
New York, N.Y. 11434

Produced by

Call now, Yule not want to miss this one.

"The First What?"

The Best of Friends bring you the first Friday and Saturday nights at

THE NEW GINZA
40 East 58th Street

Starting December 28th and December 29th and every Friday and Saturday thereafter.

Featuring the best in dancing music and your first drink free . . . You can't get a better deal!

Time – 10 p.m.   Admission: $4

The first to give you weekly discotheques in midtown.

The Best of Friends, Inc.

P.S. Check us out at the Casa Blanca on Thursdays.
253 West 73rd Street.

The awesome responsibility of being the very best.

Although we are closing our Tuesday, Friday and Sunday discotheques at La Martinique, we feel it our responsibility to give you a good replacement. We have compressed the three nights into two

Fridays and Saturdays
at
The Dom

Starting December 28th & 29th and every weekend thereafter.

Admission: $3   Time – 10 p.m.

Produced by
THE BEST OF FRIENDS &
INTERSTATE PRODUCTION

To Our Loyal Patrons .....

The Best of Friends have been quietly doing their
thing at the Ginza for the past few months.STOP,
If you haven't heard ,that's understandable.STOP,
Because we don't usually advertise over masss
media or stand in the front of someone elses'
discoteque passing out flyers.STOP.However,what
we do is attract the kind of people that look good,
rap well,and party hard.STOP BY...

at the

GINZA

40 E. 58th Street
N.Y.C.
HA 1-4321

Every **FRIDAY** *and* **SATURDAY**
10 p.m.–4 a.m.   10 p.m.–3 a.m.

Price: $4.00 (includes the drink of your choice)

THE BEST of FRIENDS
continue to do it Right .....

Of course we're at the CASABLANCA every Thursday Night. And watch out for a very exclusive
surprise we're going to lay on New York in July.

APPENDIX III

Top Ten Songs at Leviticus – Summer 1978

1. "Mighty Real" — Sylvester, Fantasy Records

2. "Hot Shot" — Karen Young, West End Records

3. "In The Bush" — Musique, Prelude Records

4. "Let's Start The Dance" — Bohannon, Mercury Records

5. "Runaway Love" — Linda Clifford, Custom Records

6. "You & I" — Rick James, Motown Records

7. "Shame" — Evelyn 'Champagne' King, R.C.A.

8. "Boogie Oogie Oogie" — Taste of Honey, Capital Records

9. "Instant Replay" — Dan Hartman, Blue Sky Records

10. "I'm A Man" — Macho, Prelude Records

Other Hits at Leviticus

- "After the Love Has Gone" — Earth, Wind & Fire

- "Brick House" — Commodores

- "Car Wash" — Rose Royce

- "Come to Me" —± Prince

- "Dance, Dance, Dance" — Chic
- "Do it Till You're Satisfied" — B.T. Express
- "Fly Robin Fly" — Silver Convention
- "Get Ready" — Rare Earth
- "He's the Greatest Dancer" — Sister Sledge
- "I Feel Like Dancing" — Leo Sayer
- "I Will Survive" — Gloria Gaynor
- "Ladies' Night" — Kool & the Gang
- "Le Freak" — Chic
- "Manhattan Skyline" — Kool & the Gang
- "More Than a Woman" — The Bee Gees
- "Play That Funky Music" — Wild Cherry
- "Ring My Bell" — Anita Ward
- "Scorpio" — Dennis Coffey
- "Shake Your Groove Thing" — Peaches & Herb
- "Soul Makossa" — Manu Dibango
- "Staying Alive" — The Bee Gees
- "Stomp" — Brothers Johnson
- "That's the Way (I Like It)" – KC & the Sunshine Band
- "Turn the Beat Around" — Vickie Sue Robinson
- "You Should Be Dancin'" — The Bee Gees

APPENDIX IV

Popular Drinks at Leviticus

- Blue Whale
- Boilermaker
- Brandy Alexander
- Cuba Libre
- Daquiri
- Gin Fizz
- Golden Cadillac
- Manhattan
- Rusty Nail
- Salty Dog
- Screwdriver
- Singapore Sling
- Tom Collins
- Whiskey Sour
- Zombie

ABOUT THE AUTHOR

Noel Hankin is a founder of The Best of Friends, Inc. (TBOF), a pioneering business enterprise that promoted discotheque events in New York City starting in 1971. TBOF owned **Leviticus**, **Justine's** (formerly Othello), and **Bogard's**, three of the first black-owned clubs in midtown Manhattan. TBOF also owned **Brandi's** in Brooklyn and **Lucifer's** (renamed **Trixx**) in Queens. These nightclubs paved the way for Studio 54, *Saturday Night Fever*, and the nationwide explosion of disco in the late '70s.

Hankin is a retired senior executive who managed some of the world's most successful brands at Moët Hennessy USA and Miller Brewing Company. He also wrote speeches for CEOs and has been published in *Vital Speeches*.

Hankin is a founder of the *Thurgood Marshall College Fund* and served as its Vice-Chair. Founded in 1987, the Fund has raised over $300 million and helped prepare 260,000 students for career success through leadership training and providing financial scholarships.

President Clinton appointed Hankin to his Board of Advisors on Historically Black Colleges and Universities (HBCUs), where he provided counsel to the President for seven years.

Hankin has a BA from Queens College, a Marketing Certificate from the Wharton School of Business, and an Honorary Doctorate from Medgar Evers College/CUNY.

Born in Kingston, Jamaica, Hankin lives in East Hampton, NY with his wife Gwendolyn. They have two married daughters and three grandchildren.

CPSIA information can be obtained
at www.ICGtesting.com
Printed in the USA
LVHW081736120322
R17210300001B/R172103PG712905LVX00014B/14

9 781736 614914